Afro-Realisms and the Romances of Race

Afro-Realisms and the Romances of Race

Rethinking Blackness in the African American Novel

MELISSA DANIELS-RAUTERKUS

Louisiana State University Press
Baton Rouge

Published with the assistance of a subsidy from the University of Southern California.

Published by Louisiana State University Press

Manufactured in the United States of America
First printing

Designer: Michelle A. Neustrom
Typeface: Minion Pro
Printer and binder: Sheridan Books, Inc.

Library of Congress Cataloging-in-Publication Data

Names: Daniels-Rauterkus, Melissa, author.

Title: Afro-realisms and the romances of race : rethinking blackness in the African American novel / Melissa Daniels-Rauterkus.

Description: Baton Rouge : Louisiana State University Press, 2020. | Includes bibliographical references and index.

Identifiers: LCCN 2019040499 (print) | LCCN 2019040500 (ebook) | ISBN 978-0-8071-7262-9 (cloth) | ISBN 978-0-8071-7340-4 (pdf) | ISBN 978-0-8071-7341-1 (epub)

Subjects: LCSH: American fiction—African American authors—History and criticism. | American fiction—White authors—History and criticism. | American fiction—19th century—History and criticism. | American fiction—20th century—History and criticism. | African Americans in literature. | Race relations in literature.

Classification: LCC PS153.N5 D25 2020 (print) | LCC PS153.N5 (ebook) | DDC 813.009/352996073—dc23

LC record available at https://lccn.loc.gov/2019040499

LC ebook record available at https://lccn.loc.gov/2019040500

The paper in this book meets the guidelines for permanence and durability of the Committee on Production Guidelines for Book Longevity of the Council on Library Resources. ♾

For my daughter, Angelika,

with hopes that you exceed your wildest dreams

CONTENTS

ACKNOWLEDGMENTS

Writing this book has been my most incredible journey yet. It has taken me to many unfamiliar and unexpected places, stretched my mind and my emotions, and changed me in ways that elude expression. So I will do my best to convey here just how grateful I am to everyone who supported me along the way.

I must begin by thanking the Department of English at Northwestern University, where I not only deepened my knowledge of American and African American literature, but also first developed my interests in race and realism. Many people at Northwestern helped me shape the ideas that comprise this book. Julia Stern was by far my most crucial source of inspiration. She taught me much about nineteenth-century literary history and provided me with a template for the kind of scholar I wanted to be. A brilliant writer and teacher, Julia remains an unparalleled example of intellectual and pedagogical excellence. I also have to thank Ivy Wilson and Carl Smith, who were as generous as they were rigorous, reading my work with great care and offering advice at every step of the way. For introducing me to African American literary criticism, critical theory, cultural studies, and critical race theory, I thank Jennifer DeVere Brody, Alex Weheliye, and Sharon P. Holland. I also have to thank Darlene Clark Hine for welcoming me into her "History of Black Women in the Diaspora" course and giving me a historical context for assessing the aesthetic and political work of black women writers at the turn of the twentieth century. For teaching me about the joys and challenges of navigating academia while black, I thank Dwight A. McBride, John Keene, Kevin Bell, and E. Patrick Johnson.

For making life outside of the classroom both fun and intellectually stimulating, I give a heartfelt thanks to my graduate school friends. Greg

Laski was, and remains, my favorite collaborator and one of my best readers. Wanalee Romero and Carissa Harris provided laughter and levity during our weekly wine and cheese soirees. Janaka Bowman Lewis, Tasha Hawthorne, and Crystal Sanders gave me sisterhood and support beyond my cohort and the department. Rickey Fayne read and commented on early versions of the manuscript and was always willing to help me locate an obscure source. Sonia Arora encouraged me to think about my academic goals in relationship to larger conversations about access and equity—both in the private K-12 sector and in higher education—which ultimately helped me to become a better scholar and teacher.

I am also indebted to the numerous conferences, colloquia, and professional meetings I attended over the years, where I presented various iterations of the work that has gone into this book. In this regard, I am grateful to the organizers and participants of the Literary Tourgée Conference and meetings of the Modern Language Association, the American Studies Association, C19: The Society of Nineteenth-Century Americanists, the Midwest Modern Language Association, and the Futures of American Studies Institute at Dartmouth College. More specifically, I am grateful to the wonderful scholars with whom I have had the pleasure of being on a panel, such as Donald E. Pease, Robert T. Tally Jr., James E. Dobson, Daylanne K. English, Mollie Godfrey, Deborah Whaley, and Jonathan W. Gray. I am equally grateful to the scholars who kindly agreed to serve on panels that I co-organized, including Kenneth W. Warren, Russ Castronovo, Sharon P. Holland, Soyica Diggs Colbert, John Ernest, M. Giulia Fabi, Eric Gardner, Barbara McCaskill, Caroline Gebhard, Andreá N. Williams, Shirley Moody-Turner, and Adam Bradley.

This book has also greatly benefited from the input and support of colleagues and friends at several different institutions. I extend my heartiest thanks and appreciation to the University of Southern California. I would not have been able to write this book without the generous financial assistance, course releases, and pre-tenure sabbatical that the university gave me at the time of my appointment. I owe much gratitude to my mentor, colleague, and friend John Carlos Rowe, who read multiple versions of the manuscript and offered crucial advice at critical junctures. In many ways, John deserves much of the credit for making this book what it has become. I also want to thank Dean Peter Mancall, who generously provided a grant from the USC Dornsife Dean's Office. For easing my transition into the department, I wish to thank David St. John, Dana Johnson, Rebecca Lemon, Devin Griffiths, and Elda María Román. I owe a very special thank-you to Devin and Elda María, who read and commented on parts of the manuscript. Similarly, I feel very lucky to have had Danzy Senna read both the introduction and the epilogue, and I credit her for pushing me to be brave and provocative in my thinking about black cultural politics. For their collegiality and assistance in everyday matters, I thank Emily Anderson, Aimee Bender, Joseph Boone, Leo Braudy, Ashley Cohen, Percival Everett, Kate Flint, Chris Freeman, Alice Gambrell, Larry Green, Tim Gustafson, William Handley, Mark Irwin, Zakiyyah Iman Jackson, Heather James, Anna Journey, Tony Kemp, Tania Modleski, Carol Muske-Dukes, Maggie Nelson, Viet Thanh Nguyen, David Rollo, David Román, Margaret Russert, Hilary Schor, Karen Tongson, and David Treuer. For providing administrative assistance and support, I thank Nellie Ayala-Reyes, Flora Ruiz, Jose Perez Guerrero, Lauren Terazawa, Javier Ramirez Franco, and Laura Hough.

I would also like to thank my former colleagues at the University of Alabama at Birmingham, where I started my career and first conceived of this book. I will always be grateful to them for taking a chance on me and for teaching me so much about the profession. Here, I must thank Peter J. Bellis, who recognized the potential of this project long before I did and encouraged me to secure a book contract. Thanks must also go to Alison Chapman, Cassandra Ellis, Gale Temple, Daniel J. Siegel, Kieran Quinlan, and Cynthia Ryan, who not only welcomed me to the department with open arms, but who were, and remain, excellent examples of how to effectively balance research, teaching, and service. I would not have survived the first few years on the tenure track without their assistance.

Long before I took the job at UAB, the seeds of this book were planted at Occidental College. Shortly after I advanced to doctoral candidacy, the illustrious P. Gabrielle Foreman hired me to teach my first upper-division literature seminar ("Race, Law, and Literature"), giving me solo teaching experience and an opportunity to return to my home state of California. But more importantly, she gave me permission to think about *Pudd'nhead Wilson* as a "black text"—igniting in me a passion for questions of literary classification, canon formation, and racial representation. Since our first conversation back in 2008, Gabrielle has been an important mentor and supporter of my career. Her presence in my life has been key to my progress, and I feel very blessed to have had her guide me through the difficult transition from graduate student to assistant professor.

For bringing this book to publication, I would like to give an exuberant thank-you to LSU Press. I am especially indebted to James W. Long, who believed in this project from the start and who kept me informed and optimistic throughout the lengthy submission, review, and production process. I could not have had a more knowledgeable, responsive, and committed acquisitions editor. You are the real MVP. Thank you for believing in this manuscript and in me. I would also like to express my gratitude to the anonymous reviewer whose feedback was invaluable in sharpening my arguments and helping me see the real significance of my intervention. Thank you, whoever you are, for making this book so much better! For shepherding this manuscript through the production phase, I want to give a special thank you to Catherine L. Kadair; to Susan Murray for her expert copyediting; and to Lisa deBoer for creating the index.

On a more personal note, I would also like to thank my friends and family, whose encouragement inspired me to keep going when I felt like giving up. There are far too many of you to name here, but I appreciate each and every one of you just the same. This book would not have been possible without your love and support.

Finally, I would like to thank my dear husband, Andreas, and my sweet baby girl, Angelika. I could never repay you both for all that you endured and sacrificed while I worked on this book for what must have seemed like an eternity. The two of you are my reasons for everything, and I am forever grateful for the compassion, patience, and understanding you showed when I needed it the most. *Vielen Dank. Ich liebe euch.*

Afro-Realisms and the Romances of Race

Introduction

Race, Realism, and the Problem of Literary Classification

When Jean Toomer published *Cane* in 1923, critics welcomed him as a promising new voice in African American fiction. Narrated through a series of vignettes that innovatively fused poetry, prose, and dramatic elements to eulogize the loss of African American folk culture vis-à-vis the Great Migration, the novel was marketed and hailed as an authentic account of the black racial experience in America. More specifically, critics praised the novel for going beyond the well-worn stereotypes that dominated most white-authored fictions of black life as well as the crude and flat characterizations that were a hallmark of black protest fiction. Despite *Cane*'s critical success, Toomer was personally outraged. Because he saw himself as belonging to a new multiracial group, neither black nor white but "a blend of all European, African, Asian, and American Indian cultures," Toomer objected to his book being exclusively promoted as a black novel (Kerman and Eldridge 80). In fact, in a letter to his white publisher, Horace Liveright, Toomer proclaimed: "My racial composition and my position in the world are realities which I alone may determine" (Sept. 5, 1923, qtd. in Toomer, *Letters* 171).[1] In this way, Toomer rebuffed the concept of a fixed black identity and the related idea that his work could not signify anything outside of a racial context. In terms of literary history, such thinking on the part of critics explains why, upon its publication, *Cane* firmly cemented Toomer's place in the Harlem Renaissance but did not immediately secure him a spot in the pantheon of American modernism.[2] Regardless of how we may feel about Toomer's reluctance to identify as black, the controversy surrounding the publication of *Cane* points to a significant problem in American and African American literary studies: the author-based system of racial/literary classification.

More than simply a matter of foreclosing the opportunity for self-identification, the practice of classifying literature according to this segregationist model delimits the interpretive possibilities for literary works by privileging the author's racial identity over the content of their writings. This has the paradoxical effect of reinforcing the very racial divisions that we have tried to mitigate through literature and criticism. On one level, the problem can be understood in relationship to the racism of the literary marketplace. The literary world has always fetishized black voices, and African American literature has most consistently been valued for its authenticity—that is, its ability to faithfully portray black life, as if that were monolithic and quantifiable. Such aesthetic judgments have made African American literature synonymous with race and realism. At its best, this formulation has produced insightful critiques of black racialized experience in the United States. At its worst, it has underwritten the idea that black writing must always depict the sociological truths of black reality, foreclosing a fuller and more artistic treatment of blackness. Not only has this resulted in a narrow view of African American literature that prioritizes political objectives over issues of subjectivity and aesthetics, but it has also placed the burden of racial representation exclusively onto African American writers. However, if we approach this problem on another level, interrogating our commitment, as African Americanists, to the idea of exclusive cultural property, then we have to ask, How might our deeply held assumptions and reading practices underwrite our own marginalization?

In order to fully appreciate the aesthetic and political complexity that characterizes African American literature, we must reconceptualize the relationship between race and realism. We have to resist the temptation to reify these terms as organic and intractable heuristics, considering that both are highly constructed and mutable. This requires that we push back on some of our most basic and predominant ideas surrounding authorship and authenticity. It demands that we see race in a new way. For far too long, we have primarily understood race as an identitarian formation, something that only blacks and other people of color possess. Regrettably, this has come at the expense of a larger understanding of race as a structural or institutional framework that all people, including whites, inhabit and negotiate, and in deeply personal and reciprocal ways no less. Consequently, white writers have been granted exemptions from what should be a shared responsibility to represent race in American literature and to make sense of the American racial landscape. To comprehend what it has meant, and what it means now, to write realistically about African American lives, and race more generally, we need to move beyond such restrictive thinking because it cannot fully account for the interracial exchange and textual sophistication that exemplify much of African American literature. A good place to start is with the genre of American literary realism itself, a mode of writing whose truth-telling aesthetics have always been a part of African American literature but has historically been seen, and is still seen, as a white discourse.[3]

According to most conventional American literary histories, realism was primarily a white genre—in terms of both its practitioners and its subject matter. It came into existence in the years following the Civil War and, under the deanship of William Dean Howells, emerged as the dominant mode of American writing by the 1880s. Canonical studies credit Howells, Henry James, Mark Twain, Edith Wharton, Hamlin Garland, and Rebecca Harding Davis for defining the genre's aesthetic and cultural project. Their novels sought to capture the microscopic details of everyday life as it was predominantly lived by white Americans from a variety of class backgrounds. Organized more around a general commitment to objective narration than to a set of unifying aesthetic principles, realist novels shared a common interest in the frank treatment of the quotidian and the taboo and were especially preoccupied with issues of social dynamics. In terms of subject matter, many realist novels explored issues of adultery, divorce, immigrants, the plight of the poor and working classes, money, prostitution, sex, and women's rights. But for a few novels written by Howells and Twain, it would appear that the genre had very little to say about race or African Americans. Since the 1990s, scholars have challenged this misconception by demonstrating realism's centrality to questions of black/white racial difference, but still too few have considered the influence of realism on African American writers and how they engaged with the form and made it their own.[4] Such critical neglect can be attributed to the fundamentally segregated nature of American literary culture.

In *Afro-Realisms and the Romances of Race: Rethinking Blackness in the African American Novel,* I argue that we must revise the canonical narrative that African Americans did not write American literary realism, and the inverse misconception that white realists did not make important contributions to African American literature. I take as my starting premise William Wells Brown's famous pronouncement in *Clotel, or The President's Daughter* (1853) that during slavery, black life constituted a "truth stranger than fiction."[5] What Brown meant was that the horrors of slavery were beyond intelligibility and that no purely factual account could fully describe its absurdity or the emotional and psychological truths of enslavement. In order to do so, one would have to, paradoxically, make use of more overtly fictional genres. Drawing on this idea, I examine how black and white writers such as Frances E. W. Harper, Charles W. Chesnutt, Pauline Hopkins, Mark Twain, and William Dean Howells employed both realist and romantic strategies in their fictions of black life to push past the limitations of mimetic representation. Their goal was to illustrate the falsehoods of the larger culture and render blackness as a more fluid and subjective phenomenon. Taking a broader view of black subjectivity, they conceived of racial identity as something that was shaped half by the socially constructed environment and half by individual consciousness. In the process of exploring this dynamic, they produced a distinctive style of writing that I call "Afro-realism."

As an aesthetic and political practice, Afro-realism is not so much a formal literary movement or school as it is a creative approach toward the difficult task of depicting the diverse and multiple realities of black life at the turn of the twentieth century. As black and white writers grappled with the fraught issue of race, they recognized that they needed a more malleable mode for conveying a sense of the elusive nature of race and unreality that characterized African American life in postbellum America. By combining romantic elements and genres (larger-than-life characters, labyrinthine quests and mythical histories, improbable coincidences, the tragic mulatto/a trope and the passing narrative, sentimentalism, and the Gothic) with realist technique and subject matter (a focus on interiority and the material body, the social world, empiricism, and moral ambiguity), black and white writers highlighted the extraordinary conditions under which many African Americans really lived. They also pointed to the fictionality of race and the ability of certain cultural and empirical discourses (the one-drop rule, law, and science) to render race real, while they themselves deconstructed it. In this way, their novels give us a greater understanding of the relationship between fiction and the real world, illustrating how literary forms and genres could be mobilized to address contentious issues surrounding race and racism. Yet what interests me more specifically is the catalog of themes, plot conventions, and narrative strategies that these writers utilize in their efforts to challenge popular theories of racial identity, interracial marriage, and the expectations of the literary marketplace.

Operating on multiple levels, *Afro-Realisms and the Romances of Race* asks the question, How might the reevaluation of a literary genre, in this case, literary realism, lead to a reevaluation of authorship and, ultimately, to a reconstitution of African American literary studies at large? Essentially, my argument is organized around three sites—genre, authorship, and the field itself—which, taken together, form a theoretical model for comprehending the full magnitude of black representation beyond the author-based system of racial/literary classification. When we put African American writers and racial issues at the center of mainstream American literary realism, something that is seldom done, we discover that there really is no such thing as the discrete author but rather that the work of representing race creates its own "author-function," to borrow a phrase from Michel Foucault.[6] The realist-author-function, as it is produced by race, is a discursive formation that transcends artificial and arbitrary racial identity categories. It is also a far more useful paradigm than the author-based system for measuring the scope of black representation because it unfastens race from the politics of authenticity and assigns greater importance to the depiction of race that shows up in the literature. This results in a larger archive of knowledge. Graphically, this looks like three concentric circles, nesting inside of each other, with genre forming the innermost ring, followed by authorship, and the field itself comprising the outermost ring. Like the ripples from a stone tossed into a pond, this book seeks to extend infinitely outward the boundaries of our interpretive practices by challenging long-standing ideas about authentic blackness, cultural ownership, and the purview of black writing or writing about blackness. As we contemplate the significance of these three sites, we gain greater clarity about how they operate, ultimately arriving at a more comprehensive account of the aesthetic developments and cultural discourses that have shaped and continue to shape African American literature.

Guided by the logic of literary reciprocity, this study analyzes black and white writers' mutual engagement with questions of racial representation to create both a new conception of African American literature and a means beyond a holistic American literature. My purpose is to show how such an approach helps us to reimagine the former in a novel way, without succumbing to the latter's false narrative of national coherence. Admittedly, my focus on black and white writers reproduces a schematic racial binary that many other scholars working on race and ethnicity have challenged with more multicultural approaches, but my objective is to address the default framework that gave rise to African American writing and that continues to inform how we make sense of this literature and how we classify it. In keeping with other studies on this pairing, such as Dana D. Nelson's *The Word in Black and White* (1992), Eric Sundquist's *To Wake the Nations: Race and the Making of American Literature* (1993), Ann Douglas's *Terrible Honesty: Mongrel Manhattan in the 1920s* (1995), Rafia Zafar's *We Wear the Mask* (1997), and Robert S. Levine's *Dislocating Race and Nation* (2008), to name a few, I emphasize the dialectical nature of literary invention by demonstrating how black and white writers participated in a sustained conversation about black representation and the political efficacy of fiction.

Consider, for example, the scene in *Iola Leroy* (1892) in which Marie, Iola's mother, expresses that she would rather see her youngest daughter, Gracie, die before seeing her subjected to slavery. Sharing her mother's sentiments, Iola cries: "So would I. I wish I could die myself" (82). Naturally, Marie tells Iola to take comfort in her Christianity, in response to which Iola asks, "Mother, are these people Christians who made these laws which are robbing us of our inheritance and reducing us to slavery? If this is Christianity I hate and despise it" (82). This heartbreaking exchange is followed by little Gracie's death:

> Swiftly the tidings went through the house that Gracie was dying. The servants gathered around her with tearful eyes, as she bade them all good-bye. When she had finished, and Mammy had lowered the pillow,

> an unwonted radiance lit up her eye, and an expression of ineffable gladness overspread her face, as she murmured: "It is beautiful, so beautiful!" Fainter and fainter grew her voice, until, without a struggle or sigh, she passed away beyond the power of oppression and prejudice. (83)

This scene, like so many in sentimental fiction, produces an intense emotional reaction in the reader, clearly recalling little Eva's death in Harriet Beecher Stowe's *Uncle Tom's Cabin* (1852). In a radical move, Harper casts a legally black girl in the role of moral authority, which contrasts sharply with Stowe's pejorative depiction of black girlhood vis-à-vis Topsy. Both authors blend sentimentalism and realism, insofar as they each use the politics of tears to advocate for social change in the real world, which complicates discussions about genre and categorical purity. But unlike Stowe, Harper does not place faith in transcendent moral truths; rather, she questions the moral underpinnings of the laws that sanction racial inequality in the first place, suggesting that people need to commit themselves to a program of both spiritual and social reform. In this way, Harper offers a more trenchant critique of religion and racism. Harper's revision of Stowe also invites us to consider a longer genealogy of literary reciprocity, in which Harper borrowed from Stowe, who borrowed from Josiah Henson's narrative *The Life of Josiah Henson* (1849), which was written by a white amanuensis. As other scholars have noted, such interracial collaboration was characteristic of nineteenth-century literary culture.[7] I offer this as an example of how reciprocity provides a more multifaceted account of genre, authorship, and African American literature.

In pursuit of this larger goal, I focus on the "nadir," the period following Reconstruction through the early twentieth century (1877–1919), and the novel because, as I see it, both function as crucial sites for reconceptualizing the political work and aesthetic innovation of a period that continues to be marginalized and a form that is frequently misunderstood.[8] Although the era did in fact witness an epidemic of racial terrorism and the erosion of African Americans' newly acquired citizenship rights, it also inspired some of the most groundbreaking developments in the African American novel, while laying the foundation for the future of black fiction. Indeed, Charles W. Chesnutt famously labeled this era "Post-Bellum—Pre-Harlem" in his essay of the same name, noting that his attainment of critical recognition paved the way for the emergence of the New Negro novel.[9] But as Barbara McCaskill and Caroline Gebhard explained in their landmark volume *Post-Bellum, Pre-Harlem* (2006), the literary critics who came after Chesnutt regarded the era "as a time of accommodation and passivity, of false white idols and thus a literary as well as political failure" (3). This formulation has pervaded African American literary criticism, perpetuating a very truncated view of African American literary history that privileges the antebellum period and the Harlem Renaissance as the marquee moments in black literature. Despite the appearance of studies such as McCaskill and Gebhard's, Kevin Gaines's *Uplifting the Race* (1996), Michele Mitchell's *Righteous Propagation* (2004), and Tess Chakkalakal and Kenneth Warren's *Jim Crow, Literature, and the Legacy of Sutton E. Griggs* (2013), there still remains a dearth of criticism on this crucial epoch, especially on African American literary realism and on the blending of genres in the African American novel.

As *Afro-Realisms and the Romances of Race* reveals, black and white writers frequently blurred the boundaries between realism and romance to highlight the link between the slave past and the post-Reconstruction present. While "realism had become science's counterpart in the arts," as David Shi has observed, demanding that writers abandon the hollow symbolism of the romance to accurately depict the harsh realities of modern life (77), a careful examination of the fiction studied here reveals a sustained engagement with the romance, so much so that Howells himself had to admit that deep into the nineteenth century *Uncle Tom's Cabin* was "still perhaps our chief fiction" (*My Literary Passions* 50). This "persistence of Uncle Tom," as Kenneth W. Warren has called it, shows up in the preponderance of turn-of-the-twentieth-century texts that incorporate the tragic mulatto/a trope, slavery, and stock romantic conventions into their narratives.[10] As Carla Peterson has explained, the African American novels published during this time make use of antebellum literary conventions to "establish continuity with a ruptured past, affirm group identity, and chart a direction for the future" ("Commemorative" 39).

Building on this observation, I argue that these novels deploy genre as the vehicle to perform this kind of cultural work, suggesting that the pathway to modernity, for black and white alike at the time, was through a confrontation with slavery and antebellum literary culture. Thus, while this book situates its analysis in the cultural and literary landscape of the 1890s and early 1900s, it relies upon a rear-view glance to anchor and contextualize its readings of texts within a longer view of nineteenth-century literary history. Reaching far back into the antebellum era—its genres, genealogies, and tropes—this project mirrors the temporal maneuver of the novels it examines by rejecting a linear narrative of literary progress, and offering, in its place, anachronism as a reading strategy for interpretation.[11] I assert that it is only from the vantage point of the late nineteenth and early twentieth centuries that we can truly comprehend the larger narrative that is African American literature.

By uncovering the ways in which Afro-realist representations of race mobilize the protocols of genre to deconstruct notions of blackness, this book responds to several important studies that have sought to recover and restore the expansiveness of African American literature by either looking for black texts in unconventional places or reading them in unconventional ways. In this context, *Afro-Realisms and the Romances of Race* joins the wider critical endeavor to broaden the African American literary canon and its criticism, putting it in conversation with works such as John Ernest's *Chaotic Justice: Rethinking African American Literary History* (2009), Eric Gardner's *Unexpected Places: Relocating Nineteenth-Century African American Literature* (2009), Kevin Quashie's *The Sovereignty of Quiet* (2012), Andreá N. Williams's *Dividing Lines: Class Anxiety and Postbellum Fiction* (2013), Aida Levy-Hussen's *How to Read African American Literature* (2016), and Christopher Freeburg's *Black Aesthetics and the Interior Life* (2017), to name a few.[12] All of these studies have convincingly argued that some of the most established approaches to African American literature have often advanced a settled, cohesive narrative about black literary/cultural production and its methodological practices, obscuring any sense of its real intricacy, internal divides, or ongoing construction.

As part of its larger, structural objective, this book also implements the seismic shifts that scholars like M. Giulia Fabi, McCaskill and Gebhard, and Ernest have called for in the way that we approach the work of critical appraisal, periodization, and literary classification. Fabi's work on the rise of the African American novel defended nineteenth-century black fiction's "bad reputation" against charges of literary incompetence, didacticism, and racial self-loathing by offering subversive readings of the tragic mulatto/a device and the trope of passing (*Passing* 1). Similarly, McCaskill and Gebhard's *Post-Bellum, Pre-Harlem* reappraised the nadir, rejecting aesthetic and historical assessments of the period as one of "artistic loss and setback" (Braithwaite 69) and offering, in its place, new frameworks for understanding the "aesthetic experimentation and political dynamism" that characterized the era's cultural production (McCaskill and Gebhard 2). More recently, Ernest has urged us to "look at the race that extends beyond the identity or social positions of authors, the race that is manifest in the literature and in the web of connections that both lead to and follow from the literature" (*Chaotic Justice* 7). In dialogue with this scholarship, then, this book aims to contribute to our larger understanding of the aesthetic and political value of African American literature as a whole. My emphasis on race and realism seeks to illuminate how black and white authors challenged prevailing approaches towards racial representation to grasp the complexities of black experience.

I am certainly not the first person to tackle these connections. In focusing on race, realism, and the politics of representation, my book is obviously indebted to the important scholarship that has already been done by Kenneth W. Warren, Madhu Dubey, and Phillip Brian Harper.[13] I have been especially inspired by Gene Andrew Jarrett's work, which has acknowledged how presumptions about racial authenticity, which are almost always tied to an author's racial identity, overwhelmingly determine which texts we include or do not include in the African American literary canon. As Jarrett has elucidated, by erroneously mapping authorial identity onto textual identity, we marginalize African American writers whose works do not overtly reflect the aesthetic and political concerns of what he calls "racial realism" (*Deans and Truants* 7); and perhaps more maliciously, we perpetuate a kind of literary "one-drop rule" that, in his words, "rationalizes the arbitrariness of racial identification" ("Addition by Subtraction" 318). While Jarrett's concerns clearly form the theoretical foundation of this book, my work departs from his, and others, considerably in its focus on the blending of realistic and romantic elements in fictions of black life. Throughout this book, I examine how black and white writers employed generic mixture as a way to challenge or negotiate widely accepted ideas about race and realism. My premise is that black and white writers innovatively mixed genres to exercise greater creative autonomy and to widen the possibilities for African American subjectivity and representation in fiction. In doing so, they sought to deconstruct the idea of race as an objective truth by conceding that reality was partially a matter of phenomenology and partially a matter of discourse. It was constructed and mediated by human observation as well as by systems of knowledge and power. In this way, they viewed the task of accurately depicting blackness as a representational problem that required, ironically enough, more aesthetic freedom and less verisimilitude in order to get at the complex truths of black life.

One of the goals of this book is to complicate our sense of what African American literature has been and what it can be by troubling notions of genre and racial representation, reading the blending of realism and romance as a dominant feature of African American writing within a larger American literary tradition. In the introduction to his classic study *The American Novel and Its Tradition* (1957), Richard Chase argued that the romance was the quintessential American literary mode and that "the history of the American novel is not only the history of the rise of realism but also of the repeated rediscovery of the uses of romance" (xii). Yet the canonical works upon which he based his analysis were entirely white, and his readings of texts were patently exceptionalist, as they appeared to have been motivated by a desire to define the singularity of American culture and to establish the superiority of the American novel over the English novel. Furthermore, the definition of romance that emerges over the course of the book is disengaged from issues of race or social problems, focusing instead on the "picturesque and the heroic," freedom from "verisimilitude," "melodrama and idyll," and a "willingness to abandon moral questions or to ignore the spectacle of man in society, or to consider these things only indirectly or abstractly" (ix). Considering the fundamental role that race has played in American culture since the founding of the nation, such a definition seems like a willful evasion, even in the context of the Cold War and New Criticism that gave rise to Chase's book. As Toni Morrison rightly observed in her pioneering study of the Africanist presence that pervades American literature, *Playing in the Dark: Whiteness and the Literary Imagination* (1992), "There is no romance free of what Herman Melville called 'the power of blackness,' especially not in a country in which there was a resident population, already black, upon which the imagination could play; through which historical, moral, metaphysical, and social fears, problems, and dichotomies could be articulated" (37).

That Chase could not conceive of blackness as a critical historical or rhetorical force in American life and letters underscores Morrison's point that the very construction of an American national literature depended on the denial of the presence of black people and the dismissal of race as a salient feature of the American landscape. As Morrison has explained, the romance was an integral part of this project because it gave American writers a palimpsest to sketch out their desires and fears. For a young republic, eager to cast off the weight of the European past, the romance's symbolism, morality, and quest-based plot allowed American writers to conceive of American character in terms of the "new white man," or what R. W. B. Lewis famously called the "American Adam," who had to wrestle with the *wilderness*—which was code for indigenous Native Americans and enslaved Africans—to fulfill his birthright and secure his independence (*Playing* 15, italics mine). According to Morrison, this was a racializing project in which white writers sublimated their anxieties and concerns about black people and slavery, in particular, into the symbolic realm, transforming blackness into an important signifier of difference as well as a repository for all that was unassimilable in the larger culture: "Black slavery enriched the country's creative possibilities. For in that construction of blackness *and* enslavement could be found not only the not-free but also, with the dramatic polarity created by skin color, the projection of the not-me. The result was a playground for the imagination. What rose up out of collective needs to allay internal fears and to rationalize external exploitation was an American Africanism—a fabricated brew of darkness, otherness, alarm, and desire that is uniquely American" (*Playing* 38). In this configuration, Morrison defines blackness as a discursive formation that not only rendered visible notions of freedom and enslavement but that also delineated the boundaries between self and other, giving white writers a sharper, albeit false, sense of their own superiority, inevitably producing a literature that was in its DNA preoccupied with questions of racial difference and problems surrounding African American identity—even when such concerns were not explicitly addressed in narrative form.

Informed by Morrison's remarks, my argument is in some ways a subversive revision of Chase's romance thesis. If, for Chase, the romance was an ahistorical, mythical form unencumbered by the baggage of the Old World and its class divisions, in my study, the romance is a socially engaged genre that gave black and white writers the representational power to attack the racial fantasies and mythologies engendered by slavery and that continued to exert force on African Americans well into the turn of the twentieth century. For the black and white writers whom I examine here, the romance drew its power from its confrontation with real historical and structural forces undergirding racial formation in America. Understood in this way, these writers' use of romantic conventions was specifically deployed to challenge racism, both in the real world and in fiction, and should not be confused with the racial evasions and displacements that, according to Morrison, characterize early American romances or with the openly racist representations found in Thomas Dixon's and Thomas Nelson Page's racial romances. While these writers also utilized the logic of romance, they did so either to alleviate their anxieties about social change or to portray slavery in a wistfully nostalgic way that defended the plantation system and undermined African American humanity. Ultimately, what distinguishes the writers whom I examine here from these other romancers is that they mobilized the genre in ways that sought to boldly confront slavery and to move African American representation away from the realm of racial caricature and stereotype toward greater reality.

Of course, my choice to include white writers in a study on African American literature goes against the critical grain and demands some explanation. My conceptualization of African American literature turns on what Gene Andrew Jarrett has described as the "ideological and discursive" or the "critical discourse of blackness" as opposed to the racial identity of the author (*Deans and Truants* 18). Putting racial identity aside, if African American literature can be broadly defined by its focus on the construction of black racial identity and the use of representational forms to interrogate the sociopolitical realm, then I think race novels published by Twain and Howells warrant inclusion in the African American literary canon. Although Twain and Howells are not black writers, I have chosen to read their works alongside those by black authors such as Chesnutt,

Harper, and Hopkins to bring into greater relief how they were influenced by and how they helped to influence many attributes of African American writing—for example, a focus on the popular, legal, literary, and scientific theories of race. In many respects, my rationale is rooted in Aliyyah I. Abdur-Rahman's important, but often forgotten, observation that "African American writing does not emerge in a cultural and literary vacuum but engages always intertextually with dominant writerly practices and output" (21).

During the early days of African American literary studies, it was imperative for scholars to identify African American literature as a discrete tradition. Because scholars had to fight charges of illegitimacy, they largely focused their efforts on identifying the set of shared characteristics that defined works of African American literature so that they could construct an African American literary canon and defend its scholarly merits. In the process of doing so, they advanced a definition of the field that insisted on black particularity and delimited the discipline's concerns to racial issues. Today, African American literature enjoys great mainstream visibility and academic institutionalization. And while virulent forms of antiblackness and ongoing conservative attacks on black studies programs continue to pose an ever-present risk to the field's stability, we should not be reluctant to create new methodologies for assessing shifting definitions of blackness as well as the range and focus of African American writings.

While it remains essential, both academically and politically, to appreciate the African American literary tradition as a separate and distinctive formation, it is also useful and productive to acknowledge the various ways in which that tradition intersects with and informs other literatures and cultural discourses.[14] Accordingly, I believe that we need to expand our sense of who and what should be included in discussions of African American literature. In a world structured by antiblackness, it is critical that we continue to prioritize African American writers, but we also need to move beyond segregated approaches to the work of interpretation and misguided notions of a fixed racial identity to embrace a definition of African American literature that is animated by and organized around black writers and their meditations on blackness but also porous enough to include certain nonblack writers and their representations of race/

engagement with black rhetorical forms, so that we might theorize, in more complex and sophisticated ways, the larger social order that constitutes race in America.

In some ways, the intellectual shift that I am calling for here is analogous to what Nellie Y. McKay proposed in 1999 in her essay "Naming the Problem That Led to the Question 'Who Shall Teach African American Literature?' Or, Are We Ready to Disband the Wheatley Court?" Invoking the poet Phillis Wheatley as a metaphor for the racial divisiveness plaguing literary studies, McKay argued that it was high time for all of us to discard the racial stereotypes and racial essentialism underwriting our work, perpetuating the misguided idea that African American literature is a lesser, quasi-academic discipline in which only black people can work or that it is one that does not require real training.[15] As McKay asserted, "there is nothing mystical about African American literature that makes it the sole property of those of African descent" (366). Invoking Toni Morrison, she insisted that "it can be learned" (qtd. in McKay 366).[16] As McKay rightly intuited at the time, this kind of "learning" would be crucial to the field's future. To disband the Wheatley court, McKay argued (1) that literary studies had to rectify the historical neglect and unfair criticism that black writers and scholars had suffered at the hands of white authorities by increasing the pipeline of black faculty and courses in African American literature, and (2) that African American literary scholars had to be willing to welcome nonblack scholars into the fold, particularly those who were serious about producing quality scholarship, so that the literature could, in McKay's words, "become a full member of the company of world literatures, open to all who wish to participate in its bounty" (366).

Today, it would appear that McKay's call has largely been answered. Certainly, there are more African American faculty members and university courses devoted to African American literature than there were back then (although we still need more). Similarly, the vast number of nonblack scholars and students currently working in African American literary studies underscores the fact that the field has broad appeal and has benefited from greater diversity. However, my sense is that McKay was also pushing for a larger paradigm shift. Essentially, McKay was arguing that our efforts at inclusion would prove successful when there is enough diversity in academia to decouple identity from scholarship. As

McKay ascertained, "where the faculty is reasonably diverse, the question of who has the right by ethnicity to teach what is irrelevant" (364). Twenty years later, we still are not there yet. Some still balk at the idea of a black medievalist or a black Renaissance scholar, and many black African Americanists are still suspicious of nonblack African Americanists. Such reactions reveal that in spite of our best efforts at diversity and inclusion, we still *feel some kind of way* when the unspoken rules of racial representation and cultural ownership are violated. While questions of identity are essential to the critical and necessary work of facilitating institutional equity—that is, providing equal opportunity for historically disadvantaged and underrepresented groups—they are not, and should not, serve as the sole basis for determining who can and cannot teach African American literature or which writers we should or should not include in those conversations.

Do not get me wrong. In advocating for an alternative to the author-based system of racial/literary classification, I am not proposing that we do away with African American literature or African American studies departments and programs. Far from it. In fact, I think that African American literature is an essential component of any college or university curriculum and that we need to devote even more resources and faculty-lines to these academic units. More specifically, I believe that we need to continue to address historical and institutional disparities by hiring and granting tenure to more black faculty members. But in addition to pursuing this kind of diversity, we must also think about intellectual diversity and expansiveness. We need to consider how faulty ideas about identity may hinder the development of more nuanced and forward-thinking scholarship. In this way, my argument builds on McKay's remarks by seeking to add greater elasticity to how we define African American literature in terms of its practitioners, subject matter, and methodologies. In doing so, I believe that we stand to gain more than what we think we might lose. What is at stake is (1) a more sophisticated and comprehensive appreciation of what it means to represent racial experience in imaginative writing; (2) a richer sense of the historical world from which this literature emerged as well as a thicker contextualization of it; and (3) new canons, literary histories, and syllabi for the next generation of scholars and students, which ensures the intellectual and pedagogical longevity of the field. Ultimately, what I am suggesting here is that African American literature is far more intricate and far-reaching than what we have thought and that it cannot be strictly limited to the slave narrative, the New Negro novel, or even that which has been exclusively produced by black people.

My claim about black and white writers is meant to achieve greater fluidity in African American literary studies so that we might create a new model for thinking about race. By placing the burden of racial representation onto black writers and only valuing their writings for their ability to authentically depict blackness, we reify the very racial constraints that these texts attempt to challenge. What is more, how can we concede that the preponderance of mixed-race characters and passing plots that punctuate African American literature challenge arbitrary racial divisions, on the one hand, and yet be reluctant to impose more tractable models for theorizing racial identity when it comes to the business of canon formation on the other? In actuality, such mutability was part and parcel of the era's literary thematics, as writers as diverse as Chesnutt, Twain, Harper, Howells, and Hopkins frequently explored issues of interracial intimacy and racial fluidity. Indeed, as Stephanie Li has noted, "fluidity has long been emblematic of black identity" ("What Is Twenty-First-Century African American Literature?" 631). Hence, I am in agreement with Jarrett, who has argued that we need to consider adopting "racial representation as an appropriate paradigm for determining communities of authors" ("Addition by Subtraction" 320). My own sense is that such an approach would not only generate new ways of talking about the relationship between race and realism or the politics of representation but would also create a more expansive, fuller body of literature about the construction of African American identity and racial experience in America.

In taking up the politics of racial representation, vis-à-vis form and genre, *Afro-Realisms and the Romances of Race* moves beyond skin-deep considerations of a writer's racial identity and stages a new formalist critique of race and realism, a relationship that up until now has been explored primarily through historicist methodologies. As such, this book offers what may very well be the first full-length account of how African American writers participated in and revised the dominant aesthetic practices and cultural discourses surrounding realism to address pressing issues of race in America and how white realists also played a pivotal role in this project. In returning to questions of aesthetics, then, my book reflects, more generally, the contemporary turn toward what Marjorie Levinson has called "the new formalism"—a movement animated by what she terms "rededication" to the text to challenge new historicism's neglect of form (561). Accordingly, it emphasizes close reading, the agency of the literary work, and the significance of form to contextualist and materialist critique to facilitate greater textual engagement in literary studies (560).[17] More specifically, however, my book reworks cultural materialism and new historicism to link social formations of race with issues of aesthetics, and thus might be better located within the critical sphere of race and the new formalism.[18] Appropriately, it adapts the reading strategies of what Colleen Lye has called "racial form" to theorize race in such a way that mitigates the tension between the aesthetic and the sociohistorical—which is in fact "especially severe in discussions of ethnic literature," as she puts it—by bridging the gap "between the notion of race as representation and the notion of race as constitutive of literary and other social formations" ("Racial Form" 96). The intellectual payoff is that it puts into practice an anti-essentialist theory of race that does not depend upon the authentic racial subject but on a set of aesthetic practices that also function as metacriticism of how race is constructed in the material world.

Afro-Realisms and the Romances of Race is organized so as to trace how black and white writers developed increasingly innovative methods for depicting African American experience and exploring the inner workings of race. Each chapter examines how an author deploys Afro-realism (that is, the blending of realistic and romantic conventions) to confront the slave past and make sense of the Jim Crow present, by rendering the crisis of racism through strategic reworkings of multiple genres and motifs: for example, the plantation romance and the slave narrative, the tragic mulatto/a trope, and the narrative of racial passing. What I am tracking here is the emergence of a set of plot conventions and narrative strategies for depicting and comprehending African American realities at the turn of the twentieth century. In analyzing the ways in which black and white writers have explored and attempted to come to terms with slavery and its present effects, we are able to perceive how questions of race and racial justice guided aesthetic innovation. As the book crystallizes and historicizes these plot conventions and narrative strategies, it also situates its readings of fictional texts within a larger, discursive field, circumscribed by ostensibly more factual discourses like history, law, and science, to explore the space in between the conceptual and material registers of race. Indeed, the prevalence of mixed-race protagonists, lawyers, and doctors in the fiction that I examine serves to allegorize the ways in which the empirical discourses of race work to construct racial reality and how popular fiction functions to deconstruct them. With each successive chapter, the book demonstrates how the persistence of slavery's effects demanded that writers adopt more experimental approaches to the problem of racial representation. Accordingly, the book's trajectory moves through the antebellum period to the dawn of the twentieth century, shuttling back and forth across timelines, genres, and racial divides, in an effort to disrupt traditional, overly schematic accounts of nineteenth-century cultural and literary progress, generic distinction, and racial identity.

Chapter 1, "The Long Hangover: Mark Twain's *Pudd'nhead Wilson* and the Ghosts of Slavery," opens my argument by tracing the ways in which Twain's novel destabilizes racial, generic, and temporal categories to explore the connections between slavery and post-Reconstruction racism. I argue that *Pudd'nhead Wilson* (1893–94) should be read as a work of African American literature, despite its author's racial identity, because of its formal qualities and content. I contend that the novel is a metaliterary critique of the plantation romance that utilizes both romantic and realistic conventions from the slave narrative to challenge the former's fundamental racism. To call attention to the absurdities, contradictions, and falsehoods at the center of slave culture (particularly as it is depicted in the genre of the plantation romance), Twain employs an outlandish plot that revolves around a "white-looking" baby with "black blood" substituted for the legitimate heir, and the illegitimate heir's murder of his uncle and his then being remanded into slavery. In this way, the novel's romanticized story echoes a popular refrain from the slave narrative, the idea that "truth is stranger than fiction," as it exposes the sexual and moral hypocrisy that undergirds slave society. These unveilings form the basis for the novel's realism, which largely focuses on the constructed nature of racial identity and the mechanisms by which reality is regulated—reaching its highest expression in its detective-murder plot/courtroom sequence. Here, I maintain that the novel's ironic ending—which finds the illegitimate heir outed as both a murderer and a black man before he is sold down the river to settle the debts on the Driscoll estate—functions as a commentary on the failures of Reconstruction and the criminalization of blackness in the legal system.

If Twain's novel uses the conventions and narrative strategies of antebellum literature to address postbellum concerns, then Harper's *Iola Leroy* complicates and extends this project. Chapter 2, "Reimagining the Tragic Mulatta in Frances E. W. Harper's *Iola Leroy*," explores the author's revision of Howells's *An Imperative Duty* (1891) within the palimpsest of racialized and gendered discourses that Michele Elam (née Birnbaum), has described as the "consanguinity of the 'Race Problem' and the 'Woman Question'" (*Race, Work, and Desire* 58–59). I examine the ways in which Harper's novel (which views mixed-race identity as a category within blackness) fills in the gaps in Howells's representation of the mulatta by providing a more substantive analysis of the double bind that is black womanhood. Because other critics have already addressed this textual pairing, most notably Elam and M. Giulia Fabi, both of whom have emphasized "the process of reciprocal artistic invention that links black and white writers of the nineteenth century" (Fabi, "Reconstructing" 49), I foreground Harper's text, while relatively backgrounding Howells's, to illustrate how Harper adapted and transformed certain aspects of mainstream realism to advance her own sociopolitical agenda.

In doing so, I argue that Harper balances a more modern mimetic realism with older, sentimental strategies to articulate the political significance of black women and black marriage in the work of uplifting of the race. By weaving realism and sentimentalism into a fairly conventional domestic plot, Harper creates a more specific brand of Afro-realism that I call "sentimental realism." I show how this form of generic mixture allows her to challenge traditional depictions of the mulatta's racial tragedy, which not only emphasized her inability to reconcile her two racial halves as the source of her existential angst but also portrayed her black ancestry as a cultural and legal impediment to marriage with her white suitor. I contend that Harper redeems the mulatta figure by providing her with the power to choose her own form of marital/narrative closure. In Harper's configuration, the mulatta achieves the highest pinnacle of personal and political subjectivity by rejecting her white love interest and choosing to marry another mulatto. Ultimately, Harper's sentimental realism not only undermines stereotypical and patently romantic representations of the mulatta's fate—which usually involved racial exposure, embarrassment, social castigation, and death—but it also results in a dramatic reworking of the mulatta figure, giving her greater artistic depth as well as individual agency and social consciousness.

Chapter 3, "Racial Fictions and the Cultural Work of Genre in Charles W. Chesnutt's *The House behind the Cedars*," continues my examination of Afro-realism (and also the tragic mulatto/a trope) by exploring how Chesnutt works his way through realism and romance to accurately portray the American racial crisis and offer a viable solution to the problem of racial prejudice. I argue that the novel demonstrates Chesnutt's dual commitment to depicting African Americans, particularly those of mixed race, in realistic ways, and confronting white America for its complicity in the maintenance of white supremacy. Acknowledging the limitations of a more mimetic realism, Chesnutt draws on the cultural power of sentimentalism to issue an emotional appeal to white readers about the ethical and moral hazards of racism. Chesnutt situates this appeal within a larger conversation about the fictiveness of race, as a biological and sociological construct, and the ability of literary fiction to undermine racist ideology. As his mixed-race characters make clear in their respective experiments with racial passing, literary fictions can be mobilized to create new identities that challenge the arbitrariness of the one-drop rule. For example, both of his mixed-race protagonists draw from romantic fictions to establish themselves as "new people" (57). However, Chesnutt demonstrates that white supremacy ultimately regulates and referees the larger cultural narrative surrounding racial identity. To illustrate the tragic consequences of white racism, then, Chesnutt adopts a more deterministic and naturalistic style toward the end of the novel, which culminates in the death of his mixed-race heroine. Chesnutt's point is that the biggest impediment to black life is structural racism. In this way, the novel uses mimetic and melodramatic conventions to bring attention to very real ways that racism threatens American democracy.

In Chapter 4, "The Limits of Literary Realism: Pauline Hopkins's Post-racial Fantasy in *Of One Blood*," I argue that *Of One Blood* (1902–3) marks an important shift in African American writing at the turn of the twentieth century, as it tests the limits of realist representation to contemplate the future of race and black political life. Ironically, Hopkins creates this prophetic vision by looking back to the past. In this final chapter, I explore how Hopkins envisions a postracial world, beyond the contours of the United States, by juxtaposing a more mimetic narrative about racial passing with a romantic fantasy about African return. To theorize a world in which race does not matter, Hopkins sends her black passer-protagonist to a mystical Africa devoid of colorism and racism. More importantly, she makes him a long-lost African king—giving him the social status he could never possess in America. I argue that this fantastic plot discards the temporal stasis associated with mainstream realism to construct a more progressive narrative about black life. But, ultimately, what is most fascinating to me is the way in which the novel looks forward to late twentieth-century and early twenty-first-century reassessments of race and blackness, revealing that as early as the turn of the twentieth century, African American writers were thinking about the postracial—not to issue a widespread call to abandon the category of race altogether, as the term is commonly understood, but more so to issue an important corrective to how we assign value to the category of race as a whole.

As I maintain throughout this chapter, race, for Hopkins, functions as an important reservoir for the construction of cultural identity—both in terms of the individual and the collective. It serves to give black Americans a healthy sense of self-esteem and cultural pride. Thus, far from invoking the postracial in the service of liberal color-blindness, which denies and erases important degrees of difference and negates the existence of institutional and systemic racism, Hopkins deploys the idea of the postracial to conceive of an alternative, postnational reality free from the nightmare of American racism. Ending on this note, this chapter demonstrates that the postracial phenomenon is not endemic to the age of Obama but rather that it has a late nineteenth-century legacy that we ignore to our own misfortune. As a historicizing gesture, this backward glance speaks to the whole of my project, reminding us that during the turn of the twentieth century, African American writers were themselves looking to add greater complexity to how black identity was theorized and represented in fiction and in the larger cultural imaginary. Ironically, they achieved this by confronting the slave past and remaking it so that they could visualize a more promising future.

Appropriately, then, this book ends with the question of what lies ahead for African American literature. In the epilogue, entitled "Rethinking Blackness," I turn to contemporary debates about the current status of the field, prompted by the appearance of Kenneth Warren's controversial book *What Was African American Literature?* (2011). As Brian Norman has observed, we "live in strange times" in African American literary studies—a time when some of the most provocative and cutting-edge scholarship "questions the field itself" (206). Warren's book is a key example. Although Warren's argument—which, in short, asserted that African American literature was a Jim Crow phenomenon, meaning that while one can and should study it, one cannot write it today—aimed to add greater specificity to how we define and periodize African American literature, it set off alarm bells for many because, as they saw it, it smacked of a delusional postracialism (a concept, which by the way, Warren does not endorse), which, in my opinion, is an unfair and inaccurate criticism of the book. More illuminating responses, such as Gene Andrew Jarrett's, rejected the idea that African American literature is over but conceded that what has passed are the black power politics that institutionalized the discipline. As Jarrett explained, "[W]hat's expiring isn't the literature itself but rather the traditional ways that readers have come to assess its political value and to define their own identities as agents of social change in an age of new black politics" ("African American Literature Lives On").

With these debates in mind, I argue that the way forward for African American literary studies lies in new approaches to how we read and make sense of texts as well as how we think about race and blackness. If we live in strange times when the field appears to be obsessed with its own mortality, then this is also an interesting moment to contemplate what the future entails for the next generation of scholars. Postbellum fiction, in particular, may have a special allure for those of us interested in advancing the field, considering its visionary impulses—that is, in Carla Peterson's words, the ways in which this literature "anticipate[d] the creation of 'future Americans'" or "New Negro modernity" ("Commemorative" 43). I call this forward-looking tendency the *proleptic hermeneutics* of the postbellum black novel, and I argue that it may offer an unexpectedly progressive framework for thinking about the purpose of African American literature and its political utility today.

By viewing race and racial representation in terms of aesthetic practices and thematics instead of essentialism, the postbellum black novel posits a more flexible conception of black identity that is more than skin deep and that also predates late twentieth-century and twenty-first-century reassessments of blackness such as the new black aesthetic, the postsoul, and postblackness.[19] Contrary to what is popularly thought, these are not discourses without some precedent in pre-late-twentieth-century America. As the fiction that I treat throughout this study demonstrates, during the nadir, African American writers were already experimenting with innovative narrative strategies to expand, transcend, and revise static meanings of black identity and experience—even as they suffered under or bore witness to police brutality, racially motivated violence, segregation, voter suppression, and incarceration. In many respects, not a lot has changed, considering how much today's racial landscape resembles that of the nadir. This may be, in and of itself, a compelling reason for contemporary African American literary studies to look to this literature as a way beyond a pessimistic mode of critique with very little room for aesthetic play, fluid subjectivities, and optimism. Ultimately, what I am suggesting here is that this fiction invites us to reconsider what black literature has been and what it can be so that we might create new ways of understanding the past, present, and future. I fear that if we do not become more willing to theorize blackness outside of the discourses of resistance and victimization, then we may very well succumb to the very marginalization that we seek to shield ourselves against by *keeping it real* and holding onto played-out principles like authentic blackness and the mythical, monolithic black community.

Afro-Realisms and the Romances of Race provides a vital rethinking of African American literature that I believe will help us tell a more nuanced narrative about race, literary production, and the value of black writing. I urge readers to consider how enduring misperceptions about identity undercut and obviate more imaginative approaches to the work of canon formation and interpretation. In an effort to expand our literary archive, as well as achieve a broader critique of race, I suggest, as others have done, that we pay more attention to modes of racial representation than to authors' racial identities. Instead of asking, Who has the racial authority to speak?, perhaps it is time to ask, What is at stake in representing racial experience? The novels that I examine here give us occasion to take up these questions by exploring the relationship between literary realism and African American literature. Ultimately, it is my hope that this book will make an important intervention in the field, demonstrating the creative and critical possibilities of an interpretive approach that offers a more pliable definition of both blackness and realism. Let me be clear. I do not offer this book as an authoritative prescription for reading African American literature. Neither do I seek to have the last word on these concerns. Rather, I seek to open up and extend the conversation about black representation by moving away from racial essentialism and restrictive reading practices to examine the narrative strategies that not only construct African American subjectivity but also endow it with greater individuality and humanity. Inspired by so many critics who have dared to explore and traverse the edges of blackness, this book boldly ventures off the beaten path to find new ways to think about race, realism, and African American literature.

1

The Long Hangover

Mark Twain's *Pudd'nhead Wilson* and the Ghosts of Slavery

> A person who is ignorant of legal matters is always liable to make mistakes when he tries to photograph a court scene with his pen; and so I was not willing to let the law chapters in this book go to press without first subjecting them to rigid and exhaustive revision and correction by a trained barrister—if that is what they are called. These chapters are right, now, in every detail, for they were rewritten under the immediate eye of William Hicks, who studied law part of a while in south-west Missouri thirty-five years ago. . . . He was a little rusty on his law, but he rubbed up for this book, and those two or three legal chapters are right and straight, now. He told me so himself.
>
> Given under my hand this second day of January, 1893, at the Villa Viviani . . .

In "A Whisper to the Reader," the unlikely introduction to *Pudd'nhead Wilson* (1893–94) quoted above, Mark Twain echoes a familiar refrain from the slave narrative: *written by himself.* But instead of repeating this exhortation verbatim, Twain recasts it, using a slightly different rhetoric of textual authenticity: "He told me so himself" (2). Referring to his lawyer friend, William Hicks, Twain assures us that the "law chapters" are "right, now, in every detail" because they were "rewritten under the immediate eye" of a "trained barrister" (1). In keeping with the conventions of the slave narrative's authenticating preface, Twain also affixes his name to the letter to guarantee its overall veracity. While Twain restricts the novel's mimesis to its legal narrative, the text's more melodramatic elements—babies switched in their cradles, mistaken identities, the Italian twins, murder, extortion, blackmail, blackface, and cross-dressing—

are actually quite crucial and significant to his larger realist project: unmasking the fictiveness of race promulgated by slavery. Animated by the cruelties and absurdities of that "peculiar institution," Twain's text spins a tangled web of realism and romance, creating an emotionally gripping narrative that is at once both wildly unbelievable and unbelievably true-to-life, a narrative that is emblematic of a distinctive style of writing that I call "Afro-realism."

What is more, the novel beckons us to contemplate how its antebellum setting also serves as a political metaphor for slavery's long hangover, that is, the persistence of its malicious legacies in the postbellum South. Published during the nadir—a period marked by virulent racism, lynching, segregation, and white supremacy—the book has a plantation plotline that underscores the ironic fact that the legal abrogation of slavery did very little to lift African Americans out of servitude or to improve their social conditions. Neither did it do much to alter most white southerners' ideas about race and the role that African Americans would play in the so-called New South. If anything, it only marked the beginning of a more sinister regime of racial regulation in which the divisions and hierarchies created by slavery would be reified and reaffirmed by Jim Crow—a series of state and local laws enforcing segregation that were constitutionally mandated by the U.S. Supreme Court's landmark "separate but equal" decision in *Plessy v. Ferguson* (1896). Scholars have long since recognized the significance of this history to readings of *Pudd'nhead Wilson,* but they have been regrettably slow to appreciate the aesthetic features and thematic concerns that root the novel in the African American literary tradition.

By urging critics to move beyond narrow definitions of racial identity, this chapter attempts to restore *Pudd'nhead Wilson*'s neglected textual and discursive complexity by examining the plot conventions and narrative strategies that underwrite the novel's critique of slavery as well as its representation of African American life. In doing so, this chapter lays the theoretical foundation for the rest of this book, providing not only radically new ways of understanding African American literature and literary realism but also responding to calls for broader and more historically attuned analyses of blackness and race. In her essay "Are We There Yet? Archives, History, and Specificity in African American Literary Studies,"

Xiomara Santamarina reminds us that "we need to continue to point out the failures of monolithic notions of race, as well as absolutist disavowals of racial power structures within the nation form" (314). As Santamarina proposes, "In a theoretical world where racial identity no longer offers the guarantee of either political effectivity or aesthetic value, historical specificity offers us insights into spatio-temporal configurations and the meanings of racial formations" (314). Put another way, we should continue to develop more expansive frameworks for historicizing race because these heuristics can offer us new insights on how race was constructed and comprehended in a specific time and place, as well as how it operated and continues to operate as a structural phenomenon. The benefit of such an approach is that it gives us a better understanding of the larger social order that constitutes race in America.

Focusing on questions of history and race in *Pudd'nhead Wilson,* I highlight the novel's seemingly anachronistic concern with slavery and its merger of genres past and present as an example of the temporal and textual intricacy that characterizes turn-of-the-twentieth-century African American literature. By exploring the novel's uncanny sense of historical disjuncture and its multiple uses of genre, this chapter examines Twain's elaborate take on the fantasy of racial and literary progress in the postbellum era, an especially fraught period punctuated by the loss of a number of political gains made by African Americans in the aftermath of Emancipation and a renewed national interest in romantic and sentimental fictions about the Old South in an age of literary realism. In the first section, I argue that the novel is a satire of the plantation romance and its racial logic. In the second section, I make the unique claim that the novel challenges that genre's implicit racism by employing strategies from the slave narrative to explore the constructed nature of identity categories—such as race, class, and gender—and even reality itself.[1] In the final section, I focus on the text's murder trial, reading it as a realist critique of the post-Reconstruction racial climate, which in its seeming withdrawal from the notion that identity is fluid ultimately underscores the power of the law to produce and police racial difference by defining race as a fixed, pseudobiological property.

Foregrounding *Pudd'nhead Wilson*'s juxtaposition of romantic and realistic discourses, this chapter works through the many ways Twain manipulates genre to trace the effects of slavery on the cultural and literary imaginations and intervene in the national conversation about race. To be sure, *Pudd'nhead Wilson* rests uncomfortably within a post-Reconstruction milieu that witnessed tremendous social change and conflict over the question of African American emancipation and what it would mean for the South and its racial status quo. Indeed, it is within this transition from slavery to modernity that we see the rise of the plantation tradition during the 1880s and 1890s—a genre of writing comprised mostly of popular literature written by white southerners that romanticized slavery in an attempt to bring back the Old South. According to David Blight, this literature depicted a "world of orderly and happy race relations" to mollify lingering sectional tensions over slavery and reunion (211). It is important to place *Pudd'nhead Wilson* within this context, particularly as a work that lampoons this kind of romantic racism. By focusing on the formal elements that Twain uses to undermine these depictions of plantation life—elements that have origins in antebellum African American literary culture—we are better able to historicize the novel's various strategies for representing race, approaching the work as a medium that does not passively reflect racial anxieties but rather actively works to transform them and bring about social change—so that, as Jacqueline Goldsby has suggested, "rather than read history *into* such literary texts," we can "read history *out* of them" (21).

Accounting for the dynamic interplay between romantic and realistic genres in *Pudd'nhead Wilson,* then, is more than merely an exercise in formalism; it reveals something more systemic about nineteenth-century America and the problems attending racial representation. As William L. Andrews has explained, one of the central characteristics of African American writing is the blending of "romantic-realistic elements" (*To Tell a Free Story* 271). This blending of genres was a necessary tactic for African American writers, who had to navigate a political climate that extolled the virtues of democracy on the one hand but upheld slavery on the other hand. In such an environment, African American writers needed a flexible form that could depict the falsehoods and contradictions that structured their realities. Guided by a similar logic, *Pudd'nhead Wilson* features a comparable blend of realistic and romantic genres to subvert the racist fantasies and mythologies undergirding slavery and African American identity, which is, in my opinion, a compelling reason to view the novel as a work of African American literature. Moreover, as Eric Sundquist has written, "[i]t is not insignificant" that African American authors such as Charles Chesnutt, Pauline Hopkins, James Weldon Johnson, and George Schuyler have all "responded powerfully to *Pudd'nhead Wilson*"—merging melodramatic and mimetic strategies to explore the absurdities and contradictions of race and slavery and their effects on the American and African American psyches (*To Wake the Nations* 226). Such points of convergence demonstrate how African American texts participate in a dialogue with other works, authored by both black and white writers, replying to and revising their themes and plots, and in the process creating a rich tapestry of writings, people, and historical events.

Mark Twain and the Plantation Romance

Often described as a flawed and incoherent text, *Pudd'nhead Wilson*'s seeming lack of aesthetic coherence finds a fitting analogue in the context of the novel's troubled production. When Mark Twain was writing *Pudd'nhead Wilson,* he was in his late fifties and on the brink of financial ruin. In fact, it was in an attempt to reduce his expenses that he established a residence in Florence and, during the novel's composition, traveled from Europe to America as he struggled to shape the long manuscript—which originally contained both the comedy *Those Extraordinary Twins,* and the tragedy *Puddn'head Wilson*—into something publishable. As Hershel Parker has revealed, Twain's process of composition and revision was sloppy and may have been motivated by his desperate need to make money (115–16). Indeed, the infamous "Caesarian operation" that Twain performed to separate the two stories was hastily done, leaving vestiges of conjoined twins and other aesthetic anomalies created by his chaotic and confusing compositional process. As Philip Cohen has explained, these anomalies include Roxy's uneven characterization (which is comical in some places and tragic in others), Chambers's sudden disappearance from the novel (and his brief return at the end), Tom's despair at learning he is a slave in chapter 9 followed by his senseless participation in the riot scene in chapter 11, and Twain's unsustained focus on the novel's "nature versus nurture" debate.[2] These incongruities have led many readers to question the novel's artistic value and the import of its representation of race.

A cursory glance at *Pudd'nhead Wilson*'s reception history shows that reviewers and critics alike have been divided over how to interpret the novel's aesthetic and political project. Shortly after the book was published, William Alden, writing in the *Idler*, praised Twain for his "carefully painted picture" of the "days of slavery," specifically his realistic approach toward characterization, offering that of the men and women in the book, "not one of them is overdrawn or caricatured" (222–23). By contrast, an anonymous reviewer in the *Atheneum* took issue with the novel's elaborate plot, writing that the story "rambles on in an inconsequential way" and that it is "not much credit to Mark Twain's skill as a novelist" (Rev. of *Pudd'nhead Wilson* 83–84). T. M. Parrott called the book "sordid" and "bitter" but praised it for its "ingeniously constructed plot" and "startling climax" (145–54). Bernard De Voto applauded Twain for having the "artistic courage" to write about miscegenation, acknowledging that it was a theme "completely tabooed in nineteenth-century American literature," but he criticized Twain for his portrayal of Roxy, which he believed suffered from too much "melodrama and sentimentality" (293–94). As Philip Goldstein has observed, *Pudd'nhead Wilson* received "mixed reviews" until the 1950s, when Leslie Fiedler hailed it as a masterpiece (8). In 1955, Fiedler wrote that the book was superior to *Huckleberry Finn* because it was "morally . . . one of the most honest books in our literature" (131). Similarly, Langston Hughes wrote, "Mark Twain, in his presentation of Negroes as human beings, stands head and shoulders above the other Southern writers of his time" (328). In sharp contrast to these positive assessments, Hershel Parker famously called the novel "patently unreadable" (136). However, I would argue that this was somewhat misguided and unproductive because it failed to situate the novel in its relevant cultural and historical contexts. More fruitful approaches—such as those by Shelley Fisher Fishkin, John Carlos Rowe, and Eric Sundquist—have interpreted the novel's aesthetic incoherence not as artistic failure but as what Susan Gillman and Forrest G. Robinson have described as "political symptom," that is, as a narrative feature that provides us with a portal into the uncertain and volatile world of post-Reconstruction America, which is reflected in the novel's convoluted plot (Introduction vii).[3]

Pudd'nhead Wilson is set into motion when Roxana (Roxy), a nearly white house slave, switches her baby with her master's baby to quell, once and for all, her fears of having her child sold down the river. Because no one suspects that the babies were exchanged in their cradles, Roxy's deception goes unnoticed for years and the boys grow up according to their environments. The black child, having taken the white one's name, Thomas à Becket Driscoll (Tom), turns into a dishonest scoundrel, whose favorite pastimes include gambling, drinking, and stealing. The white child, assuming the black one's name, Valet de Chambre (Chambers), turns into a submissive young man who speaks in slave dialect. Soon, Tom's penchant for petty crime turns deadly, and in a move to usurp his ill-gotten inheritance, he murders his guardian and alleged uncle, Judge Driscoll. As a result of the townspeople's xenophobia, a pair of Italian twins are wrongfully accused of the crime, and just as they are about to be convicted, a brilliant but dim-witted northern lawyer, David Wilson (Pudd'nhead), discovers the real murderer, using the newfangled science of fingerprinting, which links Tom to the crime and establishes his blackness. In a series of ironic reversals, the twins are exonerated, Chambers is freed from his unlawful slavery and reinstated as the real heir to the Driscoll estate, and Tom, who was originally sentenced to life in prison, is remanded to slavery and sold down the river, on account of the estate's insolvency and his legal status as a slave.

While *Pudd'nhead Wilson* is generally considered to be a lesser novel compared to Twain's more widely recognized magnum opus, *Adventures of Huckleberry Finn* (1885), no literary work of the late nineteenth century better exemplifies the deteriorating state of race relations at century's end. Twain wrote the novel during what Malcolm Bradbury has called his "later, darker period," and as such it reflects "deep, dividing forces of moral strain," which show up in its conflicting "modes and moods of comedy and tragedy," giving the novel an atmosphere of "artistic confusion," "incompleteness," and "ambiguity" (7). In many ways, it serves as a cynical addendum to *Adventures of Huckleberry Finn.* If it can be said that the triumph of *Adventures of Huckleberry Finn* is the crisis of moral agency that culminates in Huck's naïve but well-intentioned decision to "go to hell" for harboring a fugitive slave, then there is no such similar moment in *Pudd'nhead Wilson.* In fact, the sad absurdity of the latter novel's ending—which finds Tom harshly punished more so because he is a slave and less so because he is a murderer—appears to function as a severe censure of the earlier novel's almost childlike vision of racial reconciliation. In this way, the novel represents not only a break from the project that Twain began in *Adventures of Huckleberry Finn* but also a break from the prevailing literary trends of his era, which, driven by a romanticized nostalgia for the antebellum days, depicted slavery as a benevolent institution and the ideal system of social organization for racial harmony.

Whereas Twain satirized this racist outlook, most of his white southern contemporaries defended it by producing plantation fiction that perpetuated the myth of an idyllic Old South. As the historian David R. Goldfield has written: "White southerners elevated defeat into a heroic Lost Cause, their fallen comrades and faltering leaders into saintly figures, their crumbled society into the best place on earth, and their struggle to regain control over their lives and region into a victorious redemption. . . . Transforming defeat in a heroic cause, made more noble by loss than by victory, resolved some of the humiliation white southerners experienced in the years after the war. . . . Recasting the war, they reformulated the Old South" (20). Without question, it is within this context that several of Twain's contemporaries, such as Thomas Nelson Page, Joel Chandler Harris, and Thomas Dixon, produced some of their best-known fiction. As writings like Page's *In Ole Virginia, or Marse Chan and Other Stories* (1887) and *Red Rock: A Chronicle of Reconstruction* (1898); Harris's *Uncle Remus: His Songs and Sayings* (1881); and Dixon's *The Leopard's Spots* (1902) and *The Clansman* (1905) all demonstrate, the plantation romance featured plots, characters, settings, themes, and strategies of racial representation that mythologized the South as a peaceful, well-ordered world of race relations, a place where men were noble and their women virtuous, where slavery was a family affair, where slave masters were paternalistic figures who loved their slaves and treated them well, where the slaves were happy and better off under slavery than they would have been as free people. By the 1880s, this style of writing had become so wildly popular that Albion W. Tourgée, in his well-known essay "The South as a Field for Fiction," declared that American literature was becoming "distinctly Confederate in sympathy" (405).

But as American literature grossly distorted the truth about slavery in the name of national reconciliation, what was forgotten was any sense of the historical and political realities of Reconstruction. A time of dramatic social transformation, the Reconstruction era, which roughly spanned from 1865 to 1877, witnessed the emancipation of former African American slaves and their enfranchisement as equal citizens as well as the tragic overturning of democratic principles and ideals to reinstate the racial status quo of slavery. In many ways, Reconstruction was what W. E. B. Du Bois called a "splendid failure," because it proved, contrary to what many white politicians believed at the time, that African Americans had the capacity to create their own communities, churches, schools, and other civic institutions and participate in the political processes that underwrite democratic citizenship, in spite of white opposition to black rule (*Black Reconstruction* 708). But as African Americans secured the rights of citizenship, southern whites rushed to curtail their freedoms by placing limitations on the Fourteenth and Fifteenth Amendments, obstructing their attempts to enjoy the same protections afforded to whites and to participate in the electoral process by engaging in acts of racial violence and terrorism under the banner of white nationalism. In 1877, the newly elected President Rutherford B. Hayes ordered the withdrawal of federal troops from Louisiana and South Carolina, allowing Democrats to claim control of the state governments. As Eric Foner has explained, this singular act signaled the end of Reconstruction because it effectively announced that the "federal government would no longer intervene to protect either the political prospects of southern Republicans or the constitutional rights of black citizens" (190). For African Americans, this was an incredible betrayal that constituted a broken promise on behalf of the federal government to uphold black citizenship and other freedoms. What made this betrayal all the more reprehensible was that it provided the occasion for the North and the South to reunite on the basis of a shared investment in preserving the nation as a white polity. *Pudd'nhead Wilson* can and should be placed in this context as a work that critiques this history.

While some white writers utilized the representational strategies of plantation fiction to reimagine the Civil War as a heroic Lost Cause, *Pudd'nhead Wilson* demonstrates Twain's alignment with African American writers, such as Frances E. W. Harper, Charles W. Chesnutt, and Pauline Hopkins, all of whom I examine in subsequent chapters, and who through their fiction aimed to contest the plantation tradition's romanticized vision of slavery and the Civil War vis-à-vis literary devices such as irony and satire. As Cathy Boeckmann has compellingly argued, in *Pudd'nhead Wilson,* Twain writes a novel that, at least at the outset, appears to conform to the conventions of the plantation romance but in actuality has merely "borrowed the trappings of a sentimental genre" to submit that genre to scrutiny (107). While I agree with Boeckmann's contention that the novel's satire of the plantation romance is driven by "the assumptions about character and visual assessment contained within that genre," I believe that the novel's satire is propelled by a more general sense of contradiction and disjuncture caused by slavery and the persistence of its legacies (106). This shows up in the novel's tangle of history and genre. Not only does its satirical rendering of the past paradoxically point to the continuities between slavery and Jim Crow by underlining the ways in which the 1890s resemble the 1830s–1850s (the time span the novel chronicles), but the novel's bizarre blend of the melodramatic and the mimetic creates a cognitive gap between the romanticized and the real that throws into high relief the falsehoods at the center of southern life.

From the novel's perspective, the greatest falsehood of all is the idea that slavery was some kind of quaint and blissful institution. Right from the start of the novel, Twain sets out to unmask this myth by pulling back the veneer of civility on which the plantation romance depended in order to present an idyllic portrait of southern life. In the first few paragraphs, Twain points to the use of this façade as a strategy of representation:

> The scene of this chronicle is the town of Dawson's Landing, on the Missouri side of the Mississippi. . . .
>
> In 1830 it was a snug little collection of modest one- and two-story frame dwellings. . . . Each of these pretty homes had a garden in front fenced with white palings and opulently stocked with holly-hocks, marigolds, touch-me-nots, prince's feathers and other old-fashioned flowers. . . . [When there was a cat] that home was complete, and its contentment and peace were made manifest to the world by this symbol, whose testimony is infallible. A home without a cat—and a well fed, well petted, and properly revered cat—may be a perfect home, perhaps, but how can it prove its title? (3)

In crafting this Edenic portrait, Twain calls attention to the plantation romance's use of setting as an index of morality and its misrepresentation of slavery as a pastoral paradise. In Twain's view, this kind of distorted representation is a fallacy because it does not follow that slavery is as charming as "pretty homes" and "holly-hocks" simply because its violence is concealed by a beautiful exterior. As such, this lengthy description should be read sarcastically, as it mocks the genre's shallow use of symbolism and introduces the novel's larger concern with the discrepancies between appearance and reality.

The episode that introduces the Yankee outsider, David Wilson, echoes this critique of the dangers of accepting things at face value. Wilson is described as a "homely, freckled, sandy-haired young fellow, with an intelligent blue eye" (5). But when Wilson states that he wished he owned half of a barking dog so that he could kill his half, the townspeople fail to realize that his ironic comment is a riddle, of sorts, and they brand him a fool:

> "I wish I owned half of that dog."
> "Why?" somebody asked.
> "Because, I would kill my half."
> The group searched his face with curiosity, with anxiety even, but found no light there, no expression that they could read. They fell away from him as from something uncanny, and went in privacy to discuss him. One said—
> "'Pears to be a fool."
> "'Pears?" said another. "*Is,* I reckon you better say." (6)

Instead of searching for the deeper meaning behind Wilson's words, the townspeople search his face for something more concrete. Finding "no expression that they could read," they determine that he is not very bright. But as it turns out, the townspeople are the real fools because they are too literal to understand how Wilson's comments actually rebuke them for their complicity with slavery and the flawed logic that underwrites its racial divisions and hierarchies. As Wilson rightly intuits, the idea of owning half a dog and killing it is an illogical proposition that underscores the fundamental irrationality of slavery. Such illogicality is best expressed in a clause like the "Three-Fifths Compromise," a controversial agreement between North and South that allowed southern slaveholding states to count three-fifths of their slave populations for the purpose of determining representation and taxation. Of course, the central paradox was that slaves were not considered citizens but "chattel personal," that is, movable property, and under slave law they could not participate in political life. More devastatingly, their owners could treat them with impunity, even if that meant killing them. In this way, Wilson's ironic remark about killing half a dog is really a commentary on slavery, as it implicitly questions the rationale and ethics behind owning a human being, getting extra congressional representation for them but denying them political power, and killing them without having to face legal consequences.

Twain follows this up with the introduction of Roxy into the narrative, which is equally ironic as it underscores the incongruity between her physical appearance and her status as a slave. Roxy is presented from Wilson's point of view as he eavesdrops on a conversation taking place outside his window but out of his immediate line of vision. It is significant that Wilson hears her before he sees her because once she is finally rendered visible to him, he perceives a sharp contrast between how she sounds and how she looks: "From Roxy's manner of speech, a stranger would have expected her to be black, but she was not. Only one-sixteenth of her was black, and that sixteenth did not show" (9). Through this initial description, Twain highlights Roxy's racial invisibility while also mocking the flawed logic of racial fractions—gesturing back to Wilson's earlier remarks about killing half a dog. In the more elaborate description of Roxy that ensues, Twain plays with the concepts of racial illegibility and identity as performance:

> She was of majestic form and stature, her attitudes were imposing and statuesque, and her gestures and movements distinguished by a noble and stately grace. Her complexion was very fair, with the rosy glow of vigorous health in the cheeks, her face was full of character and expression, her eyes were brown and liquid, and she had a heavy suit of fine soft hair which was also brown, but the fact was not apparent because her head was bound about with a checkered handkerchief and the hair was concealed under it. Her face was shapely, intelligent, and comely—even

> beautiful. She had an easy, independent carriage—when she was among her own caste—and a high and "sassy" way, withal; but of course she was meek and humble enough where white people were. (9)

Roxy, obviously, does not look very black, and her carriage and demeanor are not what we would expect of a slave. Her "sassy" way around her own people suggests that she has absorbed the racism of her environment and believes herself to be superior to other blacks because she is nearly white in appearance. That she deliberately alters her haughty behavior around white people underscores her awareness of the social expectations that bound her and demonstrates her ability to perform the role of a meek slave. In this way, the passage makes the provocative suggestion that identity is not simply a matter of that which is visible or invisible, but that it is also a matter of environmental forces and deliberate self-fashioning.

Through these early passages of physical description, Twain builds the foundation for both the novel's plot and its satire of the plantation romance's strategies of racial representation. If visual cues are not reliable indicators of racial identity, then the guarantees of physical appearance are not enough to prevent identity from being deliberately manipulated. Furthermore, the concept of an innate, fixed racial identity based on blood loses its force when race is invisible. Indeed, what makes the melodramatic switched-baby plot possible is the fact that the babies look exactly alike and cannot be distinguished by any physical traits. As the narrator tells us, Roxy's baby "had blue eyes and flaxen curls, like his white comrade," and the only way that the father of the white child was able to tell them apart was by their clothes, as the white child wore a "ruffled soft muslin and a coral necklace, while the other wore merely a coarse tow-linen shirt which barely reached his knees, and no jewelry" (9). That the children must rely on clothing as symbolic markers of their different racial and social positions would appear to undermine the relevancy of the one-drop rule. As the novel seems to ask, What meaning can we really attribute to blood if some people can change their race by simply changing their clothes?

Interestingly, it is this question that sets the changeling plot into motion. Afraid that Percy Driscoll will ultimately sell her child down the river, Roxy concocts a plan to rescue him from the auction block. Taking advantage of the uncanny resemblance between Driscoll's baby and her own, she exchanges the children in their cradles:

> She began to move about like one in a dream. She undressed Thomas à Becket, stripping him of everything, and put the tow-linen shirt on him. She put his coral necklace on her own child's neck. Then she placed the children side by side, and after earnest inspection she muttered—
>
> "Now who would b'lieve clo'es could do de like o' dat? Dog my cats if it ain't all I kin do to tell t'other fum which, let alone his pappy." (15–16)

Changing the boys' clothing, and thus their identities, Roxy realizes that signs can easily be detached from their referents and manipulated to signify something else, and by switching the boys around, she refutes the mythology of innate racial difference, making her child the "usurping heir" to the Driscoll estate and the real heir a slave.

Although Roxy feels guilty about her actions, she takes comfort, ironically enough, in the notion of divine election. Recalling a sermon in which a black preacher uses the example of a servant switching babies with a queen to explain how God arbitrarily bestows the articles of grace, Roxy reasons that she is justified in exchanging the babies because "*white* folks has done it" too (16). Conjuring the critique of religion found in many slave narratives, Roxy points to the hypocrisy embedded in the fabric of the slave system and decides to manipulate Christian rhetoric to her favor. Pointing to God's providence, she concludes that he can save "anybody He please, saint or sinner" and determines that her decision "ain't no sin" (16). As Sally Ann Ferguson has explained, slavery engendered this kind of deliberate exploitation of Christian dogma, as slave masters used the idea of salvation vis-à-vis Christ's sacrifice to exculpate themselves from the sins of slavery.[4] For Roxy, such theological maneuvering not only functions as a form of resistance, but it also enables her to justify stealing back the very child that slavery stole from her without disqualifying herself from God's forgiveness.

In Roxy's retelling of the preacher's story, the changeling plot is embedded into a complex critique of race, class, and gender under slavery. By turning to a convention of romantic and sentimental fiction, she not only endows herself with greater importance and control over her circumstances, but she also challenges the dominant power structure:

> De preacher said it was jist like dey done in Englan' one time, long time ago. De queen she lef' her baby layin' aroun' one day, en went out callin'; en one o' de niggers roun' 'bout de place dat was mos' white, she come in en see de chile layin' aroun', en tuck en put her own chile's clo'es on de queen's chile, en put de queen's chile's clo'es on her own chile, en den lef' her own chile layin' aroun' en tuck en toted de queen's chile home to de nigger quarter, en nobody ever foun' it out, en her chile was de king, bimeby, en sole de queen's chile down de river one time when dey had to settle up de estate. (16–17)

Identifying with the mostly white servant, but envious of the queen's maternity and social status, Roxy decides to re-create, and thus imitate, this scene of racial theft. She appears to absolve the servant of any wrongdoing by placing the blame on the negligent queen who "lef' her baby layin' aroun'" because she expected the "niggers" to tend to him. And while this shifting of guilt evades the issue of the servant's unethical behavior, it also raises important questions about the morality of owning a human being in the first place and treating him or her like property. In the grand scheme of things, Roxy's theft ultimately registers as a petty crime in comparison to the wholesale theft of African people and the slave trade.

Reversing the terms of enslavement, then, Roxy authors a new fiction to replace the one that has rendered her and her child powerless against the forces of slavery. Reclaiming her stolen maternity, she turns this fiction into reality by calling the "real heir 'Chambers' and the usurping little slave 'Thomas à Becket,' shortening his name to 'Tom,' for daily use" (18–19). Of course, this subversive exchange of racial identities corresponds with an immediate inversion of class, as the boys' respective names suggest. For example, *valet de chamber* was the name given to royal servants during the Middle Ages, and Thomas à Becket was the archbishop of Canterbury. The obvious allusions to medieval culture are intended to be ironic, given the narrative's antebellum context and its southern setting. But the irony goes beyond mere anachronism, as the allusions to medieval culture also work to establish a connection between feudalism and slavery by highlighting the implicit racism and classism that animates the South's obsession with the medieval past and its social divisions and hierarchies. In this way, Twain echoes an argument he made in *Life on the Mississippi,* where he linked southern racism and the preoccupation with caste to bad fiction, commenting, "Sir Walter [Scott] had so large a hand in making Southern character before the war, that he is in great measure responsible for the war" (375–76).

Similarly, Roxy also comes to learn the power of fiction to influence human behavior, almost immediately changing her conduct toward the boys after the cradle switch. Even though she knows the truth about their real identities, she is nevertheless startled to "see how steadily and surely the awe which had kept her tongue reverent and her manner humble toward her young master was transferring itself to her speech and manner toward the usurper, and how similarly handy she was becoming in her motherly curtness of speech and peremptoriness of manner to the unlucky heir of the ancient house of Driscoll" (17). Pointing to an implicit paradox at the center of her masquerade, Roxy touches on the novel's famous "nature versus nurture" debate.[5] It is important to note that Twain believed that nurture was the greater determinant of human behavior, and as such, he thought that identity was the product of acquired or learned characteristics and not the result of innate properties or heredity. Interestingly, for Twain, nurture was a flexible term that included environment, experience, exposure to certain behaviors, conditioning, and habits—all of which he grouped under the name of "training." Consider the following maxim from Pudd'nhead Wilson's Calendar: "Training is everything. The peach was once a bitter almond; cauliflower is nothing but cabbage with a college education" (25). Read in this context, Roxy's involuntary replication of the master-slave paradigm is a consequence of her having been trained to act the part of subservient slave rather than an expression of an allegedly inherited racial meekness.

Although Roxy switches the babies to have greater control over her own life as well as her child's, her actions have the ironic effect of turning her own baby into her master. For Evan Carton, this becomes proof that Roxy has been conditioned to comply with slavery, positing that "her attempt to save one twin by dooming the other reiterates the structure and illusion of the society it challenges" (86). But I would argue that if we think about Roxy's feelings of powerlessness as the motivating factor in her decision to save her child, then her act becomes one of agency as opposed to complicity. From this vantage point, Roxy's choice can be understood not as a reiteration of the white power structure but as an attack on its foundations—as a form of resistance against a system that denies her maternity by denying her humanity. Through this subversive act, Roxy learns that there is no innate trait that makes one a master or a slave. Rather, the fictions of law and custom infuse these artificial designations with their cultural meanings. Acknowledging, then, that there is no organic link between race and behavior or character, the text implies that any differences between the races have more to do with training than with blood.

As such, the text shows how the "twinned" black and white babies develop very different personalities as a result of training. As a result of his privileged position, Tom becomes a spoiled brat almost overnight. Indeed, "from the very beginning of his usurpation" he learns how to manipulate people and events to get what he wants (19). He throws tantrums, begs for things only to throw them away, and openly defies authority. Despite his bad behavior, all of his demands are met. However, this incessant coddling is not without its drawbacks. As a result of all the petting he receives, Tom turns into a "sickly," "fractious," and "overbearing" child. Chambers, on the other hand, develops into a strong, "meek and docile" child (20). Although Tom tests his patience on more than one occasion, he learns that simply "bearing it" is better than fighting back (21). Indeed, after one particular incident in which Chambers does lash out at his "little master," his own father, who doesn't know it, gives him three "convincing canings," discouraging him from ever standing up for himself again (21). Not surprisingly, he learns to take "Tom's cruelties in all humility" (21). The explanation for the striking differences between the boys is simple. Far from being a matter of racial proclivities, the reason lies in their divergent upbringings.

But for Myra Jehlen, training alone does not provide a compelling explanation for why Tom turns out to be such a diabolical master. She argues that Tom comes across as more evil than the white slave masters, whom, she believes, Twain depicts as a "decent lot, . . . absurd in their chivalric poses . . . but on the whole men of integrity" (108). According to Jehlen, if we are to believe that Tom has been corrupted by his slaveholding environment and the racist training it provided, then the obvious question is, Why is Tom more debased than his fellow slave masters? (108). As Jehlen explains, the novel does not directly answer this question, but its historical context and Twain's own racism might, as Tom's depiction may have more to do with post-Reconstruction racial politics (for example, the beginnings of Jim Crow in the South) and Twain's ambivalence about racial justice (his reluctance or incapacity to create a character who would more aggressively challenge the racial status quo).[6]

Putting aside the issue of Twain's ambivalence, which has been well documented but is, in my estimation, largely irrelevant because it assigns too much meaning to biographical matters and Twain's intentions, I believe that we must understand Tom's depiction, and to a larger extent the novel itself, as a satire of race and its fictitious ideologies.[7] We must remember that it is but a fiction of law and custom that makes Tom black and that in actuality he is mostly white, thirty-one parts, to be more precise, as the novel sarcastically puts it. And as for the novel's white elites, Twain makes it clear that not only does he find their "chivalric poses" comical, but far from being "men of integrity," he suggests that they are adulterers and rapists, as it was most likely several generations of miscegenation that produced people as white as Roxy and Tom. Furthermore, it would be a mistake to associate Tom's bad behavior with his so-called black blood, considering that the novel mocks the practice of configuring race and identity in relationship to blood. The truth of the matter is that Tom is the product of a predominately white culture that condones lying, cheating, and stealing but hides behind a veneer of nobility—institutions like Yale and the First Families of Virginia. Ultimately, Tom's deplorable depiction is not so much a matter of Twain's reluctance or incapacity to imagine a less racist world, as much as it is a matter of southern culture's.

Through irony and satire, *Pudd'nhead Wilson* interrogates some of the nineteenth-century's most problematic assumptions about race and genre. At its core, the novel is interested in challenging the plantation romance's strategies for depicting slavery as an idyllic and virtuous institution as well as representing racial identity. To do both, Twain situates his narrative in a generic framework that will allow him to exploit the instabilities of ostensibly fixed moral and biological categories. While the plantation romance provides the connection between that which is made visible and that which is concealed or denied in slave culture, Twain discredits the merits of this surface-depth model by subjecting the genre to dark-comedic scrutiny. In Twain's hands, the plantation romance's use of racial symbolism is shown to be an absurdly illogical and inaccurate way of transmitting knowledge about slavery. Indeed, we can no sooner deduce that slavery was some kind of well-ordered, righteous utopia because of its outward appeals to gentility and honor than we can kill half a dog. And neither can we believe that one drop of black blood makes a person black, and thus racially inferior, in spite of that person's obviously dominant and visible white ancestry. In this way, the text reveals how the plantation romance's strategies of representation ultimately serve to defend the institution of slavery against charges of inhumanity, validate theories of racial difference, and perpetuate white supremacy. By exposing these strategies as false and unsound, the novel attempts to disrupt not only the genre's aesthetic principles but also the racial and political ideologies that underwrite them.

Slavery and the Fictions of Identity

At the center of *Pudd'nhead Wilson* is a problem of epistemology and reality underwritten by slavery. What I mean by this is that slavery created a number of cultural paradoxes—the mulatto, human chattel, and the slave master who is also father—that necessitated the development of cultural fictions like the one-drop rule, legal strictures classifying slaves as property, and *partus sequitur ventrem* (the child follows the condition of the mother) to suppress the realities of enslavement. From its farcical introduction, in which Twain assures us that the legal chapters are 100 percent accurate, to Roxy's melodramatic exchange of the black and white babies, to its tragic ending in which Tom Driscoll is sold down the river to settle the debts on the estate, the novel asks: What is the basis of knowledge and truth in a slaveholding society? And how can we trust the information that it produces? As part of its realist project, the novel is concerned with exploring these questions from a philosophical perspective—not in an effort to establish a singular, objective reality or to merely reflect the difficulties attending the work of racial representation but more so to interrogate the larger system of identity categories underwritten by slavery. As the novel meditates on the problem of knowledge in a slave society, it gradually reveals that much of what we think is real is actually a construction, if not an outright illusion.

No other genre in all of American fiction has demonstrated the startling accuracy of this phenomenon with greater acuteness and depth than the African American slave narrative. As Ellen M. Weinauer has observed, slave narratives "play on the distinction between what is real and what is apparent" because they are "interested in exploring the very idea of the 'real'—of where the boundary between appearance and reality collapses" (46). In classic nineteenth-century slave narratives, this often takes the shape of narrators deploying cross-dressing, blackface, and disguise as tropes that not only facilitate the slave's passage from captivity to freedom but that also work to unsettle seemingly settled notions of truth by denaturalizing ostensibly naturalized identity categories such as race and gender.[8] For example, in William Wells Brown's *Clotel* (1853), the eponymous heroine dons drag, appearing to be a white slave master, to bring about her escape. In William and Ellen Crafts's *Running a Thousand Miles for Freedom* (1860), which is considered by many to portray one of the most dramatic and elaborate examples of cross-dressing, Ellen passes for a white man while her husband pretends to be her slave. In *Incidents in the Life of a Slave Girl* (1861), Harriet Jacobs uses both the cross-dressing and blackface devices, disguising herself as a sailor and blackening her face with charcoal during her first escape. In all of these narratives, the use of these tropes functions as a transgressive narrative strategy that attempts to undermine the institution of slavery and the categories that support it. As slave narrators assume the clothing of the opposite sex and pass for white/black, they demonstrate the ease with which some mixed-race African Americans can manipulate identity and reality, thereby invalidating the idea that race, class, and gender are fixed characteristics that can be read on the body's exterior. Paradoxically, the illusions that they create are, in some instances, truer than the truth, suggesting that identity is not really a matter of bodily essences at all but something that turns on the specular and performative.

Like African American writers, Twain uses the tropes of cross-dressing, blackface, and disguise, more generally (which includes the concept of the imitation and the hidden racial self) to explore the complicated nature of identity and the idea of passing. As Twain suggests, identity encompasses a variety of phenomena, including the ocular, the performative, habits, training, and the assumptions that others make about the physical body. This comes through most clearly in Roxy and Tom's respective experiments with passing. For Roxy, the use of cross-dressing, blackface, and disguise facilitate her escape from slavery, but for Tom they become devices that enable him to avoid detection while engaging in robbery and murder. Despite their different moral objectives, Roxy's and Tom's experiments with passing complicate our understanding of what makes a person black or white, male or female, master or slave, law-abiding or criminal. As Roxy and Tom illustrate, passing is not about the adoption of a fraudulent identity or the rejection of a so-called true self; rather, passing is, as Elaine K. Ginsberg has explained, "about the boundaries established between identity categories and about the individual and cultural anxieties induced by boundary crossing . . . the visible and the invisible, the seen and the unseen" (2). By examining the construction of identity in relationship to passing, then, *Pudd'nhead Wilson* throws into question widely held ideas about the authentic and essential self.

Significantly, the most famous instance of cross-dressing in *Pudd'nhead Wilson* appears shortly after the switch that reverses Tom's and Chambers's racial identities, doubly underscoring the malleability of identity. While walking past his window, Wilson spots a mysterious woman in Tom Driscoll's bedroom. Unbeknownst to Wilson and to the reader, it is none other than Tom himself, dressed in drag to conceal his identity in preparation for an upcoming robbery. But what we see is a woman adorned with the traditional accoutrements of femininity: "The girl had on a neat and trim summer dress patterned in broad stripes of pink and white, and her bonnet was equipped with a pink veil. She was practicing steps, gaits and attitudes, apparently; she was doing the thing gracefully, and was very much absorbed in her work. Who could she be, and how came she to be in young Tom Driscoll's room?" (36). Building on the novel's critique of the arbitrary relationship between visual signs and their referents, the passage reveals that external markers are not always a reliable method for reading identity. In this case, gender, like race in certain instances, can be manipulated by adopting certain culturally agreed-upon conventions and behavioral norms. In having Tom wear a "pink and white" dress as he practices the "steps, gaits and attitudes" of a woman, the passage suggests that far from being a naturalized fact of our existence, gender is something that we do as opposed to something that we are.

Twain extends his critique about the malleability of identity in the novel's "imitation nigger" sequence, further exploring the complicated relationship between appearance and reality. In this provocative exchange, Chambers tells Roxy that the judge has threatened to "dissenhurrit" Tom (39). Angered by the challenge that this poses to her plans to extort money from him, Roxy exclaims: "Take it back, you misable imitation nigger dat I bore in sorrow en tribbilation" (39). In casting Chambers as an "imitation nigger," Roxy acknowledges that Chambers is not really black, at least as society would have it, being that he was actually born to white parents—making her use of the word "bore," which is the past tense of the verb "to bear," as in to give birth to, all the more ironic—and that she switched him at birth with Tom. In this way, Roxy's remark functions as an insult that likens Chambers to an imposter, suggesting that he possesses degraded value because he is a fraudulent imitation merely pretending to be her real son, Tom, who also happens to be really black, according to the one-drop rule. Amused by her remarks, Chambers replies: "If I's imitation, what is you? Bofe of us is imitation *white*—dat's what we is—en pow'full good imitation too. . . . We don't 'mount to noth'n as imitation *niggers*" (39). In referring to himself and Roxy as "imitation white," Chambers implicitly reminds Roxy that neither one of them looks very black and that it is only a fiction of law and custom that makes them so. Moreover, he rightly acknowledges that as "imitation whites" they both possess far more worth than they ever would as "imitation niggers," owing to the racial value system that privileges whiteness and downgrades blackness—raising the obvious question, What is the significance of racial authenticity if race cannot always be perceived and one can pass him- or herself off as the real thing?

Notwithstanding its awareness of the fluidity of identity, the text concedes that the grip of rigid racial thinking can be rather obstinate, if not completely impossible, to break. For example, when Tom learns the so-called truth about his racial identity, he cries:

> A nigger!—I am a nigger!—oh, I wish I was dead!
>
> Why were niggers *and* whites made? What crime did the uncreated first nigger commit that the curse of birth was decreed for him? And why is this awful difference made between white and black? . . . How hard the nigger's fate seems, this morning!—yet until last night such a thought never entered my head. (48)

Tom's lament draws an important distinction between black and white that functions to deconstruct the cultural meanings assigned to these racial designations. As Tom starts to truly contemplate what it means to be black, he wishes for death, which underscores the Afro-pessimist argument that the ontological condition of blackness is marked by "fungibility," that is, the capacity of the black body to be exchanged like a commodity, and a lack of subjectivity, or what many scholars have described as "social death," drawing from Orlando Patterson.[9] Ultimately, Tom comes to understand how blackness, in the context of slavery, functions as an inescapable natal liability and psychological burden about which white people never have to think.

Although Tom manages to escape growing up in slavery, his depression over his recently discovered blackness illustrates the extent to which he has unconsciously assimilated the bigotry of his environment and submitted to the social conventions governing racial protocol. After he learns the truth about his ancestry, he immediately changes his behavior. Terrified that others would spot his hidden racial stain and detect his real racial identity, the so-called "'nigger' in him went shrinking and skulking here and there and yonder, and fancying it saw suspicion and maybe detection in all faces, tones, and gestures" (49). Similarly, he "dreaded his meals; the 'nigger' in him was ashamed to sit at the white folks' table . . . and once when Judge Driscoll said, 'What's the matter with you?—you look as meek as a nigger,' he felt as secret murderers are said to feel when the accuser says 'Thou art the man!'" (49). Here, Twain invites us to hear Tom's inner thoughts, which reveal that he has come to think of himself as a "nigger" in both mind and body, without ever questioning the constructed nature of the term or acknowledging that he is, for the most part, still the same person he has always been.

This is why Tom eventually returns to his former persona as a white man—because he has not really changed. Once the initial shock of discovery wears off, Tom "drop[s] gradually back into his old frivolous and easy-going ways, and conditions of feeling, and manner of speech" (50). Although "his opinions were totally changed"—with regard to his uncle and slavery, owing to his fear of being sold at any moment—the "main structure of his character was not changed, and could not be changed" (50). The novel's point here would seem to be that racial fictions are inculcated by the powers of training. As a result of his cultural conditioning, Tom can never really stop being white because it is how he has been taught to think of himself. Although it is a fiction, it is ironically truer than the truth of his blackness. This is not to say that his true identity is consistent with his heredity, and thus reify a fixed conception of racial identity, but rather that he has been conditioned to behave and think in a certain way, as a result of his upbringing, and that his training in the ways of whiteness actually trumps the truth about his ancestry or his so-called black blood.

In *Pudd'nhead Wilson,* the conceptualization of race as blood is an ill-conceived fiction spread by bad training. In a much-debated passage, Roxy chastises Tom for refusing to accept Luigi's challenge of a duel. "It's de nigger in you," she cries, "dat's what it is. Thirty-one parts o' you is white, en on'y one part nigger, en dat po' little one part is yo' *soul*" (75). For many critics, this passage serves to reinforce the very racial distinctions that the novel sets out to undermine.[10] Yet, I would argue that the passage really illustrates the potency of racial thinking. In this way, Roxy's attribution of Tom's cowardly behavior to his African American ancestry is not necessarily indicative of the text's flawed and failed racial politics but rather of her culture's beliefs in the ostensible abjectness of blackness.[11] As it turns out, the novel's stance on identity is not as confusing as critics have traditionally believed. While essentialist economies of race and gender are presented alongside more fluid paradigms, the novel suggests that the latter provide the more compelling accounts of identity and that fixed accounts of personhood merely attempt to regulate social divisions and hierarchies.

In *Pudd'nhead Wilson,* the tropes of cross-dressing, blackface, and disguise boldly subvert the validity of essentialist epistemologies. Consider the following scene when Roxy confronts Tom for selling her down the river, appearing before him with a soot-blackened face and dressed in men's clothing:

> Tom found his door in the dark, and entered it and turned up the gas. When he faced about, lightly whistling, he saw the back of a man. The man was closing and locking his door for him. His whistle faded out and he felt uneasy. The man turned around, a wreck of shabby old clothes sodden with rain and all a-drip, and showed a black face under an old slouch hat. Tom was frightened. He tried to order the man out, but the words refused to come, and the other man got the start. He said, in a low voice—
>
> "Keep still—I's yo' mother!" (90)

What is significant about this passage is the way in which it sheds light on the phantasmagoric nature of how we experience race and racism. The imagery that is invoked here is dark and foreboding, obliquely conjuring pejorative ideas about black masculinity. But far from reinforcing these notions, the novel is interested in undermining them by suggesting that they are in effect cultural illusions with no basis in the body; rather, they have origins in the recesses of our individual and collective racial imaginary. Once Tom realizes that the man with the "black face" wearing "shabby old clothes" is none other than his own mother, it becomes clear that some of our most basic ideas about race and blackness are actually cultural projections fueled by fear and fantasy.

In the companion piece to this dramatic act, the novel further develops its critique of the fictions of identity by exploring the notion that character is the product of conditioning—not racial inheritance. Here, the novel shifts its focus back to Tom, whom we find in his bedroom, making preparations for another robbery. This time the target is Judge Driscoll, the man Tom has been raised to believe is his uncle. In this dramatic tableau, Tom grabs his "suit of girl's clothes from under the male attire" in his trunk—but does not put it on—and proceeds to "black[en] his face with a burnt cork" (99). Unsurprisingly, the robbery does not go according to plan. Just as Tom almost seizes the pile of bank notes, Driscoll grabs him and cries for help. Frightened, Tom stabs him with the twins' Indian knife and runs, dropping the knife and the cash. Once he reaches his bedroom, he throws on "his suit of girl's clothes, drop[s] the veil, [blows] out his light . . . [and] descend[s] the back stairs" (100). There is no denying, of course, that Twain's decision to have Tom rob his uncle in blackface, rendering visible his invisible blackness, reifies racist stereotypes about black male criminality. Similarly, Tom's use of the twins' knife not only implicates them in the murder but also introduces the racist logic of xenophobia into the plot, pointing to myths about Italian savagery and the so-called "born criminal." These racialized discourses are in fact relevant to any reading of the passage, and when we consider that Tom flees the scene of the crime in women's clothing, they highlight a stark contrast between how society views black and immigrant men and how it views women, rarely seeing the latter as perpetrators of violent crime. But rather than reinforce these perspectives, the novel mocks them, suggesting that Tom's murderous behavior is really a function of his poor upbringing among the plantation elite. Slavery has debased him. In fact, prior to his death, Driscoll insinuated as much, exclaiming: "[Tom] is worthless and unworthy, but it is largely my fault. . . . I have indulged him to his hurt, instead of training him up severely and making a man of him" (72). In doing so, Driscoll rejects popular beliefs about blood and its bearing on racial character to create a conception of identity that privileges the role that social conditioning plays in the construction of the self.

From a theoretical standpoint, then, *Pudd'nhead Wilson* entreats us to interrogate some of our most basic and deeply held assumptions about identity. Surely, if identity categories can be so easily manipulated, then we have to ask ourselves, What is the real meaning of social divisions and hierarchies? Exploiting the tensions between male and female, black and white, master and slave, the novel issues a complex statement about the slipperiness of these binaries and the shaky foundation upon which they stand. Moving beyond questions of personhood, *Pudd'nhead Wilson* opens up its critique of the constructed nature of identity to explore the construction of reality itself. Roxy and Tom's multiple masquerades not only redefine our sense of what's real or true, but they also stretch the boundaries of narrative possibility. There is a way in which their experiments with cross-dressing, blackface, and disguise enact broader textual transformations that occur at the level of genre and plot. The romantic farce that plays out in exchanged babies, mistaken identities, blackmail, and murder culminates in a realistic tragedy, morphing from an outlandish satire to a dark murder mystery, with the Yankee outsider, David Wilson, starring as detective, attorney, and scientist. As the drama turns on Wilson's ability to unravel the murder-mystery plot, the action shifts from the Driscoll household to the courthouse to underscore the role that the law plays in the discursive production of race and reality.

Natal Signatures: Race and Realism

In its closing chapters, *Pudd'nhead Wilson* merges the discourses of science and law, taking on the characteristics of a detective novel, a popular form whose preoccupation with questions of investigation and veracity mirrors realism's fixation with facts. The main action centers on resolving the mystery as to who killed Judge Driscoll. The Italian twins are falsely accused of murder, and Wilson agrees to defend them. As the trial begins, Wilson discovers that the twins' fingerprints do not match those left on the knife, and thus the technology of fingerprinting emerges as the evidentiary method by which the real murderer will be discovered. Arguably, the most fascinating aspect of the fingerprint plot is the way in which it reintroduces an essentialist account of identity that is lodged in the body. For many critics, this becomes especially problematic when the issue of race comes into play, given that both nineteenth-century science and the law often aligned blackness with criminal behavior.

Indeed, the nineteenth century witnessed the development of criminal anthropology, a pseudoscientific discourse that espoused the view that criminality was an inherited trait and that certain races were genetically predisposed to deviant behaviors. Widely considered to be the father of modern criminology, Cesare Lombroso, an Italian physician and criminologist, advanced the theory of the "born criminal," which dominated discussions about the origins of criminal behavior in Europe and in America during the late nineteenth and early twentieth centuries. Influenced by Darwin's theory of evolution, specifically the idea that certain species were more evolved than others, Lombroso popularized the idea that the criminal represented an atavistic species whose behavior was the result of primitive and inferior physiology, which in turn made him or her engage in savage acts. Drawing from developments in physiognomy, another pseudoscientific discourse, Lombroso argued that criminals could be identified by certain physical defects of their face, for example: small beady eyes, big noses, smaller skulls, large jaws, and prominent brow ridges and indentations at the back of the skull like apes. After experimenting on a variety of human subjects, Lombroso published his findings in *Criminal Man* (1876), a work so influential that it was published five times during Lombroso's lifetime.[12] Despite the fact that Lombroso's theories were completely devoid of scientific merit, his ideas shaped attitudes and beliefs about racial character, thereby contributing to the era's prevailing ideas about African American inferiority. Considering his interest in popular theories about heredity and human behavior, Twain would have undoubtedly been familiar with Lombroso's work.

As Michael Rogin has revealed, Twain was also fascinated by the newly emergent science of fingerprinting, which was developed by the eugenicist Francis Galton. While composing *Pudd'nhead Wilson* in 1892, Twain read Galton's book *Finger Prints,* which was published that same year. According to Rogin, the significance of this connection cannot be overstated, as it bears directly on the novel's racial critique. Although fingerprints "establish individual rather than racial difference," as Rogin is careful to point out, he insists that their appearance in the novel's trial sequence is no accident in light of the popularity of scientific racism (78). For Rogin, the trouble with fingerprinting is that it is tangled up in Galton's failed mission to prove that physiological features could be used to denote racial character. Because the revelation that Tom is the murderer corresponds with the revelation that he is also black, Rogin deduces that "[f]ingerprints defeat Galton because they cannot establish racial and characterological difference; they defeat Mark Twain because they can" (80). For Rogin, then, the fingerprinting plot ultimately undercuts the novel's racial progressivism, as it reifies the racially fixed model of identity on which slavery was based, regrettably supplanting the more mutable paradigm the novel creates through what he calls "storytelling and play" (84). In this way, Rogin concludes that the novel "reinstates slavery and racial difference" and ends in retreat and failure (81). But I would argue that *Pudd'nhead Wilson*'s ending does not back-pedal from its assertion that race is socially constructed, and neither does it weaken the novel's larger critique of racism. Rather, it points to the contradictory nature of race as both a socially determined category and a pseudobiological phenomenon.

As we have seen, this contradiction is at the very heart of life in the fictional world of Dawson's Landing, which, ironically enough, bears a striking resemblance to the real world of post-Reconstruction America. In the years after the Civil War, free African Americans would find themselves figuratively reenslaved and sold down the river, like Tom, as a result of a series of legislative acts that curtailed, or in some cases revoked altogether, the rights gained through the passage of the Civil War Amendments and the Civil Rights Act in 1866.[13] Although slavery was technically over, it was reenacted with greater fervor and violence vis-à-vis Jim Crow, which legally sanctioned not only segregation but also new forms of racial oppression: sharecropping, the convict-labor system, mob rule and lynching, and voter suppression. Predicated on the premise that segregation was necessary to preserve white supremacy and racial purity, Jim Crow laws also worked to adjudicate notions of racial difference that drew their force from the rhetoric of blood, heredity, and innate racial characteristics and instincts. One of the most controversial examples of such racial adjudication was *Plessy v. Ferguson,* where the Court upheld the constitutionality of a Louisiana state law that enforced racial segregation in public facilities as well as the practice of defining race in terms of blood and ancestry. In the language of the Court, Homer Plessy's "one-eighth African blood" was "not discernible in him," but it was within the jurisdiction of the states—not the federal government—to determine the "proportion of colored blood necessary to constitute a colored person" (*Plessy v. Ferguson* 42, 51). If we read *Pudd'nhead Wilson* in this context, then the novel's bitter ending is not a concession to the notion of race as a fixed, biological property but rather a reflection of how the judicial system employed such notions to construct and maintain racial divisions and hierarchies—in effect, making them real in an empirical way.

Consider Wilson's court presentation on the inalterability of the fingerprint. Before he presents the direct evidence that will expose Tom as the murderer, he delivers testimony on the witness stand, and thus under oath, that has the strange effect of authenticating the legal narrative that follows, lending it an additional layer of veracity. Because the prosecution has determined that it will try to convict the twins using circumstantial evidence, Wilson sets out to discredit the speculative account of the murder by turning to the epistemology of the body:

> Every human being carries with him from his cradle to his grave certain physical marks which do not change their character, and by which he can always be identified—and that without shade of doubt or question. These marks are his signature, his physiological autograph, so to speak, and this autograph cannot be counterfeited, nor can he disguise it or hide it away, nor can it become illegible by the wear and the mutations of time. This signature is not his face—age can change that beyond recognition; it is not his hair, for that can fall out; it is not his height, for duplicates of that exist; it is not his form, for duplicates of that exist, also, whereas this signature is each man's very own—there is no duplicate of it among the swarming populations of the globe! (114)

Interestingly, Wilson describes the fingerprint as a scriptive mark that is comparable to an individual's autograph or signature. Unlike most forms of documentation, the fingerprint cannot be replicated, making it one of the most authentic indicators of identity. Because most bodily characteristics change with time and are prevalent among the general population, Wilson deduces that the fingerprint is an unchanging truth—a fixed, physiological feature. While it may seem rather suspect on Twain's part to make the fingerprint the scientific technology that will expose Tom as a murderer, and a black man to boot, these aesthetic choices are not at all inconsistent with the historical reality of race in American jurisprudence. The novel's seemingly racist ending would seem to suggest that it is par for the course.

The fingerprint evidence does not prove that Tom is black so much as it proves that the laws governing racial identity are just as ridiculous as the confusing legal acrobatics that he goes through to convince the jury that baby A "was put into B's cradle in the nursery," making B "a negro and a slave" and A "a usurper" (118–19). In reality, Wilson's so-called direct evidence is not really direct at all. In actuality, it is the most interpretive and subjective kind there is, as an expert reading of the fingerprint relies upon a visual methodology susceptible to error and only as meaningful as the law makes it. Indeed, as Susan Gillman has explained: "Fingerprints appear to be the one measure of unique, noncontingent individual identity, but are in practice relational indices that must be read in and against the context of other sets of prints. . . . [F]ingerprints tell us nothing

. . . significant about either A or B as individuals, much less about the lives of 'Chambers' or 'Tom.' What they prove, in fact, is that one can be interchangeably 'white and free' and 'a negro and a slave'" ("Sure Identifiers" 99). In this way, Wilson's appeal to the indexical logic of the fingerprint does not lead to a transcendent, fixed, biological account of identity; rather, it points toward the ways in which identity categories are socially determined and legally enforced.

Moreover, Wilson's reading of the print can only make sense in a legal system that attaches racial meaning to physiological signs, thereby naturalizing the relationship between external and internal traits. No moment better illustrates this than the dramatic scene in which Wilson names Tom as the murderer:

> "The murderer of your friend and mine—York Driscoll, of the generous hand and the kindly spirit—sits among you. Valet de Chambre, negro and slave—falsely called Thomas à Becket Driscoll—make upon the window the finger-prints that will hang you!"
>
> Tom turned his ashen face imploringly toward the speaker, made some impotent movements with his white lips, then slid limp and lifeless to the floor.
>
> Wilson broke the awed silence with the words—
>
> "There is no need. He has confessed." (119–20)

Applying the same indexical logic that he uses to decipher the fingerprint, Wilson reads Tom's "ashen face" and "limp" "lifeless" fall to the floor as signs that point to his guilt, invoking the doctrine of *res ipsa loquitur* (the thing speaks for itself). These gestures might appear to be incriminating or self-evident, as Wilson seems to think they are, but in fact his reading is purely subjective. In the final analysis, Wilson gets as much wrong as he gets right. Tom is the murderer, but his face and faint do not prove it. The rationale by which Wilson establishes Tom's guilt is not direct, but interpretive. Only in a legal system where black criminality is viewed as an a priori truth can Tom confess without so much as saying a word. Even more ironic than this, however, is the loophole that nullifies his original sentence of life in prison by granting the creditors permission to remand him to slavery to settle the debts on the Driscoll estate, clearly highlighting the cruel absurdity of a legal system that punishes a man more harshly for being black than for committing murder.

If *Pudd'nhead Wilson* appears to end in failure, then it may have more to do with the failures of Reconstruction and race relations, more generally, than with Twain's aesthetic choices or political beliefs. There is no denying that the novel's final pages challenge the fluid critique of identity that structures the first three-quarters. However, I would argue that the novel urges us to consider the ways in which this departure from a more malleable conception of race only underscores what so many postbellum writings make overwhelmingly clear: the legal abrogation of slavery did not eradicate the racial divisions and hierarchies that supported the system; rather, it reinforced them vis-à-vis scientific, legal, and cultural fictions. In many respects, the novel's return to the logic of racial essentialism illustrates this very paradox, which also happens to be an organizing feature of the narrative. As we have seen, this is a novel fraught with tension. From its very first page, it enacts competing impulses toward romance and realism, tragedy and farce, disclosure and secrecy. Its ending is no different. The novel's resolution does not really resolve anything at all. In one turn, it reveals a bitter truth of race, and in another it almost suppresses it. And yet the bitter note on which the novel seems to end does not diminish the force of its racial critique. If anything, it makes it all the more powerful, as it depicts with alarming precision the preposterousness of the laws governing racial identity. Although Wilson's victory appears to overshadow Tom's misfortune, and perhaps to a certain extent, the novel's antiracist message, there is a way in which Tom's tragedy is also Wilson's. In the end, neither one of them is really free. Wilson turns out to be a slave to convention, while convention turns Tom into a slave. Finally, then, what this ostensibly incomprehensible narrative may make all the more comprehensible is that there is no essential, stable truth about race; it is as Stuart Hall has described it, a "floating signifier," and its logic is not indexical so much as it is interchangeable, like the infamous cradle-switch that made the black baby white and white baby black.[14]

Perhaps it is fair to conclude, then, that *Pudd'nhead Wilson*'s seemingly incoherent and flawed portrait of race and slavery may be more coherent and masterful than what critics have generally recognized. Buried in its tangle of realism and romance is an implicit understanding that the truth about race and slavery in America really is stranger than fiction. In many ways, the novel's outlandish plot reflects the outlandishness of slavery. By adapting and transforming certain mimetic and melodramatic conventions and strategies from African American writing, the novel crafts a version of realism that is uniquely suited to explore the fictiveness of race and slavery as well as the devastatingly real consequences of mythologies of racial difference. In exposing the absurdities, falsehoods, and contradictions at the center of southern life, the novel not only undermines the plantation romance's flat, one-dimensional, romanticized representation of slavery, but it condemns the larger society for what it had done and was still in the process of doing to African Americans at the time of the novel's publication. In this regard, the novel successfully fuses issues of aesthetic representation with the imperatives of racial equality. By focusing on the convergences between slavery and Jim Crow, the novel poses a fundamental question about the incompatibility of racism with democracy and social progress, a problem that black and white writers would continue to grapple with as the nineteenth century drew to a close.

2

Reimagining the Tragic Mulatta in Frances E. W. Harper's *Iola Leroy*

In Frances E. W. Harper's novel *Iola Leroy* (1892), a nearly white mulatta rejects her white doctor-suitor's marriage proposal on the grounds that their union might produce dark-skinned offspring who cannot pass for white. Iola suggests that not only is this a real possibility but that it also frustrates the romantic assumption that love conquers all:

> "Doctor," she said, and a faint flush rose to her cheek, "suppose we should marry, and little children in after years should nestle in our arms, and one of them show unmistakable signs of color, would you be satisfied?"
>
> She looked steadfastly into his eyes, which fell beneath her truth-seeking gaze. His face flushed as if the question had suddenly perplexed him. . . .
>
> "Ah I see," she said, "that you are puzzled. You had not taken into account what might result from such a marriage. I will relieve you from all embarrassment by simply saying I cannot be your wife. . . . I have resolved never to marry until I have found my mother. . . .
>
> There was a deep shadow of sorrow and disappointment on the face of Dr. Gresham as he rose to leave. . . . No quivering of her lip or paling of her cheek betrayed any struggle of her heart. Her resolve was made, and his words were powerless to swerve her from the purpose of her soul. (90)

In this pivotal exchange, Iola raises the specter of atavism to test Gresham's affection for her so as to determine if his love would endure the weight of public scrutiny. That his eyes fall under the pressure of her "truth-seeking gaze" implies that it would not. For Iola, Gresham's reticence confirms her doubts about interracial marriage. Although the doctor's face is full of "sorrow and disappointment," Iola remains firm in her decision to decline his offer and resolves to never marry until she finds her mother. This statement symbolizes her desire to preserve her African American heritage. Of course, once she does, she marries a mulatto physician, Dr. Frank Latimer, and the two go down to the South, dedicating their lives to elevating their people. As epitomized in this scene, *Iola Leroy*'s unique form of Afro-realism utilizes the logic of sentimentalism—with its emphasis on heightened emotions and domestic concerns such as courtship, marriage, and family—to underscore the importance of black matrimony and kinship to the social project of racial uplift. In the process of doing so, the novel dramatically rewrites the tragic mulatta trope and her narrative end, resulting in a more autonomous female figure and a dynamic critique of racial representation in American fiction.

In terms of literary history, Iola's justification for rejecting Gresham and her subsequent narrative trajectory constitute a significant break from the prevailing aesthetic paradigms of the nineteenth century and point to a crisis of representation in post-Reconstruction American fiction. As a stock figure in the romantic and sentimental traditions, the tragic mulatta was an outdated, melodramatic caricature in great need of revision. Dating back to the earliest antislavery novels, Richard Hildreth's *The Slave, or Memoirs of Archy Moore* (1836), Harriet Beecher Stowe's wildly successful *Uncle Tom's Cabin* (1852), and Dion Boucicault's *The Octoroon, or Life in Louisiana* (1859), the tragic mulatta was almost always portrayed as the beautiful victim of her own perverse breeding. What made her tragic was the curious set of reversals that usually led to the discovery of her so-called dreaded one drop, her subsequent remandment to slavery, and her broken engagement to a white man, who almost always abandoned her after learning about her alleged racial stain, leaving her to commit suicide or to die of a broken heart.[1] In the wake of Emancipation, such representations not only seemed archaic, but they also problematically rearticulated the racist ideologies and power structures of slavery. For black postbellum writers, the tragic mulatta trope, as it existed in its antebellum iteration, was an inadequate construct for depicting contemporary life on the color line or for addressing pressing issues of racial justice in an era of shifting social dynamics and emergent black political power. As African Americans struggled to achieve greater autonomy, African American writers sought to create more empowered and self-actualized characters who could better represent the race's fitness for the rights of full citizenship as well as dramatize the racial obstacles barring them from obtaining and enjoying democratic freedoms.[2]

In *Iola Leroy,* Harper achieves this by reimagining the tragic mulatta of sentimental fiction in more realistic and politically conscious ways. By juxtaposing the melodramatic elements of this trope—the moment of racial discovery, the ill-fated interracial romance, and the concept of self-sacrifice (that is, the sentimental expectation that the mulatta must relinquish her white lover once she learns the truth about her blood)—with realistic accounts of slavery, Reconstruction, black folk culture, and the black middle class, the novel fashions a more sentimental form of Afro-realism that endows the mulatta with greater narrative purpose and substance. This generic merger gives Harper the representational power to portray the mulatta as a more fully realized character who finds salvation in her black ancestry and in the black community. In doing so, Harper aims to validate blackness and to inspire black solidarity, without alienating potentially supportive white readers. With this in mind, Harper deploys the figure of the mulatta as "a device of mediation," as Hazel V. Carby has described it—one that enables white readers to identify with the mulatta and sympathize with her plight, and thus by extension, the plight of all African Americans (*Reconstructing Womanhood* 89). So rather than discarding sentimental affect in her realist revision, Harper reconfigures it to portray the American racial crisis as an intense emotional affair so as to highlight the real effects of racial injustice on the individual, the family unit, and society. In this way, the novel focuses on interiority—human emotions, conduct, and morality—while also offering a more realistic approach to characterization, narrative description, and the difficult task of developing viable solutions to the race problem.

The confluence of literary and political goals in *Iola Leroy* demands that when assessing the novel's aesthetic merits or its cultural work, we should pay particularly close attention to the ways in which the novel adopts and adapts certain aspects of mainstream literary fiction to create its own vision for black writing and racial justice. *Iola Leroy* is striking in this regard because it mobilizes the tension between realism and romance to endow the stock figure of the tragic mulatta with greater agency, thereby critiquing and expanding the narrowly drawn parameters of black female subjectivity in nineteenth-century fiction. For Harper, the mulatta provided an opportunity to challenge the era's prevailing myths about racial identity, discrediting specious claims about black racial inferiority and the related idea that intermarriage would solve the race problem. Although Harper successfully undercuts these views by having her mulatta reject her white love interest and marry a fellow mulatto instead, there are some clear limitations to her project, as it does not completely dismantle racial distinctions as much as it simply reverses the logic that gives them meaning—changing the mulatta from a sad, self-loathing woman to a fierce racial activist. Nevertheless, by not killing off her mulatta and giving her the power to choose her own narrative end, vis-à-vis marriage and work, Harper offers a provocative portrait of a legally black woman who, of her own volition, consents to cast her lot with one of her own kind rather than avail herself of the opportunity to marry outside the race, pass for white, and enjoy greater social mobility. Harper's narrative choice not only aims to make this option look less attractive, but it also deliberately goes against the grain of tragic mulatta fiction to push back on narrow definitions of blackness and black identity.

In what follows, I argue that *Iola Leroy* should be read as a critical intervention that helped pave the way for more complex and more realistic depictions of mixed-race black women in American fiction. To properly assess the merits of *Iola Leroy*'s deconstruction of race, readers would do better to historicize and contextualize Harper's bold and transgressive narrative choices in relationship to the literary trends and the politics of her day. Regrettably, this kind of nuance is missing from analyses of the novel's various uses of genre, which has had the effect of simplifying or dismissing Harper's challenges to the literary establishment and to the racial order. In my reading of *Iola Leroy,* I aim to recuperate an understanding of the novel's groundbreaking deviation from the dominant discourses surrounding race and racial representation in nineteenth-century fiction, with the specific goal of highlighting its formal and political complexity and unsettling traditional approaches to canon formation and criticism in literary studies.

Critics have either condemned the novel for pandering to white readers or lauded it as a forward-thinking attempt to elevate the black image in popular fiction.[3] For example, Houston Baker famously excoriated *Iola Leroy* for its valorization of mulattoes, its idealized portrayal of the black middle class, and its condescending attitude toward the black poor. As Baker explained, the problem with the novel is that "characters do not act, they talk. . . . What emerges from their polemics . . . is an essentially conservative appeal to white public opinion" (*Workings of the Spirit* 32) over the course of its "endless pages of exposition . . . lofty sentiment . . . and entirely predictable plot" (31). Taking issue with Carby's reading of the mulatta as a figure of mediation, Baker posited that the mulatta figure was an "implicit approval of white patriarchy" that privileged Anglo standards of beauty (25). In a more flattering appraisal, Mary Helen Washington defended black woman writers, such as Harper, who, in her words, "wrote under great pressures: to a white audience whose tastes were honed by the sentimental novel and whose conceptions of blacks were shaped by *Uncle Tom's Cabin;* to a limited black audience who desperately needed positive black role models; and to an audience whose notions of female propriety and female inferiority made it nearly impossible to imagine a complex woman character" (75). While clearly differing in their sentiments, Baker's and Washington's remarks point to a larger problem of interpretation in studies on black postbellum fiction, underlining the difficulties scholars have had in assessing the aesthetic and political efficacy of these works. As Baker's comments indicate, the dominant interpretive models that scholars have most consistently used to make sense of this fiction have been inadequate and ahistorical, often resulting in facile analyses that erect the authentic/inauthentic racial binary, which, as Frances Smith Foster and Kim D. Green have explained, presupposes that "authentic" African American literature "genuflects to the gods of Ancient Africa" and is "instructive, motivational, and mimetic," whereas "inauthentic" literature "portrays racial ambivalence, Anglophilic aspirations, and insufficient subversion or protest of values routinely attributed to American mainstream culture" ("Ports of Call" 47). To advance a new reading of *Iola Leroy* that moves beyond this binary, I examine how Harper weaves from the "threads of fact and fiction" a narrative that transforms the tragic mulatta trope from a melodramatic plot device, rooted in racial fantasy and scientific racism, to a symbol of black women's political significance in the race's larger struggle to achieve respectability and rights (*Iola Leroy* 215).

An Imperative Revision

One year before *Iola Leroy* appeared, William Dean Howells published a short race novel with a very similar plot. Published serially in *Harper's New Monthly* magazine in 1891, *An Imperative Duty* tells the story of an ostensibly white woman named Rhoda Aldgate who discovers that she is 1/16th black and has a hysterical breakdown of melodramatic proportions. But in keeping with Howells's realist agenda, Rhoda is not hysterical for long. Dr. Olney, a specialist in nervous conditions and the text's resident realist and voice of scientific reason, soon falls in love with her and proposes marriage. Rhoda accepts Olney's proposal, and in the end, they move to Italy, where she passes for Italian and they presumably live happily ever after. Implicit in the novel's plotline is an understanding that marriage is an inherently political act with major implications for race and national identity. This tacit awareness can readily be seen in the novel's sarcastic critique of "duty." In Howells's novel, duty refers to white people's cultural obligation to preserve racial purity by policing the boundaries of sexual desire. For example, the novel's central conflict revolves around Rhoda's aunt, Mrs. Meredith, who feels that it is her moral duty to tell her niece's white suitors the truth about Rhoda's blood. But Olney, Howells's realist talking head, mostly makes fun of Mrs. Meredith's racial anxieties and dismisses her fears about atavism, declaring the older woman a "morbid sentimentalist with a hypochondriacal conscience" (67). Through it all, Olney retains his cool, analytical composure. He falls in love with Rhoda after he learns the truth about her blood and determines that he will marry her despite her aunt's ridiculous fears of racial reversion. In this sense, *An Imperative Duty* deconstructs pseudoscientific notions of race at the same time that it endorses realism as the more racially progressive genre.

For all his boasting about literary realism's superiority over other forms, it comes as no surprise that Howells would take up the tragic mulatta trope, and, as Edwin Cady put it, "let the romantic steam out of" it (159). For Howells, such romantic rubbish needed to be discarded or rewritten from the realist's point of view. Because Howells was fluent and fascinated with popular race theories such as atavism and hypodescent—theories the scientific community of his day vehemently debated—this latter option was most appealing. Though regarded as taboo or distasteful, tragic mulatta fiction presented Howells with an opportunity to revise some of the romantic and sentimental traditions' racial theorems, as well as some of its most tedious narrative conventions. If the tragic mulatta's representation suffered from an excess of womanly emotion and sentiment, Howells no doubt believed that scientific objectivism and masculine proprietorship of a female-dominated genre would improve depictions of mixed-race women in fiction. As Debra J. Rosenthal has written, in *An Imperative Duty,* Howells discovered a way to "bang about" the "babes of Romance," challenging and rewriting "their romantic worldview from his realist's perspective" (496).[4]

Despite Howells's earnest belief in his ability to revise the tragic mulatta trope and undermine dominant notions of race, the novel does not provide a definitive, clear-cut statement about the meaning of race or the ideal solution to the race problem in America. In fact, critics are largely divided on whether or not Rhoda emerges as an autonomous female character and the degree to which the novel succeeds in debunking the very discourses of romantic racialism and racist science that it seeks to unsettle. Most troubling for critics is the novel's seemingly absent social-political program, its gratuitous use of racial stereotypes and clichés (which are in my opinion mostly sarcastic), and its ending, which finds the interracial couple married and living abroad in Italy, where Rhoda "is thought to look so very Italian that you would really take her for" one (121).

In what could be classified as an evasive, utopian dénouement, Olney establishes a medical practice, the couple makes friends, and they both agree to keep her racial identity a secret. In this sense, Howells does free the mulatta from the generic imperatives that would have resulted in her death or abandonment; however, he does so by robbing her of her culture, her history, and her identity. In choosing to expatriate to Italy and keep her mixed racial ancestry a secret, Rhoda loses both her American and African American heritage and settles for a life lived behind the mask. Such an ending demands that we ask a few questions: Does the novel's conclusion suggest that Howells cannot conceive of interracial marriage in the United States? Why is there no mention of the couple having children? Might this imply that Howells was unable to countenance the idea of mixed-race children who might look black? Finally, why have the couple flee the United States for Italy, leaving the problem of antimiscegenation laws for successive generations to solve?

Despite the novel's reluctance to answer these questions, it would be a mistake to condemn it because of its problematic ending or to dismiss its racial critique, which is praiseworthy for its bold attempt to undermine racial stereotypes and theories about African Americans as well as defend interracial marriage. As Paul R. Petrie has reminded us, contemporary critics tend to forget that when Howells published *An Imperative Duty,* "he was both courting controversy and taking a serious professional risk" (9). The celebrated novelist and editor was a highly influential arbiter of critical and popular taste in American literary and cultural circles. In writing a novel that challenged prevailing ideas about racial difference and intermarriage, Howells stood to not only incite the ire of his peers but to also lose the support of his readership. Logically, we must acknowledge that by nineteenth-century standards, *An Imperative Duty* was not just "decidedly liberal," as Petrie has described it, but that it was really quite radical (18).

For Howells, the challenge for democracy was racial justice for African Americans, the true test of which hung on their ability to enjoy the same civil rights as whites and be treated as equals. *An Imperative Duty* attempts to theorize what this will entail in the context of interracial marriage, viewing it as the ultimate battleground between civil liberties and restrictions on human rights. That Rhoda and Olney do not stay in America to work this out but flee to Italy reveals Howells's doubts about America's readiness and willingness to address its race problem on any large, national scale involving public policy. Thus, the novel tries to do this kind of progressive cultural work within the private realm of romantic love. And while Howells seems to believe, as Michele Elam has argued, "that mutual silence . . . ensures that miscegenation will 'not infringe on the rights of others' . . . and that private contracts *fulfill* public responsibility, that [Rhoda and Olney's] *marriage* is racial uplift," the novel does make the progressive and pragmatic claim that individuals can tackle racism in meaningful ways in their everyday lives through personal choice and in their private relationships (*Race, Work, and Desire* 70). In terms of genre, the novel also acknowledges that revisions to conventions of racial representation can also do the important work of moral and social reform.

Certainly, in taking up the question of African American representation, vis-à-vis the tragic mulatta trope, Howells honed in on a subject about which some would say he had no authority to write because of his whiteness. Anna Julia Cooper, perhaps one of Howells's toughest critics, so much as said so in her review of the novel when she asserted that Howells "does not know what he is talking about. . . . [The novel] lacks the earnestness and bias of a special pleader. . . . [He] merely meant to press the button. . . . The Kodak does no more; it cannot . . . solve problems" (201). While Cooper's suggestion about the role of personal experience with regard to imaginative writing is not without its merits, as lived experience is an invaluable source of cultural knowledge, her comments inaccurately liken Howells's realism to the reproductive technology of the camera. Because the camera can only reflect an image, and not reconstruct it, such a comparison misses the mark when we consider how much of Howells's revision is focused on changing the way we conceive of the mulatta and race. Furthermore, her critique seems to suggest that Howells could not possibly have had anything meaningful to say about race because he was not black. This assumption, rooted in ideas about racial authenticity, is at the center of many criticisms of the novel and ignores the book's representation of race altogether. In fact, I would argue that Howells's whiteness gave him a special insight into the inner workings of antiblackness in the white imagination. Who better than a privileged white man would comprehend white bigotry? But the real question is not whether Howells had the authority to write about race but whether his whiteness must invariably undermine the force of the novel's racial critique.

To be fair, *An Imperative Duty* does not attempt to really reproduce the external racial world as much as it tries to deconstruct it from a realistic perspective and in deliberate fashion—a feature that is characteristic of much turn-of-the-twentieth-century African American literature. W. E. B. Du Bois acknowledged as much in his review when he wrote: "[Howells] has not hesitated to be truthful. . . . With lies and twistings most Americans seek to ignore the mighty and portentous shadow. . . . But Howells

. . . faced our national foolishness and shuffling and evasion" ("Howells and Black Folk" 338). For Du Bois, that Howells was even willing to tackle the highly controversial topic of interracial marriage in a realistic way was a literary and a social accomplishment—one that belonged to African Americans and white Americans. In sharp contrast to Cooper, Du Bois was able to see the aesthetic and political value of *An Imperative Duty* because he was more concerned with Howells's representation of race and his realist strategies than with the question of Howells's racial identity or his racial authority. In this way, Du Bois affirmed the power of imaginative texts to transcend their authorship, engage in the work of social critique, and traffic in a wider sphere of cultural influence.

Accordingly, the remarkable similarities between *An Imperative Duty* and *Iola Leroy* compel us to reconsider the criteria by which we determine what locates a work within the African American literary tradition as well as the conventional wisdom about literary production. As M. Giulia Fabi has noted, "Although there seems to be no currently available evidence that Harper and Howells knew each other or wrote about each other's work, their parallel revisions of the popular literary trope of the (tragic) mulatta are to be read as part of the process of reciprocal artistic invention that links black and white writers of the nineteenth century" ("Reconstructing" 48–49). By bringing these kinds of interracial literary genealogies into greater relief, we can create an alternative literary history that acknowledges that literary production does not occur in racially segregated silos but rather that it is inspired by a variety of factors and influences, and that literary works freely circulate in a discursive and symbolic field. Moreover, by examining the generic innovations by which African American writers approached the work of racial representation, we can trace how they engaged with dominant literary practices and how they altered them to reflect and articulate their own unique needs. In this regard, we can better assess and appreciate how Harper took up and transformed certain aspects of Howellsian realism, romantic and sentimental genres, and how she understood the relationship between literature and the social world.

When Frances E. W. Harper published *Iola Leroy,* she was sixty-seven years old and had already established herself as an activist, essayist, orator, and poet. Her literary contributions included two volumes of poetry,

Forest Leaves (1845) and *Poems on Miscellaneous Subjects* (1854); multiple speeches, which were reported in the *Boston Journal* and the *Baltimore Sun;* and more than a dozen short stories, including "The Two Offers" (1859), which appeared in the *Anglo African Magazine* and is considered by literary scholars to be the first short story published by an African American woman. In 1869, she published *Moses: A Story of the Nile,* a lengthy retelling of the story of Moses from the Old Testament, which served as an allegory of sorts for African American political leadership and racial solidarity. Between 1869 and 1889, Harper published three serialized novels in the *Christian Recorder: Minnie's Sacrifice* (1869); *Sowing and Reaping: A Temperance Story* (1877); and *Trial and Triumph* (1888–89), all of which were rediscovered and republished by Frances Smith Foster in 1994. Committed to the *Christian Recorder*'s mission, which, as Eric Gardner has described it, entailed "facilitat[ing] diverse political and theological commentary, highlight[ing] the struggles of newly freed African Americans in the South, and assert[ing] an important place for literature in black political and cultural life," Harper viewed the periodical's political platform as an expression of her own ideological position on the question of African American enfranchisement and spiritual development (56).

Also during this time, Harper increasingly turned her attention to social justice work, as she labored to develop and defend various civic organizations designed to procure and protect African American rights and freedoms. As Harper engaged in this more direct form of social work, she also utilized her imaginative writing as a platform to address the most pressing issues facing her post-Reconstruction African American audience, such as the legacies of slavery, the need for racial uplift, suffrage, family, temperance, religion, education, community organizing and outreach, and morality. *Iola Leroy* reflects the intersection of Harper's social and literary activities. It is also her most famous and best-known work, reflecting her philosophy about the ideal merger of art and activism. Indeed, as Hollis Robbins has noted, "Harper believed that a book was needed to inspire a new generation of blacks to commit to ethical and intellectual leadership" (Introduction xx). And as Harper herself explained in a note at the end of the novel, her objective in writing the book was to inspire African Americans to "embrace every opportunity, develop every faculty, and use every power God has given them to rise in the scale of character and condition, and add their quota of good citizenship to the best welfare of the nation" (215).

The significance of *Iola Leroy* cannot be overstated, as the novel represents both a critical and a commercial victory for African American literature. As Frances Smith Foster has observed, *Iola Leroy*, "while not the first [novel] by an African American woman, did firmly establish the novel as a viable genre in African American literature. And in modifying the depiction of the tragic mulatto and introducing heroic folk characters into the written African American literary tradition, her work paved the way for the later, very popular fiction of Charles Chesnutt" (Introduction 4). Arguably, Harper was able to achieve such visibility in the novel and alter the direction of black representation because she strategically negotiated the expectations of her black and white readership, using the mulatta as both a facilitator of sympathetic identification with whites and as a symbol of black progress. This may explain the novel's success with readers and reviewers alike. As Koritha Mitchell has noted, *Iola Leroy* was so popular and sold so well that it was "reprinted four times in four years" ("Why Americans Know Frederick Douglass but Not Frances Harper"). According to Mitchell, as a "bound book" *Iola Leroy* was far more likely to "land in the hands of non-black readers as well as those who might avoid religious outlets," and in this way, the novel "benefited the race by targeting the widest possible audience *while maintaining* a community-centered perspective (Introduction 14).

While readers no doubt appreciated the novel's entertaining mixture of melodramatic and realistic elements, reviewers often praised the novel for its historical and sociological value. For example, the *Christian Recorder* commended the novel for its "credible" representation of slavery and Reconstruction but criticized it for looking backward, proclaiming that "[w]e live and fight for the future, rather than the past" (Rev. of *Iola Leroy*). The *Nation* wrote: "The present generation can hardly be reminded too often of what slavery was, that they may better understand what emancipation is, and what reconstruction should be. 'Iola Leroy' tells again the shameful story, and brings the scene through the war days into the time of higher education and professional callings for the colored people. . . . The book derives added interest from being written from an inside point of view by one of the race, long known as an ardent worker in the cause of her people" (Rev. of *Iola Leroy* 146–47). Similarly, the *Friends' Review* noted: "Whil[e] this book is classed as fiction, it is so full of historical facts" and unlike "its distinguished predecessor, *Uncle Tom's Cabin,* it does not give the hideous details of those evils, now so happily relegated to the past, and it is, on the whole, pleasant reading" (Rev. of *Iola Leroy* 758). Clearly concerned with the promise of emancipation and the evolution of the race, such present- and future-oriented reviews encourage us to appreciate *Iola Leroy* as a document of a post-Reconstruction America in transition.

In spite of persistent racial oppression, violence, and limited political power, the post-Reconstruction period was for African American writers a time of possibility and innovation. Although African Americans continued to grapple with the effects of slavery, the race also embraced notions of progress as many activists and intellectuals advocated for racial reform and racial justice vis-à-vis civic and political engagement as well as through imaginative writing. Indeed, *Iola Leroy* rests within this history and is part of a genealogy of African American novels from this period that sought to bring about greater political representation by addressing issues of racial representation in fiction. To counter charges of racial inferiority and unfitness for the rights of citizenship, African American writers produced novels, like *Iola Leroy,* that, in Claudia Tate's words, focused on issues of domesticity, for example, "courtship, marriage, and family formation," to highlight the race's "moral development, spiritual maturation, professional aspirations, and economic advancement" (4, 11). In this vein, *Iola Leroy* gave rise to Charles W. Chesnutt's *The House behind the Cedars* (1900); Pauline Hopkins's *Contending Forces* (1900); James Weldon Johnson's *Autobiography of an Ex-Coloured Man* (1912); and the "New Negro" ethos of Nella Larsen's *Quicksand* (1928) and *Passing* (1929), initiating a second revival of the African American novel, a form that was created forty years earlier with the publication of William Wells Brown's *Clotel* (1853). As all of these novels demonstrate, after Reconstruction, African American writers became increasingly concerned with the weight of the slave past and the prospect of moving past it so as to imagine themselves as full citizens in an egalitarian society.

But as a cursory glance at the American scene in the early 1890s makes clear, American society was undergoing rapid and extensive changes that gave African Americans hope but also pause about the future. Embodying the contradictory impulses of the Gilded Age and the Progressive Era, American culture showed signs of upward mobility and social decay. In the year that *Iola Leroy* appeared, the *Baltimore Afro-American* newspaper published its first issue, beginning what would become its long tenure as an important vessel for racial justice in Baltimore and eventually on the national level. In the Upper New York Bay, Ellis Island opened its doors to new immigrants from Europe, giving the "tired," "poor," and "huddled masses yearning to breathe free" an opportunity to achieve the American Dream (Lazarus, "New Colossus"). In the business world, Andrew Carnegie distinguished himself among the new tycoons, buying out competing steel companies and creating a monopoly with the formation of Carnegie Steel—giving additional power to the proverbial "bootstrap myth" inculcated by Horatio Alger's wildly popular novel *Ragged Dick* (1868). If these events symbolized the successes of democracy, then other events in 1892 would point to its failures. In Nashville, Tennessee, Ephraim Grizzard was lynched in front of a mob of more than ten thousand people on suspicion of having had sexual relations with a white woman—a horrific act of white supremacist violence that would become a national epidemic in the years after Grizzard's murder. In Louisiana, Homer Plessy was arrested for sitting in a whites-only train car, precipitating the chain of events that would culminate in *Plessy v. Ferguson* (1896). Reflecting Harper's concern with racial reform and black empowerment, *Iola Leroy* embodies the ethos of this transformative period in American culture and is, in this regard, similar to other social-problem novels of the era, including Mark Twain's *The Gilded Age* (1873) and *Huckleberry Finn* (1885); William Dean Howells's *The Rise of Silas Lapham* (1885) and *A Hazard of New Fortunes* (1890); Jacob Riis's *How the Other Half Lives* (1890); Stephen Crane's *Maggie: A Girl of the Streets* (1893); Frank Norris's *McTeague* (1899); Booker T. Washington's *Up from Slavery* (1901); W. E. B. Du Bois's *The Souls of Black Folk* (1903); Upton Sinclair's *The Jungle* (1906); and Edith Wharton's *The House of Mirth* (1905).

More specifically, *Iola Leroy*'s preoccupation with the question of interracial marriage also reflects the era's hysteria over miscegenation and efforts to adjudicate sexual conduct. During the late nineteenth century, most states had antimiscegenation laws in their constitutions. According to such prohibitions, not only were interracial marriages considered null and void, but couples who were found guilty of breaking the laws were subject to heavy fines or imprisonment—not to mention extralegal violence. In the landmark U.S. Supreme Court decision *Pace v. State of Alabama* (1883), the Court upheld the constitutionality of Alabama's interracial marriage ban, thus sanctioning racial discrimination thirteen years before *Plessy v. Ferguson.* The case involved Tony Pace, an African American man, and Mary Cox, a white woman, both of whom were arrested in 1881 for violating Alabama's antimiscegenation law. Although they were not married, the state indicted them for "living together in a state of adultery or fornication" and sentenced them to two years' imprisonment in the state penitentiary (*Pace v. State of Alabama*). On appeal to the Alabama Supreme Court, Pace argued that the law under which he was indicted and convicted was unconstitutional because it violated the final clause of the first section of the Fourteenth Amendment of the U.S. Constitution, which asserts that no state shall "deny to any person within its jurisdiction the equal protection of the laws" (U.S. Const. amend. XIV, § 1). However, the Alabama Supreme Court upheld the conviction. On further appeal to the U.S. Supreme Court, the Court ruled that Alabama's prohibition against interracial marriage did not conflict with the "equal protection clause" of the Fourteenth Amendment because the law punished blacks and whites in equal measure for committing the crime of engaging in interracial sex. In this way, the Court affirmed notions of racial difference as well as its right to intrude in the private affairs of citizens. *Iola Leroy* must also be placed in this context and viewed as critique of the laws banning interracial marriage. Although it stops short of condoning such unions, preferring to advocate for intragroup marriage and black self-determination instead, the novel employs the trope of mixed marriage to refute theories of black racial inferiority and to provide a counter-representation to the racist depictions of African Americans that had dominated American fiction since the antebellum days.

Shadows Uplifted

Focusing on the situation of the black family in the aftermath of slavery, viewing it as a metaphor for racial equality and social possibility in the United States, *Iola Leroy* is a historical and an imaginative work that contemplates the question of what it means to be an African American in the domestic and national spheres during the late nineteenth century. The novel opens on the eve of the Civil War and closes in the midst of the post-Emancipation era, chronicling its heroine's journey from racial unawareness to the discovery of her black ancestry and her gradual emergence into black social and political life. This process begins after Iola's wealthy white father dies and his cousin discovers flaws in her mother's marriage and manumission papers and sells Iola and her family to slavers. While in bondage, Iola endures sexual victimization but maintains her integrity, declaring: "I was abased, but the men who trampled on me were the degraded ones" (88). After the war breaks out, Iola is rescued by northern troops, becomes a nurse for the Union soldiers, and eventually meets Dr. Gresham. The benevolent but slightly bigoted white doctor discovers Iola's racial secret but falls in love with her anyway and eventually proposes marriage. In a move that reverses her mother's marital choice—and the plot of *An Imperative Duty*—Iola rejects Gresham's proposal and chooses to live her life as an openly black woman. Toward the end of the novel, she meets Dr. Frank Latimer, a fellow mulatto equally committed to black education and social justice, and the two soon fall in love. In the novel's closing pages, Iola and Dr. Latimer unite their activist efforts in holy matrimony, dedicating their lives to a program of racial uplift in the South.

Largely situated within the domestic sphere of the home, *Iola Leroy* deploys the construct of the family as a microcosm for the nation. Linking the household unit to larger social institutions such as advocacy groups, church, schools, and civic organizations, Harper theorizes familial and community forms of affiliation in the context of political life and membership in American society. In this way, *Iola Leroy* is what Claudia Tate has called a "domestic allegory of political desire."[5] Buried in its sentimental rendering of Iola's evolution into womanhood and political consciousness is a story about a young black woman's search for familial belonging and the protections of formal citizenship, rights that were historically denied to African Americans and that remained tenuous after Reconstruction. As Russ Castronovo has pointed out: "[T]he acceptance [that Iola] hopes to find comes at the hands of kin and community, not the state. It is this critical difference that makes Harper's novel not just an allegory but an allegorical critique of a formal citizenship created by the Fourteenth Amendment" (221). Building on Tate and Castronovo, then, I would argue that Harper addresses the limitations and failures of the Fourteenth Amendment vis-à-vis literary genres, using sentimental realism to conceive of black citizenship as an inalienable birthright and to reimagine the ideal African American polity both in terms of the family and the larger community.

As a number of critics have defined the genre, sentimentalism is chiefly concerned with the inner life of emotions, morality, and values. In its portrayal of human conflict and dilemmas, sentimental fiction seeks to instruct by cultivating notions of absolute truths and higher laws. This is often achieved through the use of a "conversion scene"—a powerful and dramatic moment in which a crisis of large proportions triggers a surge of feeling in a character, suddenly revealing to him or her the right thing to do or the right way to feel about a problem. This conversion, which undoubtedly draws from the discourse of religion, initiates a moral revolution that transforms the individual, and presumably the reader too, into a better and more sympathetic person.[6] As Nina Baym has shown, the typical sentimental plot revolves around an orphaned young woman who must navigate the cold and unfeeling world without the support of a loving family. This young woman is depicted as a heroine, and her narrative trajectory chronicles her journey toward self-possession as well as the development of moral sentiments. If she remains virtuous and committed to a program of thrift, industry, modesty, and chastity, then she is rewarded with marriage to an equally deserving suitor who will provide her with family and security (Baym, *Woman's Fiction* 37–38). In this way, the sentimental plot upholds women's roles as custodians of moral order and reifies normative cultural values surrounding gender, family, and marriage. Because sentimentalism was, in the mainstream sense of the term, a white woman's genre, it privileged white femininity over other forms of female subjectivity and reinforced a white hegemonic view of society.

Accordingly, African American writers reshaped the sentimental formula to represent their own struggles for identity, family, and respectability. Beginning with Frank J. Webb's novel *The Garies and Their Friends* (1857)—which explores African Americans' efforts to achieve respectability and economic security in Philadelphia—African American writers increasingly adopted and reformulated the sentimental novel's elements and themes to advocate for racial uplift. Obsessed with the concepts of upward mobility and social advancement, African American writers linked theories of racial uplift with the sentimental novel's concern with moral development. As a result, racial progress and moral improvement were one and the same. *Iola Leroy* clearly represents a continuation of this project, as it fuses the discourse of racial achievement with moral refinement, offering its readers both a practical and a spiritual set of tools to fight racial discrimination and secure greater civil rights.

As Jane Tompkins has elucidated, there is a long tradition in American literary history of women writers mobilizing the discursive power of sentimentalism to reconstruct the social world. In her landmark study *Sensational Designs: The Cultural Work of American Fiction, 1790–1860,* Tompkins challenged the way that critics have historically approached women's domestic fiction by shifting the conversation away from aesthetic judgments and considerations of formal merit toward the social conditions that gave rise to the literature. Tompkins's point was that the critical tendency to value the literary work as an art object overwhelmingly privileged a select group of grand narratives and limited our appreciation of how sentimental fiction "offer[s] powerful examples of the way a culture thinks about itself, articulating and proposing solutions for problems that shape a particular historical moment" (xi). In specifically addressing women's sentimental writings, which have consistently been viewed as "sensational or propagandistic," Tompkins aimed to recuperate the underassessed and misunderstood political dimensions of these works. For Tompkins, the social force of such writings resided in their much-denigrated didacticism, which sought to "teach readers what kinds of behavior to emulate or shun," making these works more pedagogical than "mimetic" and providing a "basis for remaking the social and political order in which events take place" (xvii). Interestingly enough, such a function is not at all incompatible with the goals of literary realism. Indeed, as Amy Kaplan has written, "Realists [did more] than passively record the world outside; they actively create[d] and criticize[d] the meanings, representations, and ideologies of their own changing culture" (7).

In this way, realism was not just a matter of mimetic representation and objective narration, but it was also a form of social intervention and critique. As William Dean Howells conceived of it, realism was a means of addressing growing class and racial divisions in postbellum America, and he believed that the genre could create a more cohesive and egalitarian society. In his realist manifesto *Criticism and Fiction,* Howells described the political project of realism as teaching people that they "are more like than unlike one another . . . [to] make them know one another better, that they may be all humbled and strengthened with a sense of their fraternity" (188). While the romancers and sentimentalists that he famously criticized also aimed to do this kind of cultural work, Howells felt that the best way to accomplish this task was to appeal to the intellect as opposed to emotion alone. By adopting an objective and unbiased approach to narration, as he defined the terms, Howells strove to present the facts of daily life, as most Americans lived it, with the hope that this narrative strategy would achieve a true "democracy in literature" (*Criticism and Fiction* 187). Hence, Howells advocated for a detached, scientific approach toward the business of novel writing. From his editor's chair he crafted a definition of realism that celebrated the many different class identities, styles of speech, and geographical regions that made up modern America. Yet there were limitations to his realist program of representation. While realism demanded that writers portray people and events objectively and authentically, the genre paradoxically exaggerated and overstated certain forms of cultural, racial, and social difference. In this regard, highlighting these differences often undermined the genre's objective—to bridge the gap between various Americans—by confirming people's suspicions that such distinctions were real and that they could not be transcended or assimilated into a common American culture. With this in mind, African American writers sought to downplay notions of difference to portray blacks as fully human and equally deserving of the rights of citizenship.

For African American women writers, in particular, the tragic mulatta device was a highly effective narrative strategy. To be sure, white women's ability to identify with the mulatta on the basis of color, gender, and class made it easier for black women novelists to discuss difficult topics uniquely affecting them, such as rape, concubinage, and other forms of sexual abuse. Because black women novelists were under tremendous pressure to assemble their plots in such a way that they did not violate white women's standards of propriety or the tenets governing "true womanhood," they often submerged their narratives of sexual harassment and violence within the genteel parameters set by the sentimental novel.[7] Following this strategy, then, *Iola Leroy* uses the tragic mulatta trope to help suture the racial divide, while also distinctly locating issues of women's rights within what John Ernest has described as an "African American mode of understanding" ("Mysteries" 500).

To its credit, the novel uses the tragic mulatta trope in cutting-edge ways. Anticipating later developments, Harper views mixed-race identity less as a liminal category that exists in between dominant and established racial groupings, and more as a narrative device rooted in blackness. Consider, for example, Michele Elam's study *The Souls of Mixed Folk: Race, Politics, and Aesthetics in the New Millennium.* In Elam's own words, her book examines "late-twentieth-century and twenty-first-century works that call on much earlier uses of mixed race in the African American literary tradition, not as an identity category with its own lost tradition but as a powerful trope to engage issues of civil rights and social change" as well as explore representations of mixed-race identity that are "continuous with, rather than parallel to, a capacious African American tradition" (15–16, xvi). In this way, Elam locates more contemporary depictions of mixed-race identity within a longer genealogy of African American representation, situating the figure of the mulatta/o in an expansive continuum of black experience. Although this broader and more fluid approach to race is not something that we typically ascribe to late nineteenth- and early twentieth-century works, I would argue that *Iola Leroy* stands as an early example of how African American writers radically redeployed the trope of the mulatta/o to add greater elasticity to how we conceive of blackness and to revise standards of femininity. By presenting readers with a mulatta who self-identifies as black, Harper subverts the traditional mechanisms by which we assign value to race and gender. Far from being a passive capitulation to the logic of the one-drop rule or the old adage from slavery that the child follows the condition of the mother, Harper offers Iola's choice as a self-directed act of female autonomy that reverses the conventional polarity of inferiority, making black womanhood a superior form of subjectivity and positioning whiteness as a less desirable mode of being.

Beginning with her title, Harper sets out to alter the image of the tragic mulatta figure. Using what P. Gabrielle Foreman has identified as a "homonymic" and "histotextual" association, *Iola Leroy* aligns its heroine's struggle for freedom, family, and community with the bold and unapologetic political activism of Ida B. Wells (90). As Foreman has noted, "Iola" was the pen name that Wells used in her "fiery" political journalism (92–93). Foreman has also offered the year 1892, the mutual publication date of Wells's most popular book, *Southern Horrors: Lynch Law in All Its Phases,* and Harper's *Iola Leroy,* as a point of convergence for *Iola Leroy,* making Wells's work an important political context for reading Harper's. As Foreman has revealed, Wells and Harper were close associates, and in 1892, while on a trip together, angry whites destroyed Wells's Memphis office because of an article she published denouncing the lynching of three of her friends who were accused of raping a white woman (93). In offering this history, Foreman underscores Hazel V. Carby's important observation that "black women like Frances Harper, Anna Julia Cooper, and Ida B. Wells were not isolated figures of intellectual genius; they were shaped by and helped to shape a wider movement of Afro-American women" (*Reconstructing Womanhood* 115). Such historical connections invite us to situate black women's activist and imaginative labor within a larger sphere of political activity and cultural production. By naming her female protagonist after Wells, Harper locates her heroine within a longer genealogy of black feminist thought that challenges the traditional depiction of the tragic mulatta. In this way, she also reverses and revises the racial politics governing Howells's novel. As Debra J. Rosenthal has argued, by "titling her novel after her heroine rather than a duty larger than the individual, Harper announces the importance of a single character, and a woman no less" (511).

In naming her novel after her heroine and presenting most events from her point of view, Harper emphasizes the importance of Iola's autonomy to the novel's revision of the tragic mulatta trope. Presenting the question of Iola's racial identity as a matter of choice rather than a question of duty, the novel discards biological definitions of race at the heart of Howells's novel and erects in its place a social constructivist model. Unlike Howells,

Harper gives her protagonist more latitude. She can choose to be black or white without surrendering to some culturally prescribed or self-imposed notion of duty, like Rhoda does. As a traditional sentimental heroine, once Rhoda discovers that she is black, she feels that it is her obligation to relinquish Olney and go live among her own people (a premise that the novel makes fun of because Rhoda has been raised white and does not know the first thing about being black). As Howells depicts it, Rhoda's thinking is driven by romantic and sentimental conventions and is completely devoid of a political program. Iola, on the other hand, is not restricted by Rhoda's ridiculous appeals to duty and is clearly motivated by political considerations. Indeed, if Iola has any duty, it is to select the race with which she will identify, using her own decision-making powers and not those of her white doctor-suitor (as Rhoda does). And although Iola ultimately decides to cast her lot with the poor and undereducated African Americans in the South, with whom she too shares little in common, she chooses to do so of her own volition, having already experienced the perils of passing for white in her brief experiment North after the war.

Unlike *An Imperative Duty, Iola Leroy* does not present passing as a viable solution to the race problem. In fact, Harper's novel issues a scathing critique of the passing phenomenon, condemning its logic of cultural and racial erasure and promoting in its place personal responsibility and integrity. For example, while in the North, Iola seeks employment and works a series of jobs that require her to pass due the pervasiveness of northern bigotry. Each time her secret is discovered she is discharged from her duties. As an authorial choice, this allows Harper to instill a sense of moral order into the novel's fictional universe, punishing Iola for her deceit. In fact, Iola does not succeed at work until she finds an equitable employer with whom she can be honest about her racial identity. In Mr. Cloten, Iola finds such a man, and she flourishes while in his charge. If Iola's northern experiment teaches her anything, it is that passing will only cause personal pain, as it will require her to live under a perpetual storm cloud. In this way, the novel lifts the shadows cast on blackness and underscores the importance of honesty and personal pride in the race's collective effort to achieve respectability. In a more specifically gendered context, Iola's northern experiment also highlights the significance of work to the development of female autonomy. In linking women's work to female empowerment, the novel challenges the idea that intermarriage is the only viable means of achieving upward mobility.

Like Rhoda, Iola is also given the opportunity to marry white and conceal her black ancestry, as Gresham longs to "win [Iola] for his bride, bury her secret in his Northern home, and hide from his aristocratic relations all knowledge of her mournful past" (47). Despite the implicit racism inherent in such a desire, Iola admires Gresham for his manliness and his character, which is supposed to indicate to readers that he is not a staunch racist but a mostly sympathetic figure who just so happens to be racially ignorant. Nevertheless, Iola understands that she cannot marry him. Viewing Gresham's proposal as an invitation to pass for white, one that would require her to silently endure racial abuse, Iola decides to honor her black ancestry and live her life in the open: "Doctor, were I your wife, are there not people who would caress me as a white woman who would shrink from me in scorn if they knew I had one drop of negro blood in my veins? When mistaken for a white woman, I should hear things alleged against the race at which my blood would boil. No, Doctor, I am not willing to live under a shadow of concealment which I thoroughly hate as if the blood in my veins were an undetected crime of my soul" (177). As Iola implies, marrying Gresham and passing for white would not only be a betrayal to her heritage, but it would also be a betrayal to her race. In no uncertain terms, she tells him that she refuses to live a lie and accept white supremacist claims about black inferiority. In this respect, Iola drastically differs from Rhoda (and almost all of the tragic mulattas before her). Whereas Iola interrogates whiteness, finding fault with its implicit racism, Rhoda capitulates to it. In this way, Iola's assertive rejection of her suitor's invitation to marry and pass for white represents a radical departure from the tragic mulatta paradigm, standing in sharp relief to what Ann duCille has called the "Victorian fragility" that animates Rhoda's meek concession to Olney's pleas (161). Unlike Howells, Harper privileges the black heroine's autonomy and decision-making ability. In this respect, Iola Leroy "rewrites and subverts Howells's racist construction" (duCille 161).

Promoting the project of racial uplift over intermarriage and passing, *Iola Leroy* presents activism and education as the keys to black progress. After Iola rejects Gresham's proposal, the novel takes on a decidedly more

African American focus. In the chapter entitled "Friends in Council," the novel invites readers to attend a *conversazione* comprised of prominent black activists, educators, and professionals. These men and women, who come from a variety of disciplines, including medicine, history, religion, and letters, gather to present papers on a number of issues of special importance to African Americans, such as emigration, education, patriotism, morality, and enlightened motherhood, which is also the subject of Iola's essay.[8] As Harper's description of the group reveals, the "select company of earnest men and women deeply interested in the welfare of the race" (187) constitute that special class of African Americans whom Henry Lyman Morehouse first called the "Talented Tenth."[9] In an 1896 essay of the same name, Lyman—a white patron and pioneer of African American education—argued that an "ordinary education" would suffice for men and women of "mediocrity," but for the small group of elite thinkers at the top of the intellectual hierarchy, such an education would be a "prodigious mistake" because their "superior natural endowments" would be a "mightier influence" and a "greater inspiration to others" than the collective contributions of those below them (183). In many respects, Harper's depiction of the *conversazione* reflects this elitist attitude, adopting a condescending tone toward the black laborers and the black poor, who are noticeably missing from the discussion of racial progress and who are cast as lowly and in need of moral and social refinement. Consequently, the problematic vision of racial uplift that emerges at the end of the novel is one in which the best and brightest blacks save the clueless masses.

Even as the project of racial uplift reinforced lower class blacks' social marginalization, it also positioned literacy and literary activities as vehicles for upward mobility. Interestingly, the *conversazione* features a poetry reading and prefaces Dr. Latimer's suggestion that Iola "write a good, strong book," strongly suggesting that literature was, for Harper, an important vehicle for carrying out the work of social and political activism (199). For Harper, literature existed as a heightened form of political crusading because it gave African Americans an imaginative tool by which they could chronicle and disseminate a written record of the race's history and achievements, inspiring other African Americans to strive for greatness. Through literature, Harper believed, African Americans could refute all of the various racial stereotypes and misrepresentations that maligned black character, and thus take greater control over their own representation in the real world and in fiction. Harper also believed that as African American readers consumed these representations, they would in turn experience a shift in their thinking about themselves and what it means to be black broadly construed, becoming more empowered and enlightened and furthering the cause of African American advancement.

However, Harper also acknowledged that African American writers faced special challenges that white writers did not, as a result of limited social and economic opportunities, and that these disparities hindered the development of a black literary tradition. For example, after Dr. Latimer proposes that Iola take up the pen, she states that one needs both "leisure and money to make a successful book," to which Dr. Latimer tells her: "[O]ut of the race must come its own thinkers and writers. Authors belonging to the white race have written good racial books, for which I am deeply grateful, but it seems to be almost impossible for a white man to put himself completely in our place" (199). Harper's point here is that African Americans cannot afford to concern themselves only with practical matters such as industry and remunerative activities. The race needs to develop its own intellectuals and writers so that they can narrate their stories and represent themselves in the best possible light. Not only is this an obvious reference to white authors, such as Harriet Beecher Stowe, Mark Twain, and William Dean Howells, who attempted to write sympathetically on behalf of black Americans and condemn racial injustice, but it also draws an important distinction between the noble and necessary work of racial representation and the crucial significance of self-representation. Harper's observation here is profound, as it recognizes the need for both forms of expression. Contrary to what many may think, the two modes are not necessarily incompatible with each other and may even serve mutual ends. As Harper seems to acknowledge, white writers did in fact play an important role in bringing greater awareness to racial issues in fiction, but if African Americans are to direct and shape their own depictions, and they must, then they have to develop themselves the writers who will best benefit the race by writing about black experience in more expansive and positive ways.

In this deliberately metaliterary way, the novel positions literature and literary practices as critical conduits of knowledge and power. By reading and writing literature, African Americans can transmit information of lasting importance to the race and reconstruct the terms of their representation. Not only does this radically alter individual and group identity, but it also brings about increased personal pride and collective racial consciousness. As Elizabeth McHenry has argued, *Iola Leroy*'s depiction of literary work underscores the important role that literature has consistently played in African American reform efforts.[10] In linking the novel's fictional portrayal of a literary society to the rich history of African American literary associations and book clubs, McHenry ascribes greater mimetic and political power to Harper's representation, elevating the function of imaginative writing in African American culture from art to social critique. In doing so, McHenry provides a theoretical foundation for viewing the novel as an episteme unto itself, inhabiting the middle ground in between history and fiction and complicating traditional notions of genre. Fusing questions of fictional representation with political representation, *Iola Leroy*, as McHenry suggests, provides readers with a practical model for developing the discursive strategies that will articulate the race's desires for individual and collective agency.[11]

For Harper, African American women were critical to this project, and in publishing *Iola Leroy*, she helped usher in the black clubwomen's movement. As Hazel V. Carby has illuminated, the "decade of the 1890's was a time of intense activity and productivity for Afro-American intellectuals," and we must situate *Iola Leroy*'s depiction of black feminism within this history ("On the Threshold" 264).[12] Locating the novel in this genealogy necessitates that we read its story of female maturation and intellectual development as a manifesto of sorts for the movement. Reflecting Harper's philosophy about black women's roles in the fight for equality, *Iola Leroy* does not aim to merely entertain as much as it endeavors to inspire black women to take up the difficult work of challenging racism and sexism. Understanding that racism and sexism were interlocking forms of oppression, Harper crafted a novel that utilized sentimental discourses to show how black women were doubly discriminated against in a patriarchal system where white males wielded all the power and traditional ideologies of womanhood valorized white women. By affirming their social roles as wives and mothers, this system reinforced laws and policies designed to maintain the racial and gendered hierarchy. In placing a politically engaged black woman at the center of the domestic plot, Harper suggested that black women's intellectual activities were essential to the reordering of the social world.

Indeed, it is this world of black feminist activity that the novel engages most forcefully in its closing chapters. For example, in the character of Miss Delany, Iola's eventual sister-in-law, and the female embodiment of Martin Delany, Harper presents her idea of the ideal black woman.[13] As Harper describes her, she is "brave, intellectual, and religious," and "[n]either hair nor complexion show the least hint of blood admixture" (184, 152). Put in Iola's path as a model of what she should aspire to become, Miss Delany functions as Harper's mouthpiece in the discussions of black uplift in "Friends in Council." In response to a paper on patriotism, Delany argues that activism and social work are the answers to black disenfranchisement. A fiery teacher and speaker, she passionately proclaims: "We have been aliens and outcasts in the land of our birth. But I want my pupils to do all in their power to make this country worthy of their deepest devotion and loftiest patriotism" (190). In this way, Miss Delany issues a subtle endorsement of birthright citizenship—a protection afforded under the Fourteenth Amendment—and rejects black emigration and colonization as solutions to racial discrimination, suggesting instead that African Americans need to participate in civic life to make the country deserving of their love and respect. Harper complements this portrayal of Miss Delany with Iola's presentation of her paper, entitled "The Education of Mothers," shifting the group's focus from national politics to domestic politics. Emphasizing the importance of home life and familial relations, Iola argues that enlightened motherhood is critical to the development of the race. As she argues, black women need to nurture their children, physically and spiritually, to instill in them a sense of self-love and Christian values, insisting that "if we would have the prisons empty we must make the homes more attractive" (193).

As "Friends in Council" symbolizes, Iola's participation in the politics of uplift represents the culmination of her development as a black woman. Her political involvement signifies her maturation into full subjectivity, as it allows her to merge all of the various aspects of her identity as an activist and intellectual, a burgeoning writer, a woman, and as an

African American. As an integrated self, Iola moves beyond the scope of the tragic mulatta trope and becomes an autonomous female character. Through her civic endeavors, Iola finds identity, family, and community, affiliations that, taken together, work to reverse the social destruction slavery wreaked upon her life. In Miss Delany, Iola gains a sister and a mentor. In Dr. Latimer, she acquires a lover and the consummate colleague and friend. From a moral standpoint, the novel's restoration of old family ties and its creation of new ones underline the importance of both family and community in the struggle to elevate and advance the race. The dual nuptials that close the novel—Iola and Dr. Latimer, Harry and Lucille Delany—strongly suggest that marriage is the vehicle by which the race will arrive at knowledge and respectability.

In ending the novel this way, Harper presents black love as the cure to white racism and self-hate. Iola echoes these very sentiments in her anti-passing proclamation toward the end of the novel, which rather obviously alludes to Howells's novel with its invocation of "duty." When Iola applauds Dr. Latimer for refusing his grandmother's offer to pass for white, he replies, "I only did my duty," to which Iola says: "[W]hen others are trying to slip out of the race and pass into the white . . . I cannot help admiring one who acts as if he felt that the weaker the race is the closer he would cling to it" (200). Positioning marriage as the ultimate act of moral commitment between two people, the novel conflates romantic love and love for community, transforming both into a singular undertaking that will initiate black healing and reform. In this respect, the novel makes Iola's marriage to Latimer a symbol of cultural restoration and black progress. Despite the seemingly passionless overtones of such a marriage, the novel's ending does not suggest that passion is incompatible with social purpose; rather, as Ann duCille has argued, the novel's resolution "encode[s]" sexual desire into the "much safer realm of political zeal and the valorized venue of holy wedlock" (45). As such, *Iola Leroy* successfully rewrites the canonical tragic mulatta narrative by replacing its sensational depiction of interracial desire and its attending reinscription of whiteness with a parable about the sanctity of black marriage and its transformative power to heal the wounds of slavery and uplift the race.

Underscoring this message are the novel's final images. As Harry and Lucille join Iola and Latimer in wedded bliss, the novel endorses the idea of ancestral return. For example, Harry's decision to marry the dark-skinned Lucille revokes the currency of light-skinned privilege and denotes his racial affiliation. Cast as his symbolic acceptance of his black blood, Harry's decision to wed Lucille and become one flesh with her resonates as a desire to embody blackness and undo the miscegenation that produced him. Through marriage the two legitimate their sexual desire for each other by sublimating it into intellectual labor. In this way, they share their love for one another with the community. At the end of the novel, Harry and Lucille are at the head of a "large and flourishing" school, "lifting up the homes of the people" (213). As Harper writes, Harry is neither sad nor regretful of his decision to reject the white world. In fact, his happiness hinges on the "improved condition of his pupils and the superb manhood and noble life which he has developed in his much needed work" (214). Demonstrating Harry's commitment to educating the folk, his decision to share his talents with those less fortunate than him confirms the necessity of social justice work and cross-class alliance in the project of community building. Restoring Uncle Daniel, Robert, Marie, and Grandmother Johnson to the plot, the novel's closing tableaux features the black family, in all of its various complexions and stations of life, engaged in the work of uplifting the race.

Though successful on many fronts, Harper's novel does suffer from some clear shortcomings in its revision of the tragic mulatta trope. The racial politics driving her narrative can best be described as reactionary and motivated by a desire to wrestle away respectability from the tight-fisted grip of her white middle-class readership. This has the effect of granting her mulatto and middle-class characters greater personhood, but at the expense of the novel's black poor, who are not adequately represented and who lack agency. As Andreá N. Williams has argued, the novel's conceptualization of respectability "often relapses into the hierarchical, exclusionary social vocabularies [that] Harper aims to unsettle" (*Dividing Lines* 27). Furthermore, the novel uses a series of reversals to reconfigure the meanings of binary oppositions, but the mere rearranging of the terms of difference does nothing to dismantle the structures that perpetuate inequality and marginalization. Operating within the same rigid, overly schematic paradigm of racial representation that she seeks to critique, Harper rejects the conventional depiction of the mulatta as a tragic, sad, self-loathing woman and simply replaces it with a quasi-flat display of black femininity that gains its traction from a seemingly unified black constituency. While Harper grants Iola the agency to choose her racial identity, she short-circuits it to advance her own antiracist agenda—a strategic essentialism that endorses the politics of racial solidarity to advocate for civil rights and disprove myths of inferiority—which not only collapses the distinction between author and character but, more problematically, does little to undermine the idea of race as biological essence. This can be seen in Iola's numerous references to "blood" and her appeals to "her people." But in Harper's defense, revising the terms of the mulatta's representation constituted an important victory in its own right, and the urgencies of post-Reconstruction antiblackness necessitated that she portray the African American community as a united front, so as to give greater power to its collective demands for racial justice and the rights of citizenship.

Although *Iola Leroy*'s use of romance and sentimentalism may strike some readers as counterintuitive given its investment in presenting the mulatta in more realistic ways, its narrative strategy should be lauded as a smart attempt to navigate the late nineteenth-century minefield of race, gender, and genre. As a black woman writing at the turn of the twentieth century, Harper was in a difficult bind. Neither sentimentalism nor realism alone could have provided Harper with an ideal forum to depict the realities of black womanhood without offending certain conventions governing true womanhood and potentially alienating readers. Therefore, Harper had to strategically weave both aspects of these genres into her narrative. Sentimental realism was an expedient device; it allowed Harper to articulate black women's longings for autonomy and community while also issuing a severe indictment against racism in a palatable narrative package. Insofar as the novel successfully manages to undermine damaging stereotypes about black women's sexuality and moral integrity as well as offer a model for black civic engagement, *Iola Leroy* stands as the more progressive text. Howells's novel leaves these stereotypes intact by evading them altogether and erasing the possibility of the mulatta finding acceptance in a black social context. Moreover, Howells does not give his heroine any decision-making authority. She simply yields to her white doctor-suitor's wishes. In sharp contrast, Harper gives her heroine the power to choose her racial affiliation. In foregrounding Iola's choice, the novel attempts to theorize racial identity as a question of personal preference rather than as a simple matter of genealogy or descent. While Iola ultimately decides to honor her black ancestry, she does so by making a conscious decision based on her own values and priorities, which rather obviously reflect her creator's commitment to fostering black self-esteem and racial dignity. Nevertheless, this is a highly innovative gesture by nineteenth-century standards, anticipating more groundbreaking developments in approaches to racial identity that would emerge in the late twentieth and early twenty-first centuries, as it primarily views race as a sociopolitical construct and attempts to privilege self-identification over biological or legal definitions of race.

Taken together, *Iola Leroy* and *An Imperative Duty* offer a broader and more nuanced way of thinking about racial representation in realist terms. For Harper and Howells, the mulatta functioned as a figurative device that could facilitate a more comprehensive critique of race—both as an interior, subjective phenomenon and as a structural reality. In this sense, their revisions to the trope were really attempts to contemplate the inner life of race as well as what Shu-Mei Shih has called the "worldliness of race"—that is, the situatedness of race, the ways in which forms of racialization exist in specific times and places and institutional contexts (1349). Despite the limitations of their critiques, both novels insist on literature's dynamic relation to the real world and, as a result, posit a belief in the efficacy of literary works to enact social change. Their reciprocal revisions of the tragic mulatta trope also encourage us to abandon the insular, segregated approaches to race that continue to dominate interpretive methodologies in American and African American literary studies today. Such reading practices are limited and overdetermined, often producing their own ideologically driven analyses that reveal scholars' blind spots and biases. At the turn of the twentieth century, African American writers not only acknowledged the popularity of mainstream, white realism, but they engaged with it in highly innovative ways. By blending realism with romantic and sentimental forms, black writers could better articulate their desires for a freer and more inclusive society. In this way, African American writers participated in metaliterary dialogues with white writers and reworked established narrative forms to cultivate greater self-representation. We can hardly insist on a definition of African American literature that does not recognize that such cross-racial conversations have been central to the task of revising and expanding the possibilities for black representation in fiction. The intertextual and interracial exchange that characterizes Harper's and Howells's racial revisions urges us to reconsider what it meant to read and write African American literature in their time and what it means in our own— inviting us to reexamine our rationale for what we do or do not include in that project, why, and ultimately, what it reveals about us.

3

Racial Fictions and the Cultural Work of Genre in Charles W. Chesnutt's *The House behind the Cedars*

In a pivotal scene in *The House behind the Cedars* (1900), Judge Straight and John Warwick, the formerly black office boy turned white attorney, discuss the legal loopholes that permit his racial passing. Pleased to see his old disciple but afraid that John's stay in Patesville will compromise his new identity, Judge Straight reminds John that "custom is stronger than law" and that in matters of race, "custom *is* law" (23). Alluding to the legal technicality that makes John a white man in his new state of South Carolina (where race is determined by reputation and social standing), but a black man in his former state of North Carolina (where race is defined by fractions of blood), Judge Straight, whose name implies an honest and balanced approach to legal matters, highlights the arbitrary and widely divergent nature of the laws establishing racial identity in the South. Moreover, he suggests that when it comes to the color line, our de facto practices may carry more weight than de jure laws. This means that if John's black ancestry is revealed, then it will not matter how South Carolina defines blackness because the widely-subscribed-to one-drop rule will inevitably trump the actual law. In many respects, this critical observation sits at the center of the novel's racial critique, opening up into a broader analysis of the relationship between the social and legal fictions of race and fiction in a more literal sense. Exploring the subjects of racial passing and miscegenation through the organizing frameworks of law and literature, Chesnutt creates a haunting meditation on the American racial crisis that underscores the fictiveness of race as well as its real and tragic consequences.

In *The House behind the Cedars,* Chesnutt uses Afro-realism to illustrate the various ways in which romantic and realistic discourses can be used to underwrite and undermine racist ideology. Blending romantic conventions (the tragic mulatta motif, allusions to *Ivanhoe* and other medieval fictions, and improbable coincidences) with realistic devices (meditations on law and scientific racism, critiques of moral agency, and the naturalistic plot of decline), Chesnutt cleverly mobilizes the protocols of genre to demonstrate how literary fictions can work to establish and deconstruct racial truths. For example, both of Chesnutt's mixed-race characters draw from popular romantic fictions to construct their new identities, pass for white, and thus pursue the American Dream. But when they lose themselves in the stories they tell and the so-called "truth" about their racial ancestry comes to light, the narrative shifts to naturalism. By utilizing this deterministic form of narrative closure, the novel suggests that the biggest threat to racial equality is structural white supremacy.

That genre is tangled up in the novel's deconstruction of race suggests that literary traditions and their conventions can in fact perform important cultural work. In some ways, the novel's greatest realist achievement is its insistence that popular fiction can be deployed to bring about social change. In his journals, Chesnutt expressed this very sentiment in terms of the benefits of a realistic and romantic approach to fiction writing. As Chesnutt explained in an oft-cited passage, he intended to dispose of the "stale negro minstrel jokes" and "worn out newspaper squibs on the 'man and brother'" so as to "leave the realm of fiction" and "come down to hard facts" (*Journals* 126).[1] But Chesnutt also believed that black life was "rich in the elements of romance" and that such material could facilitate the "elevation of the whites" (*Journals* 139). In this way, Chesnutt suggested that documenting the harsh conditions under which black people lived could soften white people's feelings, raise their moral consciousness, and stamp out racial injustice.[2] In *The House behind the Cedars,* Chesnutt combines both perspectives, playing out the story of racial passing and intermarriage along generic lines, to demonstrate the power of fiction radically to alter the social and literary landscape.

In what follows, I offer a metaliterary critique of the novel's textual complexity, calling specific attention to the racial uses of genre. In a series of close readings, I explore the at times puzzling and seemingly contradictory aspects of a novel whose formal intricacies are more complex than they appear and that work together to intervene in turn-of-the-twentieth century debates about black identity and racial inferiority. Focusing on four major developments that stand at the center of the novel's deconstruction of race—the opening sequence, the tournament scene, the marriage plot, and the fatal conclusion in the swamp—I examine how Chesnutt mobilizes Afro-realism to interrogate the cultural, legal, and literary fictions of race. Accounting for the ways in which Chesnutt's characters use literature as a tool to reinvent their racial identities, I want to underscore the connections between literary fictions and racial fictions. By working through these connections, I seek to bring into greater textual relief the cultural significance of Chesnutt's aesthetic and political projects. As I will explain, the text makes the argument that the right kind of imaginative writing, which also happens to be the right kind of realism, can rid the world of racism. In many respects, this philosophical outlook informs and defines Chesnutt's realism. For Chesnutt, realism not only had the power to change the way that black identity was constructed in popular fiction, but it also had the power to alter the way that we conceived of it in the real world.

Charles W. Chesnutt: Race, Realism, and the U.S. Literary Marketplace

The House behind the Cedars represents the culmination of ten years of revisions to an early short story entitled "Rena Walden." The story was initially rejected by *Century* editor Richard Watson Gilder in 1890 on the grounds that it was, in his words, too "amorphous" (*Letters* 67). As Gilder explained, there was "either a lack of humor in the author or a brutality in the characters" that made them "uninteresting" (*Letters* 67). In a letter addressed to his mentor and friend George Washington Cable, Chesnutt admitted that his story was somewhat "amorphous," but not due to any literary deficiencies on his part but rather to society's tendency to regard mulatto people as "amorphous" in the first place (*Letters* 65). For this reason, Chesnutt concluded, "I fear there is too much of this sentiment to make mulattoes good magazine characters . . . all of the good negroes . . .

have been . . . full-blooded, and their chief virtues have been their dog-like fidelity and devotion to their old masters" (*Letters* 65).

Evidently, Chesnutt understood that most people at the time saw race in very narrow terms and that this tendency made the task of representing mixed-race African Americans difficult. Moreover, Chesnutt was aware of the racism that fueled the literary marketplace and how the appetite for so-called authentic accounts of African American life was really a desire for racist, romantic, and stereotypical portraits that reinforced white people's distorted ideas about what black people were like and how they lived.[3] Because Chesnutt saw himself as a realist, he wanted to disrupt this trend by creating more complex, more realistic, and less conventional black characters. Taking offense to Gilder's assessment of his story, he sarcastically disclosed in his letter to Cable: "I suppose I shall have to drop the attempt at realism, and try to make my characters like other folks, for uninteresting people are not good subjects for fiction" (*Letters* 66). With Cable's guidance, Chesnutt continued working on the manuscript, eventually publishing it as a novel under a new title with Houghton, Mifflin & Company.

Despite its lengthy and troubled production, *The House behind the Cedars* received favorable reviews, with most contemporary critics praising Chesnutt for his storytelling ability and his courageous approach to a taboo topic. Shortly after it was published, an anonymous reviewer writing in the *Boston Evening Transcript* exclaimed, "[N]othing in recent fiction is finer," and "its strong conclusion—the race prejudice conquered late by love—may be taken as . . . the eventual solution to the race question" (Rev. of *The House behind the Cedars* 12). Another reviewer writing in the *Zion's Herald* described the novel as a "Southern story, told with no little power and close faithfulness to life" (Rev. of *The House behind the Cedars* 1526). One reviewer in the *Peoria Evening Star* commended Chesnutt for his ornate style and thoughtfully concluded: "No one can impartially read this book without arriving at the three-fold conclusion: [f]irst, that nobility of character is not the exclusive attribute of any particular race or races, but may be and is the possession of all; secondly, that the only true and just judgment is that which is based upon the individual; and thirdly, that human brotherhood is not a theory but a fact" (Rev. of *The House behind the Cedars* 10).

Considering that so many reviewers lauded the novel for its construction and compelling antiracist message, it seems a little more than bizarre that William Dean Howells did not review the book, especially in view of the highly flattering appraisal he gave Chesnutt's short fiction in his *Atlantic Monthly* essay entitled "Mr. Charles W. Chesnutt's Stories." In this career-defining piece, Howells celebrated *The Wife of His Youth and Other Stories of the Color Line* (1899) and *The Conjure Woman* (1899) as works of realism, commending Chesnutt for his "passionless handling," "self-restraint," and "severely impartial and studiously aloof attitude" (699–700). Yet, it would appear that Howells was not equally impressed by *The House behind the Cedars*. Shortly after the novel's publication, Chesnutt sent Howells a copy of the book as well as a follow-up letter expressing his gratitude for the rave review Howells had given him just six months before, hinting that another ringing tribute would be greatly appreciated (McElrath 494). Although Chesnutt's letter to Howells is no longer extant, what has survived is Howells's reply to it, dated November 10, 1901, in which Howells thanked Chesnutt for the copy of the novel and asked Chesnutt to send him another color-line story but made no explicit reference to the possibility of him writing a review essay on *The House behind the Cedars* (McElrath 494–95).

Taking this history into account, we can assume that Howells did not approve of Chesnutt's melodramatic and didactic style. Of course, Howells's disapproval of Chesnutt's bizarre realism would soon be confirmed after Chesnutt published his second novel, *The Marrow of Tradition* (1901). Although the book was a work of realism, insofar as it was based on the Wilmington, North Carolina, race riot of 1898, it also utilized romantic and sentimental conventions. Featuring Chesnutt's signature style, which included improbable coincidences, scenes of intense emotion, compassion toward all the black characters and disdain for all the white ones, and moral sermonizing, the novel showcased a raw and rousing depiction of deteriorating race relations in the South. Howells found the book to be so very "bitter" ("A Psychological Counter-Current" 882) that after reading it he penned a letter to the Chicago novelist Henry Blake Fuller, in which he exclaimed, "How such a negro must hate us" (*Selected Letters*, vol. 4: *1892–1901* 274). Scholars have noted that Howells never wrote to Chesnutt again and that Chesnutt was deeply troubled by the unfavorable review, but Chesnutt's rejection of Howells's realist teachings would seem to suggest that Chesnutt may have been disillusioned with his mentor and that he was perhaps more controversial than readers have generally recognized.

In retrospect, Chesnutt's movement away from Howellsian realism began with the publication of *The House behind the Cedars.* To be sure, the novel reflects Chesnutt's unique style as well the influence of his relationships with Cable and Albion W. Tourgée, both of whom objected to the kind of realism advocated by Howells on the grounds that it was lacking in sympathy and moral accountability.[4] In this way, Chesnutt never really fully embraced Howells's prescriptions for the genre, as he endeavored all along to produce his own version of realism, one that could accommodate the full range of human emotions and experiences, including everything from the ideal to the real to the seemingly unreal.[5]

In a larger sense, *The House behind the Cedars* also represents Chesnutt's break from the prevailing literary trends and tastes of the 1880s and 1890s. During this period, the American literary scene was dominated by local color and plantation fiction. In chapter 1, I discussed the emergence of the plantation tradition as a response to the tremendous social and political changes brought about by Reconstruction, but what, perhaps, remains less clear is how local-color fiction was entangled within this genre. Like plantation fiction, local-color literature attempted to give a diverse American readership an authentic and credible account of a people, region, or way of life that was either unfamiliar or no longer in existence. Focusing on the dialect, customs, landscape, and other specific features endemic to a particular region, local-color fiction also reflected a nostalgic desire to return to or re-create an ostensibly simpler time located in the preindustrial past. In this way, southern local colorists sated northern readers' curiosity about the antebellum days and in some respects symbolically contributed to the larger national project of reconciliation. But the problem with local-color fiction was that it also romanticized slavery and relied on stereotypes to depict African Americans. As Irwin Russell's "Christmas-Night in the Quarters" (1877), Sherwood Bonner's *Suwanee River Tales* (1884), and the plantation fiction I mentioned in chapter 1 all illustrate, local-color fiction frequently reduced African

Americans to racial caricatures: "Sambo," the "coon," "Uncle Tom," "tragic mulatto," "Mammy," and the "black brute."

While many southern local colorists were more interested in accurately portraying slave dialect than in defending slavery, they nevertheless reinforced the racial and racist dynamics of plantation fiction. Chesnutt's dialect tales subverted these ideologies, even as they worked with the genre. As William L. Andrews has explained, Chesnutt depicted African Americans "with greater care and sympathy than any of his white fiction-writing contemporaries," and his approach to representation sought to underscore the "common humanity between blacks and whites" (*Literary Career* 58). But local color literature's short form made it virtually impossible to fashion fully developed characters. By the late 1880s, Chesnutt had grown tired of the genre and frustrated by its narrow racial logic. In 1889, he commented in a letter to Cable, "I think I have about used up the old Negro who serves as a mouthpiece, and I shall drop him in future stories, as well as much of the dialect" (*Letters* 44). Sensing the possibilities that existed outside of the limitations of dialect fiction, Chesnutt set his literary sights on expanding African American representation in fiction by taking up the longer form of the novel.

The House behind the Cedars is Chesnutt's first full-length meditation on the race problem, and out of all of his novels, it is probably the one most focused on creating complex black characters. In exploring the controversial subjects of racial passing and miscegenation, the novel attempts to humanize mixed-race people and quell fears about racial mixture by dramatizing the tragic effects of racism on the individual psyche and on society, thereby suggesting that racism is not merely a feature of the American landscape but that it is also a moral hazard. As a mixed-race African American himself, Chesnutt had a profound understanding of the complexities and difficulties of life for "mixed bloods," and *The House behind the Cedars* illustrates his developing and evolving concern with questions of racial representation in fiction, the myth of racial purity, and the social and legal construction of race. In this way, the novel continues the project that Chesnutt began in the beginning of his career with his dialect and color-line stories, the best of which appear in *The Conjure Woman* and in *The Wife of His Youth*, where in the former,

Chesnutt adopted and transformed local-color and plantation fiction's strategies for depicting African Americans and slavery, and in the latter, he explored topics like intermarriage, color consciousness, and racial assimilation. While these early collections established Chesnutt's reputation as a short-story writer, *The House behind the Cedars* catapulted Chesnutt into literary maturity as a novelist. Moreover, the novel stands as his most popular and best-received work of long fiction, as Chesnutt did not go on to garner the same commercial or critical acclaim with *The Marrow of Tradition* or his third and final novel published during his lifetime, *The Colonel's Dream* (1905), which ended his literary career and led him to logically conclude that there was not a strong demand in the U.S. literary marketplace for books featuring African Americans, or written in such a way as to challenge the racial status quo.[6] Nevertheless, *The House behind the Cedars* remains one of the most important studies of racial passing and miscegenation in all of American and African American literature to date.

Part of its enduring legacy is that the novel reflects in dramatic form Chesnutt's concern with the paradoxes of race and the future of race relations. Beginning with his first published essay, "What Is a White Man?" (1889), Chesnutt sought to debunk the fiction of race by highlighting its legal and social constructedness as well as the arbitrariness of the laws governing racial identity in the South. Chesnutt argued that racial divisions were created by man, not by God, and that the laws enacted to preserve and defend such distinctions, such as the one-drop rule and antimiscegenation laws, were essentially impossible to enforce, as intermixture was both a historical reality and a forgone conclusion in a multiracial world. That the laws differed from state to state was, for Chesnutt, proof that a large percentage of the population had "black blood" and that southern courts, aware of this fact, drew the color line in such a way as to preserve the balance of power between black and whites in their respective states. As Chesnutt saw it, amalgamation would inevitably bring about the assimilation of African Americans into mainstream American life.

In "The Future American" (1900), a three-part series of articles for the *Boston Evening Transcript*, Chesnutt further explored this idea. Here, Chesnutt argued that this process of amalgamation had already been under way for hundreds of years and that it would continue, resulting in a future species of Americans that would be an aggregate of all the various races that populated the North American continent. Chesnutt did not believe that miscegenation and intermarriage would miraculously solve the race problem, but he did believe that it would signify the waning of racial prejudice against African Americans and mark their full obtainment of the rights of citizenship. Indeed, Chesnutt concluded, "There can manifestly be no such thing as a peaceful and progressive civilization in a nation divided by two warring races, and homogeneity of type, at least in externals, is a necessary condition of harmonious social progress" (862). In this way, Chesnutt positioned racial passing as the only viable means by which some African Americans could avail themselves of the opportunities exclusively afforded to whites. Published during an era of inconsistent and arbitrary legal and social definitions of racial identity, the novel sought to undermine the saliency of racial divisions and hierarchies so to highlight African Americans' kinship with whites.

Passing as Theme and Narrative Strategy

The House behind the Cedars begins a few years after the Civil War and focuses on a pair of mulatto siblings, John and Rena Walden, who cross the color line to achieve the promise of postbellum emancipation. In the novel's opening, John, who has taken the name "Warwick," returns to his childhood home in Patesville, North Carolina, after a ten-year absence, to convince his sister to come live with him in Clarence, South Carolina, and also pass for white. It is important that John has taken this name because it is a reference to Edward Bulwer-Lytton's historical novel *The Last of the Barons* (1843), a medieval romance about the fierce competition for power between the English king Edward IV and his ambitious and influential minister Earl of Warwick, who is portrayed as a manipulative power broker. In this way, Chesnutt suggests that John's passing, albeit calculating and unscrupulous, is motivated by a very human desire for upward mobility, which is something that he wants to share with his sister. Like her brother, Rena also takes a name from a medieval romance, "Rowena," an obvious allusion to Sir Walter Scott's novel *Ivanhoe*. Of course, what makes this so ironic is that it is the name of the novel's pure Anglo-Saxon heroine, who also happens to be the true love of the brave Anglo-Saxon knight Ivanhoe.

At a tournament inspired by this wildly popular book, Rena meets a southern white aristocrat named George Tryon. He falls in love with her and soon proposes marriage. Rena accepts his offer but fails to tell him about her black ancestry. In what can only be described as a remarkable series of coincidences, he spots her at a drugstore in her hometown, discovers the truth about her ancestry, and quickly breaks off the engagement. Brokenhearted, Rena renounces passing and takes up the work of racial uplift by teaching at an all-black school. But in a deadly turn of events, she gets lost in a swamp while trying to evade George, who has had a change of heart, and her lecherous mulatto boss, Jeff Wain. A good-hearted, dark-skinned black man named Frank Fowler, who has always loved her, comes to her rescue but too late to save her life. Rena ultimately falls ill from brain fever and dies in the house behind the cedars.

Obviously, the narrative is over-the-top, but its melodramatic plot serves the realistic purpose of highlighting the complications and ironies of life on the color line. Indeed, much of the story turns on the mulatto siblings' racial indeterminacy and the ironies of how race is perceived and how it is constructed. From the start, Chesnutt sets out to undermine one of the most pervasive assumptions about race, that is, its legibility. The text's opening, in which John and Rena are first presented, dramatizes, in exaggerated form, the inaccuracy of this idea to ultimately invalidate the notion of race as a phenotypical essence. For example, John is described as "tall, dark, with straight, black, lustrous hair, and very clean-cut, high-bred features," which leads the white clerk at the hotel to assume that John must be a prominent white businessman (1–2). Moreover, John himself makes the same racial assumption about his own sister, whom he gazes at lustfully while walking behind her, having failed to recognize her after being absent for so many years:

> Warwick's first glance had revealed the fact that the young woman was strikingly handsome, with a stately beauty seldom encountered. As he walked along behind her at a measured distance, he could not help noting the details that made up this pleasing impression, for his mind was singularly alive to beauty, in whatever embodiment. The girl's figure, he

> perceived, was admirably proportioned; she was evidently at the period when the angles of childhood were rounding into the promising curves of adolescence. Her abundant hair, of a dark and glossy brown, was neatly plaited and coiled above an ivory column that rose straight from a pair of gently sloping shoulders, clearly outlined beneath the light muslin frock that covered them. He could see that she was tastefully, though not richly, dressed, and that she walked with an elastic step that revealed a light heart and the vigor of perfect health. Her face, of course, he could not analyze, since he had caught only the one brief but convincing glimpse of it. (5)

In having John notice how "strikingly handsome" his sister is as well as her "ivory" white skin, Chesnutt evokes the dual specters of incest and miscegenation. As Eva Saks has explained, incest and miscegenation were viewed as analogous crimes of amalgamation in the nineteenth-century imagination: one involving the merger of blood "too similar" and the other, blood "too dissimilar" (71). Chesnutt uses the tropes of incest and miscegenation to interrogate the scientific fictions regarding racial difference and to highlight the cultural anxieties and fears surrounding sexual desire and racial identity—emotions exacerbated by the mulatto's invisibility. But far from granting validity to such feelings, Chesnutt actually weakens them by provocatively deploying the incest and miscegenation tropes to challenge the idea of race configured as blood while making an argument for the concept of universal kinship and the notion of race as something that denotes the larger human family.

As the narrative progresses, Chesnutt gradually chips away at the impression he has created of his mulatto protagonists' whiteness through indirect cues. For example, as John follows Rena through the residential portion of Patesville, the neighborhood gradually changes from "staid respectability to poverty" (5). As he listens to Rena speak to Aunt Zilphy, he notices that her voice bears a "faint suggestiveness" of the old negro woman's accent (6). John also watches as Rena stops to pull a "half-naked negro child out of a mudhole" but fantasizes that she might be an uptown lady looking for a servant (6). Not until she reaches the familiar cedar hedge does he finally make the connection that this ostensibly white woman is his own mixed-race sister. Thus, not only do the characters engage in racial passing, but the text also enacts a form of racial concealment, which Chesnutt slowly and systematically undermines to make the connection between race and class. As M. Giulia Fabi has noted, this encounter introduces the interrelated subjects of miscegenation and racial passing as both "theme and narrative strategy" (*Passing* 73).[7]

By introducing both John and Rena in this way, Chesnutt uses ocular logic to undermine not only our assumptions about the legibility of race but also our assumptions about the relationship between race and class. As Chesnutt recognizes, markers of lower-class status, such as a poor neighborhood or a nonstandard dialect, can be attributed to racial inequality rather than to any alleged innate racial difference. Moreover, since race is not always visible, and the white-skinned but socially/legally black person has the uncanny ability to manipulate the way that racial identity is perceived, why even talk about innate racial differences in the first place? In asking and answering this question vis-à-vis John and Rena's mutual misrecognitions, as well as our own assumptions as readers, the text suggests that the mulatto siblings are essentially incapable of being viewed as anything other than white, and thus makes the attending claim that racial identity is informed by perception and environment. Thematically, then, this entire sequence works to weaken the authority of the one-drop rule and the idea of race as interior essence. That John and Rena can so easily pass for white implicitly calls into question the practice of using hypodescent as the metric by which we codify mixed-race identity.

What is more, the opening sequence suggests, too, that race is also a matter of self-identification. In the absence of any physiological features that we might recognize as black, John and Rena's cultural location—the fact that they were raised to embrace white, middle-class norms and appear to have more in common with the white elite whom they resemble both in terms of behavior and social aspirations—makes it difficult to view their racial passing as an act of self-loathing or racial treason. By rendering John and Rena in such a way where it is apparent that neither one of them comfortably fits into the African American world, Chesnutt implies that the siblings *should* have the power to choose how they will identify. The text explores this provocative idea in its passing narrative.

Cast as a tool of self-invention, Chesnutt presents passing as an imaginative act rooted in narrative, but one that is ultimately susceptible to the limitations of both gender and genre. For example, John's experiment with passing proves to be far more successful than his sister's, as he skillfully blends romantic and realistic strategies to procure and protect his assumed identity—disappearing from the narrative altogether once their racial secret is exposed. While Rena, on the other hand, collapses under the weight of the tragic mulatta motif, ultimately dying of brain fever in her mother's humble abode. Although Chesnutt portrays passing in a sympathetic way, looking to explain the causes and effects of it rather than condemning it as a form of racial trespassing, his narrative choices with regard to John and Rena's respective trajectories, particularly as they diverge along the lines of gender and genre, warrant scrutiny. By granting John and Rena very different experiences and outcomes, Chesnutt suggests that passing is riskier for black women than it is for black men. Arguably, this is because black women bear the burden of both race and sex discrimination in a society organized by racial and gendered divisions and hierarchies. In this way, John enjoys greater social mobility than Rena does because he is not restricted to the domestic sphere or subject to the same kind of social castigation for transgressing sexual norms and ideas about virtue and propriety. As Valerie Smith has observed: "Passing women characters . . . are either reeducated and returned to the bosom of home and community, or they receive some extreme form of punishment such as death or the sacrifice of a loved one" (45). In this context, we can think of Chesnutt's decision to kill Rena off at the end of the novel not as a form of chastisement but as his way of exploring the systems of racial oppression that regulate sexual difference and behavior and that undercut black female agency.

In a larger sense, Chesnutt suggests that narrative may provide a vehicle for obtaining some degree of agency and navigating the racial landscape. What is most fascinating about the novel's exploration of passing is the idea that literary fictions can be just as powerful as social fictions, if not more, in the construction of racial identity. For example, the single-most-influential factor in both John and Rena's self-making is their father's bookcase. As Richard Brodhead explains, the bookcase is a stand-in for the siblings' "absent white father" whose "literary classics" inspire them to rewrite their personal narratives (207). But out of the two, John clearly has the better handle on such fictions, having spent his entire childhood reading *Ivanhoe, Robinson Crusoe,* and the *Arabian Nights.* Chesnutt suggests that it was these narratives that authored his flight—a story, which for his mother and sister has all "the charm of an escape from captivity [and] the thrill of a pirate's tale" (15). By envisioning himself as a character in an adventure narrative, John attains a type of mythic significance that he could never possess in real life, which has the ironic effect of making his fictional story appear more real than reality itself.

For John, identity is created vis-à-vis narrative. He easily convinces his mother that Rena's future depends upon her ability to write a new story, insisting: "[S]he will have no chance here, where our story is known. The war has wrought great changes . . . but it hasn't wiped *that* out. Nothing but death can remove that stain, if it does not follow us even beyond the grave. Here she must forever be—nobody!" (17–18). As John acknowledges, upward mobility is inextricably tied to race. There is an opportunity gap that affords white people greater access to social capital and economic resources and keeps black people stuck in a cycle of disadvantage and disenfranchisement. For John, not even the promise of post-Emancipation freedom can erase the stigma of the slave past. As long as other people know their racial story, they are bound by it. In what Saidiya Hartman has called "the afterlife of slavery," the stigma of blackness is a stain that, as John suggests, can be lifted only by death but may very well continue to oppress African Americans in the afterworld.[8] John's point here is a profound one that acknowledges the ways in which the legacy of slavery lives on in the postbellum period. If Rena is to be a "somebody," as John desires, then she will have to metaphorically die and re-create herself by writing a new fiction for an all-white audience. Appropriately, she pulls her new identity from *Ivanhoe,* a romantic novel that serves as an origin story for white southerners who believe that they are Scott's descendants.

Ivanhoe Revisited

As Alide Cagidemetrio has observed, Scott's *Ivanhoe* provided much of the inspiration for Chesnutt's miscegenation plot. Pointing to Ivanhoe's love for the Anglo-Saxon Rowena and "the final casting aside of Rebecca, the beautiful Jewess, as a suitable match for the Christian hero, Ivanhoe," Cagidemetrio posits that Chesnutt uses the *Ivanhoe* narrative to explore and condemn southern attitudes toward interracial marriage (16). Translating Scott's medieval romance into a post-Reconstruction narrative, Chesnutt reconfigures the *Ivanhoe* legend to attack southern anxieties over miscegenation. If in Scott's narrative Rebecca is, as Cagidemetrio claims, "the prototype of the American Other," then in his account, Chesnutt not only positions blackness as the archetypal form of American racial difference, but he also undermines the American fiction of Anglo-Saxon racial purity by naming his heroine after Rowena instead of Rebecca (22). Obviously, if a mulatta who is rendered black by the cultural and legal power ascribed to the one-drop rule can pass herself off as a Rowena, then blood loses its saliency as a fiction of identity in the face of narrative self-fashioning.

Chesnutt also uses the *Ivanhoe* narrative to critique the southern fiction that views chivalry as a cultural virtue and to show its complicity with the white, racist power structure. In the chapter entitled "The Tournament," Chesnutt indicts the South for its veneration of Scott, demonstrating that the cultural obsession with chivalry actually underwrites racism and a number of related ills, like class inequality and misogyny. Situating his censure of Scott at the Clarence Social Club's annual tournament, an elaborate medieval contest based on *Ivanhoe,* Chesnutt shows how literary fictions may be used to defend racial privilege and reinforce cultural norms. For example, at the tournament, the people of Clarence pretend to be medieval knights and ladies from Scott's novel. Sporting cardboard armor and fancy costumes, they participate in mock jousts and swordplay. But their performances are more than mere sport. They are symbolic demonstrations of so-called Anglo-Saxon perfection that allow the people of Clarence to return to the feudal past.

As Aaron Ritzenberg has elucidated, the tournament sequence is really "a communal wish-fulfillment for a culture of nobility and honor" (57). But we might just as easily describe it as a collective fantasy for white, racial power. Indeed, Chesnutt recognizes that there is a connection between the white power structure that sanctioned slavery and the white power structure that created the social divisions and hierarchies that characterized the feudal system. As I mentioned in chapter 1, Twain made a similar observation when he blamed Scott for creating a "Middle-Age sham civilization" that "made every gentleman in the South a Major or a

Colonel, or a General or a Judge" and "created rank and caste down there," ultimately starting the Civil War (*Life on the Mississippi* 282). Building upon Twain's critique, Chesnutt illustrates the dark side of chivalry. In his formulation, it has dangerous consequences for blacks and whites alike, but it delivers its deadliest blow to African Americans. This is an idea that Chesnutt literalizes when one of his black characters is struck by a fragment from a knight's lance and bleeds without anyone caring.

Chesnutt begins his critique by giving us a brief gloss of *Ivanhoe*'s reception to convey a sense of its role in structuring southern life before and after the war:

> The influence of Walter Scott was strong upon the old South. The South before the war was essentially feudal, and Scott's novels of chivalry appealed forcefully to the feudal heart. During the month preceding the Clarence tournament, the local bookseller had closed out his entire stock of "Ivanhoe," consisting of five copies, and had taken orders for seven copies more. The tournament scene in this popular novel furnished the model after which these bloodless imitations of the ancient passages-at-arms were conducted, with such variations as were required to adapt them to a different age and civilization. (31)

As the passage indicates, the war did very little to loosen Scott's grip on the southern imagination. Postbellum Clarence is just as enchanted by *Ivanhoe* as it was before the war. Committed to keeping feudalism alive and well, the white community endeavors to re-create the novel's tournament scene so that its members can live out their collective fantasy of a culture of chivalry. Billing their reenactment as a "bloodless imitation" of the "ancient passages-at-arms," Chesnutt suggests, sarcastically of course, that the people of Clarence believe that they are the more advanced and enlightened successors of Scott's line (31).

But only the well-heeled white people can actually lay claim to this history. As a result, they get to occupy the grandstand, while the "poorer white and colored folks" watch the tournament from the bleachers (31). Ironically, John, of all people, takes his seat in the second row and proudly declares that the tournament is "the renaissance of chivalry"—revealing that he does indeed think of himself as a privileged white man (32). While trying to convince a skeptical Mrs. Newberry that Clarence's reenactment is superior to Scott's Ashby-de-la-Zouch, because it is less physical and more cerebral, John ascribes racial and teleological significance to the historical narrative of chivalry:

> [L]ike any other renaissance, it must adapt to new times and circumstances. For instance, when we build a Greek portico, having no Pentelic marble near at hand, we use a pine-tree, one of nature's columns, which Grecian art at its best could only copy and idealize. Our knights are not weighted down with heavy armor, but much more appropriately attired, for a day like this, in costumes that recall the picturesqueness, without the discomfort, of the old knightly harness. For an iron-headed lance we use a wooden substitute, with which we transfix rings instead of hearts; while our trusty blades hew their way through wooden blocks instead of through flesh and blood. It is a South Carolina renaissance which has points of advantage over the tournaments of olden time. (32)

The enthusiasm that John displays for the pageantry of the tournament reveals a great deal about how he views himself. Appropriating a cultural narrative that is not his own, he interpolates himself into the historical timeline of whiteness—a European temporal frame that begins in ancient Greece and ends with modernity—and as a result, comes to view the newfangled technologies of the reenactment as improvements that index the degree to which "his race" has evolved. Pairing the discourses of aesthetic and biological evolution, then, John suggests that their revisions to the *Ivanhoe* legend constitute a cultural victory in the name of chivalry.

But the new chivalry turns out to be just as violent as ever. No sooner than John starts to sing the praises of the new tournament's safety, a flying fragment from a lance hits an unknown black man in the head and draws blood. Fifty pages later, we learn that this man is none other than Frank Fowler, Rena's faithful childhood friend. But at the tournament he is completely anonymous. Chesnutt ventriloquizes white society's lack of regard for black life when he describes Frank's reaction as "good-natured" (33). When "seeing no great harm done," the white bystanders begin to make "witty and original remarks about the advantage of being black upon occasions where one's skull was exposed to danger" (33). Once Frank discovers that he is bleeding, he ties a red handkerchief around his head for want of proper medical attention. The white people in the audience, however, are indifferent to the extent of his injury. And they continue to enjoy their seemingly civilized display of chivalry.

The seemingly innocent and accidental nature of the injury and the unsympathetic reaction that it receives reveal a great deal about chivalry. In no uncertain terms the text suggests that its violent cultural practices disproportionately affect black people, whose lives are not considered valuable in the first place. Moreover, the flying fragment from the lance cannot be divorced from its phallic registers, as the lance symbolizes white sexual power at the expense of black masculinity. When George Tryon ties Rena's handkerchief around his lance he subtly communicates his sexual interest in her, while also adding an emotional wound to Frank's physical wound, as he is secretly in love with Rena and knows that she does not see him as a suitable romantic partner because of his dark skin and lower-class status. Chesnutt's point here is that southern chivalry emasculates black men and leaves black women vulnerable to sexual conquest at the hands of white men. At the end of the day, George wins the tournament and crowns Rena the "Queen of Love and Beauty," while Frank's injury is seen as merely incidental and does not constitute a major loss. In fact, no one even seems to care. Clearly, chivalry's moral code does not extend beyond white people. George tells Rena: "May your Majesty never abdicate her throne, and may she ever count me her humble servant and devoted knight" (42). But this remark proves to be ironic when, after discovering the truth about her ancestry, he quickly casts her aside in a most ungenerous manner, "peeling away [his] chivalrous veneer" as J. Lee Greene has described it (69–70). Ultimately, what the tournament sequence makes unmistakably clear is that chivalry underwrites racial inequality because it supports white supremacy.

The Marriage Plot and the Genres of Racial Passing

Soon after the tournament, Chesnutt introduces the marriage plot and the novel's racial tension split along the lines of gender and genre. A popular feature of romantic and sentimental fiction, the marriage plot originated in the mid-eighteenth century with the publication of Samuel

Richardson's novel *Pamela* (1740), which revolves around a wealthy landowner who repeatedly and unsuccessfully attempts to rape his fifteen-year-old servant and eventually rewards her for her virtue with marriage. Although the marriage plot has been "coded as white, female, and European," as Ann duCille has explained, it is a critical device for unpacking African American representations of love and marriage, which are often subversive critiques of the social, legal, and moral frameworks that underwrite courtship and matrimony in U.S. culture. Indeed, as duCille has observed, the marriage plot's "relationship to the African American novel has always been highly political" as African American writers frequently appropriated and subverted the device to explore and intervene in popular debates about race, sex, and family (3). Guided by a similar logic, Chesnutt adopts the marriage plot and integrates it into his generically mixed passing narrative to examine issues of race, class, and gender (specifically black female subjectivity) as well as the different pathways of mobility that marriage and passing offer men and women on the color line.

Genre provides the ground rules and conditions that organize John's and Rena's respective narrative trajectories. As Steven Belluscio has observed: "[I]f one traces the development of John Walden, [the text] has the makings of a realist narrative with the requisite plot of social adaptation and ascent. If one focuses upon his sister Rena Walden, then the details of her failed struggle with passing suggest a melodramatic, even naturalistic, plot of decline" (139). Because Rena feels the weight of her racial secret in ways that her brother does not, the sense of determinism that pervades the latter half of the novel is entirely contained within her narrative. As Rena's fears of racial discovery intensify, John emerges as the text's resident realist, dismissing her worries as the result of a "tragic view of life" and thus self-reflexively invoking the tragic mulatta trope. In calling attention to the antebellum iteration of this stock character, Chesnutt issues a metaliterary critique that acknowledges the degree to which sexism and racism have animated depictions of mixed-race women in fiction, portraying them, as I discussed in the previous chapter, as depressed or suicidal, a victim of their divided racial inheritance, sexually promiscuous, hysterical, or better off dead. With this literary history in mind, Chesnutt places John and Rena on two very different trajectories to explore some of our most basic racial and gendered narrative expectations for mixed-race characters, with the specific purpose of undermining them, while also preparing the way for his ultimate censure of white racism: George's rejection of Rena and her subsequent death.

Beginning with John, Chesnutt suggests that his social success can be attributed to a combination of good fortune and self-determination. Early on in the narrative it is revealed that during the Civil War, John had the luck of escaping military service by managing a "large estate" whose owner had died on the battlefield (15). After the war, John married the man's orphan daughter, which placed him in direct control of the plantation. "Rich in his wife's right," John attended law school and was admitted to the bar and made a career out of practicing law (15). But Chesnutt suggests, too, that John's success is also a product of his own innate rhetorical and interpretive prowess. Indeed, as William L. Andrews has observed, John "is a singular figure in the race literature of post–Civil War America" because "he is perhaps the first character in American fiction who, having been raised 'black,' decides on his own to pass for white and constructs a legal and moral justification for doing so" (*Literary Career* 164). Moreover, as Andrews also notes, John is the first black character to successfully pass for white by marrying a white woman (*Literary Career* 153).

While still a boy, John visits Judge Straight and announces his intention to become a lawyer, and Judge Straight reminds John that he is black and therefore unfit in the eyes of the law to be admitted to the bar. In this way, Judge Straight invokes a definition of race that is rooted in legal precedent, calling to mind the *Dred Scott* decision (1857), in which the majority opinion held that because Dred Scott was a slave, and not a citizen of the United States, he could not sue the federal government for his freedom. In a similar way, Judge Straight tells John that he cannot be a lawyer because he is "black" and "not free" (113). In an antebellum context, this means that John cannot travel without papers, secure accommodations at white facilities, vote, be out past curfew, or testify in court (113). In short, Straight's point is that, like Scott, John has no "rights which the white man is bound to respect" (113). But John argues that the Court's decision does not apply to him. He agrees that the law may be true but suggests that the truth is ultimately a matter of interpretation. He reminds Judge Straight that a "negro is black" and that he is clearly white in appearance (113). Invoking the same argument that Homer Plessy did in *Plessy v. Ferguson*

(1896), John lays claim to his whiteness as a form of property by reversing the logic behind the one-drop rule, asking, "Why shouldn't it be the other way, if the white blood is so superior?" (113). When the judge tells him, "[I]t is more convenient as it is—and more profitable," John concludes that, "It is not right," making a crucial distinction between natural law, that is, those rights endowed by nature or God, and positive law, which refers to man-made laws (113).

Perhaps owing to his legal training, John takes a more logical approach than his sister to the business of marriage and passing. He argues that marriage is a contract for the future and that it does not require disclosure of previous events: "We are under no moral obligation to inflict upon others the history of our past. . . . Still less are we bound to bring out from this secret chamber the dusty record of our ancestry" (54).[9] In dismissing the significance of the past, John revises a key component of the tragic mulatta narrative. As I discussed in chapter 2, according to the traditional formula, the mixed-race heroine is expected to relinquish her white lover and dedicate her life to the project of racial uplift once her secret is exposed. But John rejects this sentimental configuration of duty and self-sacrifice by suggesting that Rena's real obligation is to give up her silly and potentially destructive desire to tell George the truth. In this respect, John supplants Rena's romantic and sentimental notion of moral responsibility with the realist's worldview, defending the individual's right to make his or her own decisions, or what critics of realism call moral agency.[10]

Insisting that a revelation of this nature would only do George unnecessary damage, not to mention affect a number of other people, John asks Rena: "Would you not be willing, for his sake, to keep a secret—your secret and mine, and that of the innocent child in your arms? Would you involve all of us in difficulties merely to secure your own peace of mind? Doesn't such a course seem just the least bit selfish? (56). John's realist calculation of the collateral damage that would ensue in the wake of a revelation deeply affects Rena since "it had never before occurred to her to regard silence in the light of self-sacrifice. It had seemed a sort of sin; her brother's argument made of it a virtue" (56). This line of reasoning convinces Rena that right and wrong is largely a matter of perspective, which helps her "bury the past in forgetfulness" and, at least temporarily, live in the present moment (59).

But as Chesnutt illustrates, vis-à-vis a series of improbable coincidences, "[t]he past is never dead. It's not even past."[11] Shortly after Rena decides to keep her and her brother's secret, she dreams of her mother's illness for three nights in succession. Because Rena believes that a dream repeated three times "was a certain portent of the thing defined," she leaves for Patesville on the eve of her wedding (62). But before she does, she stops by the post office, where she finds a letter from her dear old mother confirming her worst fears: her mother is in fact desperately ill. Strangely enough, this grave message compels Rena to revert back to her tragic imagination: "The thought that her mother might die without the presence of any one who loved her pierced Rena's heart like a knife and lent wings to her feet. She wished for the enchanted horse of which her brother had read to her so many years before . . . that she might fly through the air to her dying mother's side" (64). With this in mind, Rena succumbs to this romantic vision and boards a train home.

John, however, remains firmly entrenched in the realist's position. After learning that George will be in Patesville at the same time as Rena, he attempts to "balance" the "probabilities" that the two lovers will run into each other. He reasons that he "may easily be in [town] for a day or two without meeting her" because she will more than likely "spend most of her time at mother's bedside, and he will be occupied with his own affairs" (69). But he also contemplates the worst-case scenario, thinking that if George "should meet her—well, he was very much in love, and he had spoken very nobly of birth and blood," insisting that it did not matter, as he himself was the descendant of a convicted felon (69). Having determined that there is a 50 percent probability in either direction, John takes a coin from his pocket and spins it on the floor, proclaiming: "Heads, he sees her; tails, he does not" (69). John's young son Albert, fascinated by the shiny, whirring disc, catches the coin before it can touch the floor, which serves to dramatize the unpredictability of everyday life. Not even a shrewd realist like John can always predict the outcome of an event, as Chesnutt suggests that destiny is partially shaped by chance and partially shaped by choice.

Demonstrating that even the best-laid schemes go wrong at times, Rena runs into George on the third day of her stay in Patesville. Inevitably, George discovers the truth about her ancestry, despite several attempts by John, Judge Straight, and Frank to forewarn her of her fiancé's presence in town. Underscoring his consternation, George cannot reconcile the fact of Rena's blackness with the fiction of whiteness that she led him to believe was true. Having lost his ability to see her as a white beauty, his first feelings are of "anger and disgust" (95). The trauma of discovery soon causes him to succumb to "illness" (95), as he feels that he is the innocent "victim" of a "fraud" (96). Predictably, George quickly calls off his engagement to Rena. But oddly enough, he does so in a letter addressed to John, in which he writes: "I shall never be able to think of you as other than a white man," but "I cannot marry your sister" (102–3). Such a dreadful double standard begs the question of how George can continue to view John as a white person but not Rena. Arguably, George can accept John's decision to pass for white over Rena's because John's passing does not pose personal complications for him in the way of sexual intimacy. Because John is not a prospective marriage partner, George need not hold him to the same level of racial scrutiny. Despite George's knowledge of the truth, he can relate to John on the basis of gender and thus view his racial passing as a form of masculine self-fashioning. But with Rena he must grapple with the so-called atavistic threat, that is the idea, at least within the racist scientific imagination, that they could produce offspring who might look more black than white, effectively shattering the illusion of white racial purity.

In this way, George's rejection of Rena harkens back to an earlier moment in the text, before the moment of racial discovery, where Chesnutt satirizes the concept of atavism. While waiting for Dr. Green to return to his office, George picks up a medical journal featuring an article on the topic. Arguing from a position of scientific racism, the article contends that "negro blood," no matter how "diluted," will always "revert [back] to the African type . . . for the smallest trace of negro blood would inevitably drag down the superior race to the level of the inferior" (71). George concludes that the article is "well-considered, albeit a trifle bombastic" (71). In having George arrive at this opinion, Chesnutt suggests that George is indeed prejudiced, but that he is not really a racist in his heart of hearts, as his ability to see that the article is slightly overblown distinguishes him from the flaming racist and makes him a moderate by the standards of his time. Chesnutt's point here is that most white people are like George.

In abstract, they may hold bigoted views, but upon developing a more intimate association with a black person they come to see them in more sympathetic ways. This is why George does not change his opinion about John, and why even after calling the engagement off he has second (and third) thoughts about Rena and attempts to win her back.

Interestingly, John and Rena react very differently to George's goodbye letter. John, the cold, calculating pragmatist that he is, does not take this rejection personally. While he attempts to assuage his sister's feelings of grief with a few sympathetic words, he suggests that she adopt a more practical view of the situation by trading in her pain for reason: "[D]o not despair; all is not lost. . . . Come back and try again" (119). Viewing love in a purely utilitarian light, John suggests that Rena forget about George by setting her sights on a new unsuspecting target. Rena, however, is unable to share John's businesslike approach toward marriage and passing. Highlighting the differences between the sexes, she argues, "A man may make a new place for himself—a woman is born and bound to hers" (121). John attaches no weight whatsoever to his sister's argument and vanishes from the narrative altogether, presumably to take his own advice and go pass for white elsewhere, leaving his sister to navigate a racial land mine that he put her in the way of for his own selfish purposes.

That John and Rena have radically different narrative arcs invites us to see how gendered expectations underwrite generic outcomes in the marriage plot and in the passing narrative. By making their respective points of view a function of gender and genre, Chesnutt not only adds greater complexity to our understanding of attitudes and beliefs about interracial marriage and miscegenation at the time, but he also troubles our assumptions about the ethics and political efficacy of an ostensibly more masculine, pragmatic realism and the alleged vacuity of feminine sentimentalism. As Chesnutt illustrates through John's and Rena's narrative arcs, both genres have their advantages and their limitations. While John is clearly the more logical character, Rena is more emotional and concerned with others' feelings. In this way, Chesnutt suggests that John's pragmatist realism is too inward-looking and that his success comes at the expense of others' misfortune, while Rena's more romantic imagination keeps her bound to social conventions to the detriment of her own personal happiness. Chesnutt's point seems to be that either extreme is problematic and that a more balanced approach toward both gender and genre might yield better results in popular fiction and in the real world.

The Quagmire of Race and Gender

After breaking off the engagement, George has a series of changes of heart and seeks contact with Rena. At one point he writes her a letter, asking for an interview, but she rebuffs his proposal on two counts: race and respectability. Rena argues that there would be no point in meeting since George has already drawn the color line: "You are white, and you have given me to understand that I am black" (172). And she points out that they would not be able to meet without controversy: "As a white man, this might not mean a great deal to you; as a woman, shut out already by my color from much that is desirable, my good name remains my most valuable possession" (172–73). In this pivotal exchange, Rena acknowledges her vulnerable position as a woman of color. And a critical late scene in the novel concretizes this vulnerability, as she finds herself faced with a literal and metaphorical fork in the road, with George on one path, and Wain on the other.

In this scene, Chesnutt adopts the naturalistic plot of decline—a sequence of events that illustrate a character's gradual deterioration or progression toward death—to highlight the ways in which Rena's racial reality is, in Ryan Simmons's words, "relatively bound by her environment" (69).[12] As Simmons has explained, in the latter pages of the novel, roughly chapters 21 through 33, Rena's "behavior is not biologically driven—as [George] assumes it has been . . . but it is constrained by historical circumstances"—for example, race, class, and gender (69). When Rena comes to the fork in the forest, all of these forces collide, and she is literally bound by her surroundings. Because she has free will only within the parameters that her culture has delineated, she must make the most of her limited options. Chesnutt prioritizes Rena's limited choices to explore the question of moral agency. As a realist, Chesnutt wants to give Rena the ability to make her own decisions. But he also wants to show how her decisions are restricted by the constraints of race and gender. Like John, Rena could continue to pass in some new setting where she is not known, but instead, Chesnutt has her teach at an all-black school to make fun of, and thus subvert, a contrived plot point to highlight her lack of options. Chesnutt's point is that Rena's social circumstances render her relatively powerless. If she continues to pass, she might get caught, and who is to say that the next white man will be as discreet as George? If she goes back to George, she will presumably have to pass for the rest of her life or live in secrecy as his black mistress. If she chooses Wain, she risks physical abuse and sexual degradation. Ultimately, then, what the final section of the novel demonstrates is how Rena's race and gender place her in a vicious moral quagmire that Chesnutt literalizes in the swamp sequence.

In this gripping scene, Rena, eager to get home before an impending storm arrives, decides to take the shortcut near the swamp. In the fierce winds, she loses sight of her youthful companion, Plato, whom George has bribed with a dollar to reunite them in the forest, and finds herself at a fork in the road:

> Her forward step had brought her to the junction of the two paths, where she paused doubtfully. The route she had been following was the most direct way home, but led for quite a distance through the forest, which she did not care to traverse alone. The intersecting path would soon take her to the main road, where she might find shelter or company, or both. Glancing around again in search of her missing escort, she became aware that a man was approaching her from each of the two paths. In one she recognized the eager and excited face of George Tryon, flushed with anticipation of their meeting, and yet grave with uncertainty of his reception. Advancing confidently along the other path she saw the face of Jeff Wain, drawn as she imagined in her anguish, with evil passions which would stop at nothing. (181)

Chesnutt literally positions Rena at the forefront of two divergent paths that symbolize two radically different fates. On the one hand, there is George, the would-be noble knight, and on the other, Wain, the mulatto scoundrel. The former represents the white romantic fantasy, whereas the latter epitomizes the bleak reality of her current social position.

Chesnutt makes it very clear that both men and both paths are fraught with danger. Rena cannot be too certain as to George's real intentions, in light of his fickle behavior toward her. And neither can she ignore the fact that Wain is an abusive womanizer. Thus, the fork in the road symbolizes the twin hazards of her precarious position:

> In the two conflicting dangers she might have found safety. The road after all was a public way. Any number of persons might meet there accidentally. But she saw only the darker side of the situation. To turn to Tryon for protection before Wain had by some overt act manifested the evil purpose which she as yet only suspected would be, she imagined, to acknowledge a previous secret acquaintance with Tryon, thus placing her reputation at Wain's mercy, and to charge herself with a burden of obligation toward a man whom she wished to avoid and had refused to meet. If, on the other hand, she should go forward to meet Wain, he would undoubtedly offer to accompany her homeward. Tryon would inevitably observe the meeting, and suppose it prearranged. Not for the world would she have him think so—why she should care for his opinion, she did not stop to argue. She turned and fled, and to avoid possible pursuit, struck into . . . a clump of prickly shrubs and briars. (181–82)

Interestingly, Chesnutt entertains the idea of Rena finding "safety" in the two contradictory paths but undermines the likelihood that this will come to pass by referencing the "darker side of the situation." Operating on two levels, this evocative phrase not only describes Rena's deteriorating mental state under the pressure, but it also delivers a metalevel critique about the tragic turn that the novel has taken in relationship to genre. The tragedy of Rena's predicament is that no matter which path she chooses, she runs the risk of ruining her reputation (the most valuable thing she has), which really does not leave her with much of a choice at all. Acknowledging the powerlessness of her position, Rena creates a third option by jumping into the briars, which causes her to get lost in the swamp and subsequently die of a combination of exposure and mental derangement.

For many critics, Rena's death ultimately reads as a romantic construction that reinforces the tragic mulatta stereotype and undermines the novel's antiracist message. As Steven Belluscio has noted, "One would be hard-pressed to find a more self-consciously melodramatic ending" (218). Chesnutt's "racial romanticism . . . undercuts both the aesthetic and political project of his work" (Belluscio 145). To be sure, Rena's plot does reflect certain aspects of the tragic mulatta narrative. Not only does she renounce her white lover, but she also appears to spiral into mental illness after realizing that her racial identity prevents her from being with the one man whom she really loves. In a particularly theatrical scene she laughingly cries: "[D]ear George, do you love me? How much do you love me? Ah, you don't love me! . . . I'm black . . . you despise me!" (192). Moreover, she succumbs to brain fever and dies before George can declare his love for her and reverse his attitudes about race. Certainly, if Chesnutt really wanted to debunk the fictions of race and elevate white people, then would it not make sense to have the lovers marry?

In my estimation, Chesnutt does not allow the marriage to occur to achieve a more important aesthetic and moral goal. In ending the novel as he does, he highlights Rena's lack of alternatives. As a woman on the color line, Rena occupies an ambiguous space that puts her at a cultural and social disadvantage. There really is no place for her in the Jim Crow South. Because her identity is constructed by the social and legal discourses of race and gender, she has very little agency in determining her life's course. As Cathy Boeckmann has argued, "When [Rena] rejects both men and both paths and sets off into the uncharted swamp, she succumbs to the powerlessness of her gender position and the liminality of her racial identity" (166). But in some respects, Rena's rejection of both men and both paths actually registers as an act of agency for a woman whose choices are limited by both her race and her gender. While it remains true that her ending is tragic, her story is different from that of most nineteenth-century fictional mulattas. As M. Giulia Fabi has explained, "Rena's death results not from some Howellsian aimless self-sacrifice but from an effort of self-preservation" (*Passing* 84–85). In the final analysis, Chesnutt uses a romantic construction to make a realistic argument: the fiction of race can have devastating consequences.

No moment better illustrates this than the scene in which George learns of Rena's illness and sets out with Godspeed to visit her. His belated recognition of the role that he has played in her emotional and mental decline is the final and most powerful gesture in Chesnutt's struggle to depict the moral hazards of racism. As the narrator remarks,

> If anything could have taken more complete possession of George Tryon at twenty-three than love successful and triumphant, it was love thwarted and denied. Never in the few brief delirious weeks of his courtship had he felt so strongly drawn to the beautiful sister of the popular lawyer, as he was now driven by an aching heart toward the same woman stripped of every advantageous advantage and placed, by custom, beyond the pale of marriage with men of his own race. Custom was tyranny. Love was the only law. Would God have made hearts to so yearn for one another if He had meant for them to stay forever apart? If this girl should die, it would be he who had killed her, by his cruelty, no less surely than if with his own hand he had struck her down. (194)

In having George realize, all too late, that he loves Rena enough to reject the cultural taboos and laws surrounding miscegenation, Chesnutt asks white people to try to relate to his character's internal battle. By foregrounding George's perspective, Chesnutt urges white readers to reevaluate their racial attitudes and to adopt a more compassionate stance to his fictional characters, and by extension, real people, who, like Rena, are injured by racism. In so doing, Chesnutt places the onus on whites to give up their white privilege and see African Americans as fellow human beings. Speaking through his narrator, Chesnutt leaves us with the moral of his story: "Custom was tyranny. Love was the only law." As Rena dies of heartbreak and George loses his one true love as a result of his own cruelty, the novel makes the argument that racism ultimately hurts both blacks and whites alike, albeit not in equal measure.

If true love evades George and Rena, then it also escapes Frank Fowler—the novel's real romantic hero. By the end of the book it becomes undoubtedly clear that he is Rena's truest and purest suitor. For example, when on her deathbed, she cries, "[D]ear George, do you love me?"—Frank says: "Oh, my honey, my darlin' . . . Frank loves you better'n all de worl'" (192). Similarly, in their last exchange, when Rena finally realizes that Frank was her "best friend" and "loved [her] best of . . . all," he confesses that, "I'd 'a' died, fer you, Miss Rena" (195). Frank's unwavering love for Rena obviously raises the question of why he is never presented as a viable romantic option? Arguably, it is because he is not a realistic choice for her, given his dark skin, his occupation as a laborer, and that he speaks in the black vernacular. For a woman of Rena's in-between racial and class status, combined with her social aspirations, someone like Frank would not be a suitable marriage partner, as her light skin and boarding-school education would have afforded her a certain kind of cultural privilege.[13] In many respects, this intragroup racial discrimination makes him the other tragedy at the novel's centerpiece.

Trudier Harris has argued that Rena's inability to view Frank in a romantic light proves that "Chesnutt [was not] able to lift himself far enough above his own prejudice"—as he too was a member of the mulatto class to which his heroine belonged (228). As Harris reads it, Chesnutt's decision to have Rena die rather than unite with Frank ultimately compromises the novel's racial politics, as it points to a blind spot in Chesnutt's progressive vision. Although I agree with this reading to a certain extent, I also think that Chesnutt chose to end the novel with death, as opposed to a validation of black love, because he wanted to indict white people for their racism and illustrate, in dramatic form, the terrible consequences of racial hatred. How would having Rena take up with Frank change white people's views about racial identity and deeply personal matters of the heart like love and marriage? Had Rena ended up with Frank, the novel would have lost its shock value, its ability to appeal to a broader white audience, and its cross-racial critique—all of which it achieved, judging from the reviews it received at the time of publication.

In terms of narrative strategy, the final third of the novel urges us to sympathize with Rena by acknowledging the impossibility of her situation. When Rena finds herself at the fork in the road, pursued by George on one path and Wain on another, the reality of her vulnerable position as a mulatta woman is brought into high textual relief. Not only does her gender place her at the mercy of each man's desires, but her race also renders her powerless against the threats of moral condemnation and sexual degradation. When Rena rejects both men and wanders off into the swamp, she chooses to exercise what little agency she actually has to maintain her virtue. That this decision also precipitates her untimely death reveals the extent to which, at the time, black women were at a special disadvantage when it came to choosing their own destinies and thus creating their own identities. The naturalistic plot of decline underscores this ugly truth, illustrating how Rena's racial environment determines what decisions she can make. The novel's tragic ending is designed to wake white readers up from their racial complacency and inspire them to do that which George failed to do before it was too late: show black people mercy and love.

The Cultural Work of Genre

In the fictional world of *The House behind the Cedars,* the quagmire of race and gender finds ample expression in the merger of genres. In Darryl Hattenhauer's words, the novel is a mixed-genre work in which the "sentimentalism and melodrama overlaying this text are underlaid by the thematic complexity of realism and tragedy" (43). Acutely aware of the important cultural work that genre could perform, Chesnutt approached his first novel as an opportunity to present white readers with an illustration of black life that not only captured its difficulties but also illustrated its possibilities. To achieve this dual vision of realistic and romantic representation, he revisited what would have undoubtedly been familiar textual territory for his late nineteenth-century readership: the tragic mulatta trope. In doing so, Chesnutt appropriated a seemingly simple and noncontroversial figure to explore very taboo topics: passing and miscegenation. Looking to give greater emotional complexity and psychological depth to one of the most widely recognized, parodied, and stereotyped figures in all of American fiction, Chesnutt deployed a contrived plot device to make a cynical and optimistic point: racism kills, but literature can pave the way toward greater understanding.

As he expressed in his journals, Chesnutt believed that race and genre were deeply connected and that fiction was the ideal forum for exploring the relationship between politics and aesthetics. *The House behind the Cedars* reflects this philosophical view perhaps more so than any of his other novels, demonstrating that solutions to social problems could be explored and theorized in imaginative writing. Convinced that it was the "province of literature" to prepare the way for "social recognition and equality" as well as guide white people "step by step to the desired state of feeling," Chesnutt mobilized the protocols of narrative to open the door for marginalized African Americans who were, for the most part, outside of mainstream America's visual field of focus (*Journals* 139–40). And, as Brook Thomas has explained, he relied on "as much logos as pathos" to create sympathetic characters who would ultimately "alter people's feelings" about race and racism (*American Literary Realism* 182).

The fullest and most compelling expression of this narrative strategy is the novel's shift from its opening statement that "custom is law" to its closing corrective: "Custom was tyranny. Love was the only law" (23, 194). These two phrases encapsulate the two radically different views about race that are present in the novel. Whereas the first embodies the spirit of the one-drop rule, the second speaks to the power of sentiment. When Judge Straight asserts that "custom is law," what he is truly saying is that our cultural beliefs and practices are powerful forces that organize our reality. Put another way: "We make our customs lightly; once made, like our sins, they grip us in bands of steel; we become the creatures of our creations" (24). But by the end of the novel, Chesnutt reverses this perspective with the real takeaway of the novel, a truth that gains much of its potency from the tragedy that produces it: love is stronger than custom. In the final analysis, Chesnutt's point is that love is the solution to the problem of racism.

By lodging this sentimental truth in a work of fiction, Chesnutt was able to issue an antiracist message in a narrative package that could be easily digested by white readers and that would also do justice to black people. As an African American writer, Chesnutt knew that his greatest obstacles were his race and the deeply held prejudices of his largely white readership, and he used genre as a way to overcome these hurdles. Wanting to write a novel that was at once realistic, at least as he defined it, and yet not so abrasive as to risk alienating his intended, white audience, who, as he suggested, needed to be lifted up from their racial ignorance, Chesnutt decided to manipulate well-known literary traditions and their conventions to communicate his feelings about the moral and social hazards of racism in a way that would appeal to the common humanity of both blacks and whites. In the process of doing so, he crafted compelling, politically conscious metaliterary statements about the purpose of fiction. Recognizing the relationship between racial fictions and literary fictions, Chesnutt used his novel as a sounding board for the virtues of an Afro-realism. Combining romantic and realistic genres, in their broadest terms, he successfully made the case that fiction was perhaps our greatest weapon in the fight to create a more equitable social and literary landscape.

4

The Limits of Literary Realism

Pauline Hopkins's Postracial Fantasy in *Of One Blood*

> Fiction is of great value to any people as a preserver of manners and customs—religious, political and social. It is a record of growth and development from generation to generation. *No one will do this for us; we must ourselves develop the men and women who will faithfully portray the inmost thoughts and feelings of the Negro with all the fire and romance which lie dormant in our history,* and, as yet, unrecognized by writers of the Anglo-Saxon race.

In the preface to her first novel, *Contending Forces,* an excerpt of which appears above, Pauline Hopkins offers a critical assessment of the cultural stakes of fiction. According to the prolific writer and editor, fiction and history should serve mutual ends: the uplifting of the race. Pointing to the artistic and archival merits of both disciplines, Hopkins implores her fellow African Americans to take up the pen. As Hopkins suggests, fiction's primary power lies in its pedagogical potential. Fiction has the ability to educate African Americans about their rich and painful past, and this past can in turn enrich literary production, as it is replete with material that might easily be adapted for the sake of artistic development and political agitation. Addressing African Americans specifically, Hopkins indicates that it is the responsibility of the race to produce the writers who will narrate this past "with all the fire and romance" that it deserves, thus calling for a fiction of both mimetic detail and romantic affect, or what I have called, throughout this book, "Afro-realism."

In *Of One Blood, or The Hidden Self* (1902–3), Hopkins uses Afro-realism to explore issues of ancestry, miscegenation, slavery, broken kinship, and the legacies of the antebellum past on the postbellum present.

What is more, the novel surveys a vast field of nineteenth-century cultural discourses on identity, including anthropology, ethnology, Ethiopianism, the new psychology, and double-consciousness. It also draws from several literary traditions: realism, the gothic novel, the adventure narrative, and the speculative genres of utopia and fantasy. And it adopts a bifurcated plotline that splits the novel into two separate sequences, one set in America, and another in Africa. The first part focuses on the protagonist Reuel Briggs's racial passing. The second part focuses on his discovery of a hidden city that not only doubles as a metaphor for his hidden identity as a long-lost African king but that also subverts the racial divisions and hierarchies of postbellum America. Taken together, both the American and African narratives form a realistic and a romantic meditation on blood, identity, and genealogy that functions as a fantasy of racial transformation, one, that, in Paul Gilroy's words, "points towards the possibility of leaving 'race' behind, of setting aside its disabling use" (29).[1]

In what follows, I argue that *Of One Blood* should be read as a postracial fantasy.[2] Exploiting the tension between realism and romance, the novel attempts to envision a world beyond the racially inflected contours of the United States. Far from abandoning racial thinking or the plight of black Americans, the novel revises the racial fictions—the one-drop rule, polygenesis, and myths of innate savagery—that relegated blacks to subhuman status. To subvert these fictions and imagine an alternative topography for turn-of-the-twentieth-century African Americans, Hopkins destabilizes the concept of race. Beginning with her deliberately paradoxical title—*Of One Blood, or The Hidden Self*—Hopkins discredits the idea of multiple distinct races, but she resists the wholesale cancellation of race to preserve culture. This allows her to endorse the notion of the single racial family (thereby contradicting polygenetic claims about separate racial lineages and African American inferiority), while simultaneously maintaining black cultural distinctiveness.

From here, Hopkins adopts various generic traditions to frame her deconstruction of race, reminding us that the work of racial revision is often a question of representation, best addressed by form. To combat racism at home, she replaces the more mimetic narrative of racial passing with a melodramatic counternarrative that looks toward Africa and its past as a source of cultural pride. Not only does this shift constitute a generic dislocation, but it also represents a temporal one, making the premodern past contemporaneous with Reuel's life as a black man during the nadir. More importantly, Hopkins uses these displacements to create another paradox central to the novel's racial critique: *race matters* and *race does not matter.* In the American narrative, *race matters* insofar as it is a totalizing discourse that organizes all social interaction. But in the African narrative, *race does not matter* in the same way, as it functions as a reservoir of cultural worth. For example, in Telassar, Reuel discovers a hidden city—free from racial segregation and hierarchy—along with his royal bloodline, which makes him not only king but also heir to a rich legacy of African achievement. A story rarely, if ever, told in nineteenth-century American fiction, *Of One Blood* has a fantastic plot that pushes past the limits of realist representation in the service of creating a more progressive narrative about black life.

Realism, as it was practiced by white writers such as Henry James and Edith Wharton, was mostly concerned with white life among the middle and upper classes. In fact, James and Wharton were considered "high realists" because they concentrated their efforts on dramatizing the internal conflicts felt by aristocrats and the nouveau riche in a rapidly changing America and Europe. As they did so, they constructed a portrait of the external world that excluded the poor, the working class, and people of color, reinforcing their class and racial privilege and leaving social divisions and hierarchies firmly intact. In this way, realism was, for them, a means of expressing what Phillip Barrish has called "cultural prestige"—that is, one's social status and knowledge about exalted and exclusive forms of cultural production and enjoyment such as art, fine dining, classical music, and literature (*American Literary Realism* 6). In this manner, their aesthetic choices about narration, characterization, language, and form were really aesthetic and cultural judgements about how society should look and function. Consequently, the definition of realism that emerged in their writings made the genre synonymous with the attitudes, customs, and beliefs of the upwardly mobile and the cultural elite. In short, their realist writings ultimately worked to glorify whiteness and wealth.

Cognizant of the fact that such a genre did not reflect her subjectivity, Hopkins altered the form. To achieve her aesthetic and political goals,

Hopkins changed the genre's focus and loosened its mimetic grip. By foregrounding African American characters and utilizing more romantic and speculative devices, Hopkins was able to reimagine black experience outside of the contexts of turn-of-the-twentieth-century racial violence and discrimination. Departing from these expected forms of social documentation, Hopkins sought to create a version of realism that portrayed African Americans as the inheritors of an ancient and venerable African nobility, thus modeling the political and social potential of blackness. In this way, Hopkins's break from the prevailing literary mode was really an attempt to move away from the grim realities of black life in America and toward an ennobling fantasy of black social and political achievement. Hopkins's generic innovation not only illuminates the political stakes of imaginative writing and literary genres, but it also demonstrates that as early as the turn of the twentieth century, black writers were already theorizing what we now call the postracial to conceive of life beyond the color line.

Pauline Hopkins, the *Colored American Magazine*, and *Of One Blood*

Of One Blood was published serially in the *Colored American Magazine* from 1902 to 1903. By this time, Hopkins had already established herself as a staunch advocate for African American rights and as a prominent writer of race literature, much of which appeared in the *Colored American Magazine*. As an editorial announcement from its first issue in May 1900 proclaimed, the monthly periodical sought to "offer the colored people of the United States a medium through which they can demonstrate their ability and tastes, in fiction, poetry, and art, as well as in the arena of historical, social, and economical literature" (Elliot, "The Story of Our Magazine" 60). As Lois Brown has revealed, soon after the first issue left the press, Hopkins turned her attention to "political and writerly reclamations of Africa" (387). For Hopkins, this meant soliciting prospective articles from "Africans active in the international conference movements and African expatriate press" in addition to writing fiction and nonfiction that could contribute to the "growing pan-Africanist movement" (Brown 387). Looking to connect African Americans to their African ancestors,

Hopkins defined race in terms of the diaspora and focused on highlighting the achievements of all black people to revise the dominant narrative about the role that they played in world history (387). Just before *Of One Blood*'s first installment appeared, Hopkins completed two biographical series, "Famous Men of the Negro Race" (1900–1901) and "Famous Women of the Negro Race" (1901–2). As Hazel V. Carby has explained, the purpose of these works was to "teach her black readership" that they were "the descendants of a great and ancient civilization" in Africa (Introduction xliv). For scholars, however, these biographical series provide a critical framework for understanding the social context and intellectual history that gave rise to *Of One Blood,* as they reflect an important shift in Hopkins's thinking about racial justice from a domestic concern to an international one.

Of One Blood's plot reflects Hopkins's evolving global consciousness, particularly her sense that racial progress could be achieved vis-à-vis imaginative writing. This is perhaps best expressed by the novel's creative merger of the political aims of Pan-Africanism with the aesthetic principles of speculative fiction, trading in the American racial nightmare for a mythical and triumphant Africa where black people are fully vested members of social and political life. As a black bildungsroman, the novel traces its protagonist's development from passer to prophet. Reuel, whose name means "friend of God" in Hebrew, is a brilliant, but poor Harvard medical student passing for white. He marries Dianthe Lusk, a beautiful mulatta suffering from amnesia but quickly loses her to his best friend, Aubrey Livingston. Determined to steal Dianthe at all costs, Aubrey sends his impecunious friend on a lucrative expedition to Ethiopia. While Reuel is away, Aubrey uses mesmerism to seduce Dianthe, who is susceptible to suspended animation. Reuel returns to America to rescue his wife from Aubrey's clutches. To his horror, he arrives too late to do anything other than watch her die. Afterward, he learns that he, Aubrey, and Dianthe are all "of one blood"—siblings born to Mira, a former slave who frequently appears in phantom form as a haunting reminder of slavery's continued presence in the Jim Crow era. Distraught by the news of his incestuous relations, Reuel determines that there is no happy ending to be had in America and returns to Africa to serve as king, achieving a political victory that could never be realized in America. Although the narrative is at times "grotesque" and "morbid," as Claudia Tate has described it (207), its movement away from the American racial scene carves out the visionary space to imagine what Yogita Goyal has called "black political futures" (29).

Without an extant reception history, it is difficult to ascertain how Hopkins's contemporaries responded to *Of One Blood* both during and after its serialization. But modern-day criticism has most consistently focused on the novel's impressive catalogue of nineteenth-century racial theories and debates, its back-to-Africa plot, as well as its use of romantic and speculative genres to dramatize the effects of slavery and Jim Crow on the African American psyche and on the African American community. For example, Susan Gillman has shown how the novel engages "scholarly and popular discourse on mind and race," exploring the sciences of ethnology, Egyptology, and Ethiopianism alongside "political issues of black leadership, Pan-Africanism, and the African-origins-of-Western-civilization thesis" (*Blood Talk* 32). Acknowledging that Hopkins's objective in raising these concerns was less to advocate for actual emigration and more to inspire a general sense of black pride, Eric Sundquist has described the novel as "patently escapist fiction meant to flee the brutality and racism of American history in favor of lost history of great wealth, material achievement, and intellectual superiority" (*To Wake the Nations* 569).[3] In response to this reading, black feminist critics and diaspora scholars have pointed to the ways in which the back-to-Africa plot performs meaningful intellectual and political work. In this manner, Daphne Brooks has argued that in the figure of Dianthe Lusk "black nationalism is reconstituted through the politics of black women's performances" and that the text "imagines performance as the insurgent site for dismantling imperialist and patriarchal discourses" (292).

In underscoring the role of black womanhood in the Pan-Africanist project, Brooks has made a significant revision to the dominant, masculinist narrative surrounding black nationalism. Her remarks provide a basis for Robert S. Levine's observation that by the late nineteenth century, African American women writers such as Hopkins "were boldly enunciating a gendered black literary nationalism" that drew its force from Ethiopianism ("African American Literary Nationalism" 131). Dana Luciano has perceptively described this gendered black literary nationalism as "racial melancholia," arguing that the novel "narrates the unspoken and as-yet-unrecognized trauma of historical and racial separation" and that Hopkins's intent to explore the inner workings of the psyche took her "well beyond the conventions of realism, since neither canonical realist literature . . . nor contemporary psychological theory offered a sufficient model" (149). With its labyrinthine plot and aesthetic complexity, *Of One Blood* continues to generate a variety of critical readings. My own reading of the novel has been influenced by all of these critical responses, but it departs from them to explore how Hopkins deploys Afro-realism to contemplate African American subjectivity, both inside and outside of race, ultimately fashioning a postracial portrait of black political possibility.

By most critical accounts, *Of One Blood* stands out among Hopkins's writings because it is in many ways her most innovative and poignant work. Hopkins began her literary career in 1900 with the publication of "The Mystery within Us" (a short story that many critics consider to be the inspiration for *Of One Blood*), which appeared in the inaugural issue of the *Colored American Magazine.* During the brief five-year period in which Hopkins worked at the magazine—initially as a staff writer, followed by a stint as the literary editor, and then as editor in chief—she published four novels (three of which were serialized in the *Colored American Magazine*), seven short stories, two biographical series, and numerous commentaries and editorials. In all of her writings, Hopkins demonstrates her commitment to "rais[ing] the stigma of degradation from my race," but it is in her fiction, particularly in her novels, where she intervenes most effectively and forcefully in the national and international debate about racial justice and black empowerment (Preface to *Contending Forces* 13).

Hopkins's best-known work and initial contribution to this project is *Contending Forces* (1900). A long and sweeping historical romance, the novel traces the effects of slavery on the Montfort family, beginning with its tragic breakup in antebellum North Carolina and ending with its bittersweet restoration in postbellum Boston. If *Contending Forces* represents an attempt on Hopkins's part to give her turn-of-the-twentieth-century black readership a master narrative about the historical roots of their present-day suffering, then her magazine fiction constitutes an effort to make this origin story accessible to a popular audience. Shaped by the conventions and demands of the monthly periodical and serial publication formats, Hopkins's magazine fiction shows signs of lightning-speed composition and an increasing reliance on popular fictional formulas such as melodrama, the ghost story, adventure, suspense, the cliff-hanger, and fantasy. All of these narrative elements are present in *Of One Blood* and are woven into its more overtly political and didactic critique of individual and collective racial trauma. Of all her magazine fiction, *Of One Blood* is perhaps Hopkins's most aesthetically ornate and politically explicit statement about the need for panracial unity and group pride. In offering the ancient African past as the source material for these goals, Hopkins historicizes black identity. This enables her to locate modern-day African Americans on a longer timeline that predates slavery and Jim Crow but also extends into the future, where the abjectness brought about by racial oppression no longer exists.

In light of its forward-looking vision of blackness, *Of One Blood* can and should be placed in the context of speculative fiction. This is a capacious category that includes science fiction, fantasy, horror, futuristic writings, and utopian, dystopian, and supernatural writings. In many respects, speculative fiction has a long genealogy in American literature, which can be traced all the way back to the emergence of the American novel and the rise of the romance as a literary genre. As Nina Baym has explained, the romance was the default mode of the antebellum American novel, so much so that the terms "novel" and "romance" were virtually indistinguishable from each other during this time ("Concepts of the Romance" 438). Hence, in the romance lie the antimimetic seeds of speculative fiction, with the latter sharing many traits with the former, including astonishing and supernatural events, improbable coincidences, larger-than-life characters who possess almost superhuman abilities, and otherworldly or gothic elements.[4] Over the course of the nineteenth century, African American writers adapted and transformed these features of white American romances. By the 1850s, black authors had largely moved away from the autobiographical slave narrative toward what William L. Andrews has described as "the novelization of voice"—that is, fictive narration that incorporates multiple voices other than that of the narrator ("Novelization" 24).[5] As Carla Peterson has explained, fictional novelization gave African American writers the representational power to create "alternative worlds . . . that, unlike history and autobiography, permitted projections into the future and the possibility of narrative closure" ("Capitalism" 563). In this specific context, Martin Delany's *Blake, or The Huts of America* (1859) represents one of the earliest examples of black speculative fiction, taking as its subject a successful slave revolt that leads to the creation of a sovereign black utopia in Cuba.

After the Civil War, African American writers turned increasingly toward speculative fiction to revisit and revise the historical narrative surrounding slavery. In looking backward to better assess their postbellum present, African American writers were trying to construct a usable past that could not only function as a narrative of collective struggle and survival against all odds but that could also help guide them to the future as free and empowered citizens. Consider Sutton Griggs's *Imperium in Imperio* (1889); Charles W. Chesnutt's *The Conjure Woman* (1899); Frances E. W. Harper's *Iola Leroy* (1892); and Edward A. Johnson's *Light Ahead for the Negro* (1904). Griggs's novel focuses on the operations of a covert and sovereign African American organization based in Waco, Texas, whose sole function is to protect and defend black Americans. Chesnutt's collection of tales features seemingly unintelligent slaves outwitting their slave masters with the power of voodoo. Harper's idealized portrait of an upwardly mobile and progressive black intelligentsia anticipates later movements. Johnson's highly innovative narrative features a racially indeterminate protagonist who in 1906, before going to teach at an all-black school in the segregated South, is involved in a midair crash, which he survives, preserved in a state of suspended animation for one hundred years, after which he wakes up in postracial America. While all of these narratives, to varying degrees, lack regard for plausibility, their racial critiques are nevertheless compelling confrontations of the American racial crisis and the legacies of slavery on modern African Americans. What all of these narratives make unmistakably clear is that less mimetic genres provided African American writers with greater artistic flexibility. Such creative freedom was essential for African American authors seeking to rewrite the past to produce a more inspiring history, transcend present-day realities, and make optimistic projections about the future of race and African American identity.

Realism Reconsidered

While many critical readings of Hopkins's *Of One Blood* have focused on the novel's more speculative elements—its bizarre blend of gothic, adventure, and utopian conventions—very few accounts have specifically examined the novel's engagement with literary realism. There is no denying that the novel's preoccupation with mesmerism, ghosts, archaeological expeditions, and imagined worlds clearly defies realism's demands for mimetic accuracy, but it is also true that the novel does not completely reject realist subject matter or technique. As Valerie Rohy has rightly argued, *Of One Blood* "does not abjure realism," and in "fundamental ways" it is "a realist text," a text "at any rate, with stubborn aspirations to realism" (77). But I would go so far as to argue that not only is *Of One Blood* a realist text, but it is a realist text that creates and adheres to its own vision of what the genre can and should be and how this offers African American writers and readers a more creative form of racial justice. In its endeavor to deconstruct the fictions of race and black inferiority, the novel rehearses and refashions some of mainstream realism's signature moves. Not only does this add greater elasticity to the genre's repertoire of representational concerns, but it also constructs a more accurate and multifaceted depiction of black identity.

By and large, *Of One Blood*'s realism hinges on the project of interrogating racist science and history and modifying the rules of the realist novel. After all, it is no mere coincidence that the novel's racial critique is lodged within a scientific subplot featuring a black doctor passing for white. As a signifying strategy, this gives Hopkins greater ground to attack scientific racism. But more importantly, it demonstrates the degree to which *Of One Blood* is entangled with realism's greater critical agenda: exposing the facts, establishing empirical knowledge, and exploring social problems. In many respects, the novel performs realism's cultural work, setting the record straight on slavery, miscegenation, and racism amid a sensational and episodic plot that thrills readers with its use of popular and established conventions from dime novels and story papers (Carby, Introduction xxxvi). Recalibrating realism's aesthetic microscope, the novel focuses its objective lenses on black subjectivity. Equally noteworthy is the novel's engagement with several scientific discourses: medicine, psychology, history, and archaeology. Not only does it respond to these disciplines' fraudulent claims about black inferiority, but it also converts these methodologies to its own use as it crafts an alternative narrative of black experience.

Despite its deviation from strict mimesis, *Of One Blood* begins in traditional realist mode. Hopkins takes her time in establishing the details of the scene at hand. As in any realist novel, such descriptions are key to creating an accurate portrait of the world as we know it, but in Hopkins's case these identifiers function as important cultural signifiers that situate the novel in a discursive debate over the meanings of race. As Deborah E. McDowell has explained, in setting the novel in Boston, Hopkins "clos[es] in on one of the nerve centers of the U.S. cultural debate on 'blood,' bloodlines, and the roots of the 'human family'"—evoking Louis Agassiz's polygenetic campaign vis-à-vis Harvard University (Introduction x). And her verisimilitude does not stop here; outlining the spatial terrain in which the novel's race drama unfolds, the opening introduces place, protagonist, and scientific subplot, while capturing a sense of the gloominess that plagues Reuel's Briggs's life as a black man passing for white in post-Reconstruction America:

> The recitations were over for the day. It was the first week in November and it had rained about every day the entire week; now freezing temperature added to the discomfiture of the dismal season. . . . The east wind for which Boston and vicinity is celebrated, drove the sleet against the window panes of the room in which Reuel Briggs sat among his books and the apparatus for experiments. The room served for both living and sleeping. Briggs could have told you that the bareness and desolateness of the apartment were like his life, but he was a reticent man who knew how to suffer in silence. (441)

Saturated with dreariness, this passage portrays Reuel as a lonely and hardworking scientist subsisting on the margins of Harvard society. Drawing a comparison between his bleak dwelling and his bleak emotional state, the passage positions him as a depressed young man consumed by intellectual labor. Aside from divulging critical expository information, the opening passage also performs an important structural function, as it shifts the narrative's focal point from external phenomena to mental interiority, producing a type of psychological realism that remains palpable throughout the novel.

Hopkins further develops this psychological thread by adopting the realist novel's crisis of moral agency to speak to the problem of black suffering while simultaneously positioning passing as the ultimate ethical dilemma. In this same opening scene, Hopkins invites readers to observe Reuel's fragile mental condition. When read with his mixed-race heritage in mind, the passage takes on additional meaning, suggesting that his depression stems from the racial angst brought on by passing. Plagued by morbid thoughts, he wonders: "To what use all this persistent hard work for a place in the world—clothes, food, a roof? Is suicide wrong?" (441). Here, Reuel not only implicates upward mobility as the motivation for passing—what Adenike Marie Davidson has called "racial uplift gone awry" (79)—but he also questions the fruitfulness of the American obsession with social climbing and material goods. As Reuel weighs the decision to work hard or not, to pass or not, to commit suicide or not, the reality of his existential crisis comes into greater narrative relief. The novel, in turn, achieves a greater degree of realism by illustrating the challenging emotional and social terrain that modern black Americans, like Reuel, must navigate as they struggle to define themselves outside of white America's prejudiced lens and achieve the American Dream in a world dominated by Jim Crow.

In many respects, Hopkins's frank treatment of Reuel's inner turmoil is more realistic than it is melodramatic or sentimental. As part of the project of representing character truthfully, the realists, contrary to popular belief, did not shy away from human emotions. Rather, they approached the inner life of feeling as analysts. As Melanie Dawson has explained, the realists were interested in "analyzing and intellectualizing emotion," and paradoxically they "sought not to represent emotions *emotionally;* rather, they attempted to demonstrate that a modern approach to emotional understanding could be achieved in part through observation and categorization" (11). In other words, the realists aimed to chart the details and facts of feeling without giving into the emotional excesses of melodrama and sentimental fiction. Viewing these latter genres as representational modes dominated by hyperbole, the realists concerned themselves with empirical accounts of interior experience, treating some of the more vulgar aspects of human emotion—rage, sexual desire, and depression—with what they considered to be detached, scholarly interest. I would argue that Hopkins's approach to representing Reuel follows suit, demonstrating her serious interest in black interiority.

In her portrayal of Reuel, Hopkins explores the more clinical side of human behavior, drawing on the discourse of neurasthenia that George M. Beard popularized in the 1880s.[6] A trendy psychological disorder, neurasthenia was a condition characterized by nervousness, which often took the shape of anxiety, fatigue, and depression. Linked to modern civilization's increasingly competitive and sedentary business culture, neurasthenia disproportionately affected white Americans of the middle and upper classes. As Tom Lutz explains in *American Nervousness,* neurasthenia gave white elites a certain kind of smug self-satisfaction about their racial and class superiority, as the illness was viewed as a badge of accomplishment (6–10). Hopkins, however, takes an unconventional approach to the illness by placing a poor black medical student, who happens to be passing for white, at the center of the neurasthenic phenomenon, thereby signifying on the illness's pathological script, both in terms of race and class. This important revision to the canonical medical narrative should be viewed as a type of realist intervention in its own right. Not only does it recuperate African Americans from the margins of psychology, but it also challenges the widely accepted and erroneous belief that black people could not suffer from depression because they lacked mental development and were naturally happy. Of course, this latter idea was birthed in slavery and popularized by nineteenth-century plantation fiction and minstrel shows, both of which frequently depicted blacks as lazy, childlike buffoons who were content with their enslavement.

Hopkins subverts this kind of malignant thinking by drawing on the conventions and strategies of the gothic novel. To invalidate the idea that African Americans lacked mental interiority and the related myth that slavery was some kind of benevolent family affair, Hopkins uses the gothic to explore the uncanny effects of slavery and racism on the black psyche. To illustrate the psychological and emotional trauma caused by slavery, Hopkins incorporates apparitions and acts of mesmerism to exhume and exorcise the ghosts of the slave past as well as comment on the ways in which slavery continues to haunt the Jim Crow present. In this way, Hopkins turns away from the more traditional realism with which she began the novel and increasingly toward the paranormal realm to highlight how the racial and sexual trauma engendered by slavery still oppresses modern-day African Americans. This abstraction shows up in the novel as perverse supernatural phenomena. This shift produces a text that locates the psyche as the ultimate site of gothic horror, as opposed to some medieval castle in a mythical and desolate world. Put another way, Hopkins trades the "romantic chasms" and "labyrinthine dungeons" of gothic fiction in the style of Edgar Allan Poe for what Fred Botting has called the "murky recesses of human subjectivity" (11).

While it might seem counterintuitive to adopt a gothic framework to make a serious statement about the continuities between slavery and Jim Crow, I would argue that there is no more suitable genre in all of American literary history. As Leslie Fiedler opined in his classic study *Love and Death in the American Novel,* "Only the American tradition of symbolic gothicism, which from Poe and Melville to Twain and Faulkner has never ceased to confront the problem of the Negro, has proved in an age of realism adequate to the complexities of life in the American South" (449). By tracing the gothic tradition back to its mid-nineteenth-century forefathers, Fiedler showed how the gothic had always been the preferred mode for depicting all of the dark and unspeakable things that were suppressed in American culture. Not only was the gothic, in some ways, more socially attuned than realism, but it was also uniquely equipped to accommodate the excesses of southern culture. Of course, in the years since Fiedler's book appeared, numerous other scholars have elaborated on this idea, most notably Teresa A. Goddu, who has posited that the "benighted South is able to support the irrational impulses of the gothic that the nation as a whole, born of Enlightenment ideals, cannot" and that the "gothic's focus on the terror of possession, the iconography of imprisonment, the fear of retribution, and the weight of sin provided a useful vocabulary and register of images by which to represent the scene of America's greatest guilt: slavery" (*Gothic America* 4, 133). In many ways, *Of One Blood*'s gothic subplot reflects all of these themes, using the genre's conventions and narrative strategies to specifically highlight how slavery terrorized African American women, thus issuing a black feminist critique in a veiled form.

In the Hallow-eve sequence, Hopkins uses this disguise to tell a black story in whiteface. The episode begins with a ghost story about a mysterious lady in white who haunts the Hyde house every Hallow-eve. As Hazel V. Carby has elucidated, this technique serves to introduce the novel's white characters and to depict whiteness "as a systemic set of social forces, through accounts of the experiences of Hopkins's black characters" (Introduction xxxvii). The story is told by Molly Vance, an affluent and happy-go-lucky white girl, who along with her brother, Charlie Vance, makes up part of Reuel's privileged social group at Harvard. Of course, the irony of it all is that neither the white characters or Reuel and Aubrey themselves know that they are half siblings and that they are both passing for white. In this way, the novel enacts the very form of racial concealment that it seeks to explore. Although Molly's rendering of the story does not reveal the race of the characters involved, it should be viewed in the contexts of slavery and rape, as it features "an unfaithful husband, a wronged wife and a beautiful governess" (458). As Molly goes on to explain, the apparition was the niece of a man who murdered a guest in his home. Having discovered "blood stains on the door of the woodshed," the niece confronted her uncle about the guest's disappearance (458–59). The uncle, in turn, admitted his guilt and secured his niece's silence. Together, the two of them kept the secret until they died. But even in death, they were chained to the murder. The niece's ghost was released on the condition that she give a public confession. After doing so, she was never heard from again. But according to urban legend, she visits the Hyde estate every Hallow-eve in observance of the tragedy.

Emerging from this shadowy story is Dianthe Lusk, the beautiful mulatta and jubilee singer who first appears to Reuel in the form of an apparition in the gloom of the hemlocks. As it turns out, this is the same woman "who had haunted him sleeping and waking for weeks past" (461). The product of an abusive relationship between her mother and her slave master, Dianthe embodies, as Deborah Horvitz has explained, "the sexual molestation, rape, and miscegenation endemic to slavery" (252). For Dianthe, this history registers in the form of sexual trauma, of which her predisposition to suspended animation, trances, amnesia, fainting spells, and fatigue are symptomatic expressions of her victimization. While Dianthe is mostly presented as a passive figure who is animated by or acted upon by others, especially men, through her performances with the Fisk Jubilee Singers, she achieves a form of autonomy that not only gives her a voice but that also allows her to speak for all of her sisters wronged by slavery. We see this most forcefully in her performance of the popular Negro spiritual "Go Down Moses," conveying in melodic form, "[a]ll the horror, the degradation from which a race had been delivered . . . in the pleading strains of the singer's voice" (454). In this way, Dianthe's singing functions as a form of black feminist resistance that also doubles as a revision to the tragic mulatta trope, challenging readings of the novel that posit that she is devoid of agency because she remains susceptible to suspended animation.[7] Through song, Dianthe conveys the horrors of slavery and sexual violence. By presenting this history in the form of a ghost story, Hopkins suggests that the realities of African American women's experiences in slavery are more frightening than the stuff of gothic fiction.

Merging the discourses of the real and the unreal, Hopkins follows up the Hallow-eve sequence with a bold appeal to science and the occult. Aubrey, serving as the voice of reason, orders Reuel to "[b]ring your science and philosophy to bear on this" (459). And Charlie Vance dismisses Molly's story altogether, declaring, "Reuel doesn't believe such stuff; he's too sensible" (459). But Reuel's remarks foil Charlie's expectations and reaffirm the novel's merger of empirical and speculative heuristics: "If these are *facts,* they are only for those who have a mental affinity with them. I believe that if we could but strengthen our mental sight, we could discover the broad highway between this and the other world" (459, italics mine). In a move that rejects the notion of objective truth, Reuel employs a more subjective definition of the facts that suggests that truth is not simply a matter of that which can be observed with our literal eyes but that it is also a function of that which we perceive with our mental eyes: intuition. As Reuel conjectures, intuition may be the conduit between the physical world and the spiritual world. It is hardly coincidental that this exchange occurs after the ghost story. In some ways, it serves as a manifesto of sorts for Hopkins's views on race and realism.

Standing in stark contrast to the more mimetic realism of her white contemporaries, Hopkins's version of the genre is steeped in the realm of supernatural experience. It also challenges prevailing ideas about the regressive, primitive nature of the gothic as a literary genre. In fact, Hopkins disrupts the linear timeline of evolutionary progress that locates a realism at the end of the spectrum as the most advanced literary form by subjecting the aims of realism to the narrative strategies of the gothic novel.[8] Hopkins's point is that slavery continues to afflict her turn-of-the-twentieth-century characters (and her African American readership) in very real ways. As a portal to the spiritual realm, the gothic also allows Hopkins to undercut much of the social Darwinism and racial determinism that defined African Americans at the time in purely biological and genetic terms drawn from scientific racism. As an example of what John J. Kucich has called "counterhegemonic practice," Hopkins's revision of realism pulls from the discourses of spiritualism to create an alternative model for theorizing race, one that is preoccupied with questions of consciousness and subjectivity (139). Merging scientific praxis with the occult, Hopkins's realism provides a new epistemology for representing and comprehending the after-effects of slavery as a form of individual and intergenerational trauma.

Postracial Romance

In the second half of the novel, Hopkins supplants the more realistic narrative of racial passing in post-Reconstruction America with a romantic fantasy about African return. If in the first half of the novel she uses a gothic realism to explore questions of epistemology as they relate to the slave past and contemporary racial subjectivity, then in the second half she uses the literary strategies of more speculative genres to convert this knowledge into a useable fiction for her modern-day African American audience. Ironically, it is in the name of scientific research that Reuel joins an archaeological expedition in search of the fabled Ethiopian city of Meroe. In this way, Hopkins suggests that the imaginative sphere possesses great potential for the more empirical work of scholarly inquiry because it can provide new and more creative ways of thinking about science, history, and identity itself. In moving her narrative from America to Africa, Hopkins trades realism's factual, mimetic, and temporal frame for a more malleable mode that enables her to conflate past and present so that she can simultaneously revise racist history and rewrite the cultural narrative of turn-of-the-twentieth-century black life. In Africa, Hopkins introduces the trope of excavation as a metaphor for the project of ancestral recovery. Through excavation, Reuel discovers his hidden self. But the identity that he uncovers is not an essentialized, racial self that draws it legitimacy from blood, or even a real Africa, for that matter. Rather, it is a type of subjectivity that is informed by an imagined Africa, one that Hopkins creates, and that offers Reuel both cultural distinctiveness and freedom from American racial divisions and hierarchies. In this context, the novel's vision of African return is really a postnational and postracial critique of the limitations and failures of American democracy.

There is no question that the African sequence, with its formulaic plot and exotic African setting, appears to lack a serious, political message. After all, its rapidly moving action, blatant disregard for plausibility, its exotic locale, its focus on the discovery of a hidden city and a long-lost king, its melodramatic love triangle, and supernatural occurrences more accurately resemble a Rider Haggard novel, as Thomas J. Otten has argued, than a social problem novel (246). Although *Of One Blood* incorporates all of these over-the-top plot devices into its schema, these seemingly escapist flourishes do not render the novel any less steeped in the social and political crises of its era than a more traditionally realistic novel. In fact, the highly imaginative quality of this segment only enhances the novel's political cachet. As Ramón Saldívar has argued, such visualizations facilitate the construction of what he calls "postrace narratives," stories that "perform the critical work of symbolic action, denoting the public work of the private imagination" and that "through the pathway of fantasy" construct "new political destinies" (595). As Saldívar would suggest, we should view *Of One Blood*'s outlandishness not as escapism but as a form of creative displacement that gives Hopkins the imaginative space to depict African American political enfranchisement in the age of Jim Crow.

Understood in this way, her romantic and transnational turns allow her to explore the possibilities for African American identity beyond the here and now of constitutionally sanctioned segregation in America. To realize the promise of the future in the present (and in the process, rewrite the dominant narrative about the African past), Hopkins invokes the concept of simultaneous time. In referencing Ecclesiastes 3:15—"That which hath been, is now; and that which is to be, hath already been; and God requireth that which is past"—she destabilizes the boundaries between past, present, and future (552). When Reuel arrives in Africa, he finds an ancient, supernatural world that coexists alongside his dreary life in America. And to connect contemporary African Americans to this world, Hopkins constructs an Africa that is timeless, exotic, and steeped in the occult. In our first glimpse of the African shore, Hopkins provides an Orientalist account of the continent. She mentions the "Djema el Gomgi" mosque, compares Tripoli to "Cleopatra," and describes the city as "an oasis of palms studded with hundreds of domes and minarets" (509). This Orientalist account is not meant to position Africa as primitive or preindustrial as much as it is meant to exaggerate its foreignness, challenge Western hegemony, and thus offer an African American audience a vision of black cosmopolitanism.

Indeed, in a very telling scene, Reuel and Professor Stone debate the monogenetic origins of mankind. Stone insists that the Negro is the primal race and that Ethiopia predates ancient Egypt. The implications of such a claim are not lost on Reuel, who sarcastically asks, "How can the Anglo-Saxon world bear the establishment of such a theory?" (520). Arguing that Egypt drew from Ethiopia "all the arts, sciences and knowledge of which she was mistress," Stone rewrites the narrative of Western civilization by crediting Ethiopia as the true source of its glory (521). Stone even asserts that the original color of man during prehistoric times was black. Taking it for granted that all educated people would be familiar with the fact that life began in Africa, Stone says that he was never puzzled by the origins of the blacks, but of the whites (521). By insisting that blackness is a natural condition, indeed the very color of the earth out of which God made Adam, and that whiteness is an aberration, Stone reverses an important binary at the heart of Western civilization. He makes the Ethiopian "the most ancient source" of modern life and posits that all the other races descended from the Negro (520).

The expedition sequence is rife with these kinds of historical revisions, which utilize the trope of excavation as the literal and figurative process by which African Americans (and presumably all of humanity which descends from Africa) can uncover their hidden selves. The literal excavations led by Professor Stone are in and of themselves symbolic of the processes of ancestral and genealogical recovery. During these excavations, the members of the expedition not only unearth valuable African artifacts and exotic treasures, but they also retrieve an obscured African past that forms the basis for a comprehensive sense of black cultural pride. As Thomas J. Otten has rightly observed, in "[e]xcavating the depths of black character" Hopkins "yields a Pan-African understanding of racial history" (230). This Pan-African vision connects modern-day African Americans (and all people) to their ancient African ancestors. In the novel's formulation of "one blood," (combined with its miscegenation and incest plot) Pan-Africanism is not deployed to reify racial difference but to reinforce the monogenetic idea of common origins for blacks and whites alike. That Reuel, Aubrey, and Dianthe are siblings (all three of them born to the slave Mira and her white master) and share the lotus-lily birthmark on their breasts would appear to be proof enough. Not only does the birthmark tie them to the royal line of ancient Ethiopia, erasing the degraded status associated with blackness vis-à-vis American slavery, but it also makes them members of an interracial family that serves as a synecdoche for the human family. In this way, the novel simultaneously upholds both cultural particularity and universal humanism as the keys to racial healing and racial justice.

As the novel seems to suggest, accessing the hidden self may not require actual expatriation or a formal education for that matter. In fact, Hopkins implies that this process of discovery is more of a meditative, inward-looking endeavor, as she hints that Reuel's expedition in the fabled city really occurs within the province of his own mind. As Cynthia D. Schrager has observed, this idea is "reinforced in the pivotal scene where Reuel's descent down a ruined staircase that will lead him to the hidden city is accompanied by a simultaneous descent into unconsciousness" (198). Along these lines, Dana Luciano has described the hidden city as "a perpetuated ideal, a horizon of possibility that must be continually recreated" (156). Indeed, as Hopkins writes, it is "from profound unconsciousness, deep, merciful, oblivious to pain and the flight of time, from the gulf of the mysterious shadows wherein earth and heaven are alike forgotten" that Reuel wakes up in the dreamlike, fairy-tale world of Telassar. Here, racism does not exist and cultural distinctiveness remains intact despite the obvious signs of intermixture (544). In Telassar, "[d]arkvisaged" people ranging in "complexion from a creamy tint to [the] purest ebony" live in peaceful cohabitation (545). And hair, an important signifier of racial difference in the United States, does not possess the same destructive codifying capabilities, as Reuel observes various textures from "soft, waving curls to the crispness of the most pronounced African type" (545). These phenotypical variations are clearly employed to highlight a history of miscegenation and therefore debunk the myth of racial purity. That these variations fail to signify racial difference or to legitimate racial divisions and hierarchies underscores the universal humanity of the Telassarians, and by extension, all of civilization. Accessing this knowledge simply demands that we see past such phenotypical differences and embrace our common ancestry as well as the diversity of humankind.

Hopkins follows up her critique of the ocular logic of race in America with a severe condemnation of the one-drop rule. Unlike the Americans, the Telassarians do not observe this practice. In fact, Ai (Reuel's faithful servant and mediator between worlds) is surprised to learn that in the United States it is considered a disgrace to possess even the slightest trace of black blood, given his people's belief in the monogenetic origins of humankind. As Ai explains, the Telassarians do not value race as an ontological mode of being. Instead, they assign importance to the "soul Ego," and they believe that it contains the true source of life, not blood (562). This distinction is a profound one that circles back to the novel's subtitle, "the hidden self," suggesting that it is a spiritual essence, rather than any racial essence, that exists within every human being and that ultimately forms the foundation for identity. This configuration of the soul Ego is critical to the construction of Hopkins's postracial fantasy. The spiritual and psychological connotations of the term provide her with an alternative model to theorize identity outside of the turn-of-the-twentieth-century's prevailing frameworks of biology and sociology.

In emphasizing the soul Ego, Hopkins evokes her contemporary W. E. B. Du Bois, whose theory of double-consciousness popularized this kind of spiritualistic and psychic deconstruction of race. As Cynthia Schrager has noted, Hopkins's "surface-depth model of selfhood" was more than likely inspired by Du Bois's notion of "doubleness" (190). If in Du Bois's model, the souls of black folk are split in two—"an American, a Negro; two souls, two thoughts, two unreconciled strivings; two warring ideals in one dark body, whose dogged strength alone keeps it from being torn asunder" (*Souls* 8)—then in Hopkins's fantasy they have integrated spirits and psyches endowed with the attributes of "the great Unity," which is Hopkins's concept for God or the Creator (562). In connecting black people to God or the Creator, vis-à-vis the soul Ego, Hopkins not only revises the racist rhetoric of her day that posited that blacks were devoid of a spiritual and psychological register, but she also adds greater depth to her monogenetic argument about the singular origins of humankind by making black subjectivity a sacred manifestation of divine election. Furthermore, by describing the Telassarians' religion as a belief in "One Supreme Being" who made all men "of one blood," Hopkins aligns the idea of monogenesis with monotheism to suggest that belief in the single racial family is in line with the teachings of Christianity (562). In such a configuration, not only is a racial fiction like the one-drop rule incompatible with the creation myth, but it is also a sin.

Hopkins also uses this Christian framework to locate Telassar's postracial province in the prelapsarian past, suggesting that racism is a consequence of the fall. A tour of the hidden city reveals that it is an African paradise unsullied by modern civilization. If one of the hallmarks of modernity is, as Gilroy has argued, the hypervisibility of race, which is, as he explains, a by-product of the process of making race "epistemologically correct," then Hopkins counters this discourse through her depiction of Telassar as a premodern utopia (58). Set in an ancient African temporal frame, Telassar represents a bygone era in the history of world civilizations, a time when race and racism did not exist. Along these lines, Hopkins borrows a quotation from Milton's *Paradise Lost* to compare her Telassar to Eden: "Flowers of all hue, and without thorn the rose, / [. . .] / The trembling leaves, while universal Pan, / Knit with the Graces and the Hours in dance, / Led on th'eternal spring" (550). Similarly, just a few pages before these verses appear, Reuel asks Ai: "Can it be that you are an Ethiopian of those *early* days, now lost in obscurity? Is it possible that a remnant of that once magnificent *race* yet dwells upon *old* mother Earth? (547, italics mine). Invoking the more primordial sense of the word "race"—devoid of its legal, social, and scientific connotations—Hopkins uses the term to indicate early man, suggesting that the origins of all humankind lie in Africa, thereby, in a sense, making all people African.

When Reuel is declared King Ergamenes, Hopkins's postracial fantasy reaches its pivotal climax. In Reuel's ascent to the throne, the Ethiopian kingdom is restored to its former glory, and the trope of black leadership emerges as the symbolic index of racial progress. Representing that which cannot occur in Jim Crow America, Reuel's crowning moment revises the racist script governing democratic political rule. In making Reuel king, by way of ancestry and divine right, Hopkins negates the logic of the one-drop rule, which in her Jim Crow America not only barred black men from participating in the electoral system but made it impossible for them to even logically think about achieving the highest level of political office. In this way, Reuel's coronation is also a fantasy of racial redress. As John Cullen Gruesser has argued, it offers an African American audience "a fantasy that restores to Africa its former greatness but also a more local and much needed fantasy, one in which a white American character must answer for racial prejudice and legal segregation"—as Charlie Vance is eaten alive by serpents as punishment for his bigotry (76). In making a black man king and holding a white man accountable for racism, Hopkins gives her black readership that which Reconstruction failed to provide: political and emotional reparations for slavery's wrongs.

In her progressive revision of black femininity, Hopkins makes another powerful compensatory gesture. In the figure of Queen Candace, Hopkins signifies on the trope of black leadership to tackle the issue of gender. Providing an alternative portrait of black femininity that challenges the American historical narrative of rape and sexual abuse, Hopkins presents readers with a chaste female monarch. One out of a long line of Ethiopian queens rumored to have periodically ruled over Meroe, Candace is depicted as a virginal "Venus worked in bronze" (567), and, as Susan Gillman has observed, a "reincarnation of Dianthe" (*Blood Talk* 35). Powerful and revered, Candace contradicts Dianthe's depiction as a traumatized woman susceptible to suspended animation and masculine control. But more importantly, Candace's sovereignty over the Ethiopian kingdom suggests that black women not only have the capacity for political work but that they are critical conduits of ancestral and cultural knowledge. Indeed, Candace's union with Reuel promises to "give to the world a dynasty of dark-skinned rulers" (570). And this merger sends the message that a marriage between two black equals will improve the health of the black family, on a more local level, and the nation, on a larger level. That Candace and Reuel will rule together suggests that Hopkins's postracial fantasy is a postpatriarchal one as well.

Given how improbable all of this is, it seems perfectly logical to ask, Why use the trappings of popular fiction to tell a story about genealogy and racial identity? As Deborah E. McDowell has commented, *Of One Blood* is "much less baffling when it is read as fantasy, utopian in stripe, of a fully, self-sustaining black community existing in the ancient past, meant to prefigure the reincarnation of the same such community in present-day America" (Introduction xvi). In the past, critics have not always been willing to grant the novel this kind of complexity, preferring to read it through the historical and political lenses of black nationalism and expatriation to Africa. Such readings are relevant and important, but they cannot adequately assess the radical reworking of race and genre in Hopkins's imagined Africa. I would argue that had Hopkins used a more conventionally realistic aesthetic, the novel would not possess the same political force or generic innovativeness. To measure the scope and scale of both requires that we contemplate the disjuncture between the racial reality of Hopkins's era and the more "wildly unbelievable" dimensions of her narrative, to use Elizabeth Ammons's phrase (*Conflicting Stories* 84).

In order to draw any conclusions about the novel's aesthetic or political work, we must turn to the province of utopia. As M. Giulia Fabi has observed, it "is surprising that despite the great scholarly interest in nineteenth-century African American literature . . . so little attention has been paid to African American contributions to the extraordinary outpouring of utopian fiction" that appeared at the turn of the twentieth century (*Passing* 44). This important observation reminds us that critics have been slow to view black writing in this way because of the cultural and racial baggage associated with the more canonical tradition of white utopia, for example, eugenics and totalitarianism, as well as prevailing assumptions about African Americans' inability to envision alternative worlds and sublime political futures owing to the crushing weight of their bleak historical realities and their disenfranchisement. In actuality, the dystopian nature of post-Reconstruction black life provided the perfect context for utopian imaginings. Reconstruction's failure to truly transform the American racial landscape supplied African American writers like Hopkins with a vast array of material to be translated into sociopolitical critique. What is more, the utopian form provided African American authors with a conceptual vehicle to project that which could not be achieved or realized in the real world onto the domain of fantasy.

As Fredric Jameson has noted, "the deeper truth" of utopia "lies in what it reveals about the reality principle . . . rather than in what it tells us about our wish fulfillments" (*Seeds* 75). What this means is that those things that cannot be conceived of, even within the emancipatory space of the utopian novel, are far more important than the actual fantasy itself, as it points to our own limited imagination—our incapacity to see past the conventions of our era and its inevitable expiration. This is why Jameson has also posited that the "vocation of Utopia lies in failure . . . its epistemological value lies in the walls it allows us to feel around our minds, the invisible limits it gives us to detect by sheerest induction, the miring of our imaginations in . . . the mud of the present age in which winged Utopian shoes stick, imagining that to be the force of gravity itself" (*Seeds* 75). In other words, the utopian novel performs a kind of pedagogical work that teaches us about our shortcomings and deficiencies as a society by rendering incomplete its image of perfection. Hopkins's imagined Africa may be depicted as a postracial nation in which multicolored inhabitants occupy an idyllic space free from racial prejudice and Anglo standards of beauty, but it is also a place where her mixed-race protagonist still feels the deleterious effects of American slavery and racism. In some ways, Africa does not really resolve Reuel's inner racial conflict because the novel cannot project far enough into the future to imagine the full potential of universal humanism and blackness outside of the nineteenth century's ideological matrices of race and nation. In fact, I would argue that the full potential of Hopkins's postracial fantasy lies in the realm of the *not yet here*.

To be sure, Reuel's postracial fantasy is not a pure utopia. In Africa, he learns that his wife, Dianthe, and his friend Aubrey Livingston are in fact his half siblings, as they all share the same mother, Mira, who was a slave. Thus, they are literally "of one blood," to invoke the novel's dominant trope.[9] In this way, the novel configures incest and miscegenation as the tragic and inevitable consequences of slavery because the institution gave white men permission to rape black women, while the slave market dismantled black families and destroyed kinship ties. Worse yet, Jim Titus tells Reuel that Aubrey had conspired to seduce Dianthe from the moment he first saw her and thus sent him on the expedition to get him out of the way. Jim also confesses that he is Aubrey's foster brother (which makes him a fictive sibling and adds an additional layer to the incest plot) and that Aubrey bribed him to kill Reuel and that he has already killed Molly. At Jim's urging, Reuel returns to America. But he arrives too late to rescue Dianthe from Aubrey's clutches. Not only has Aubrey seduced her, but he has also poisoned her. Guilty of murder, Aubrey is forced to commit suicide according to Ai's command. The one silver lining in all of this, if it can be described as such, is that Reuel is reunited with his long-lost grandmother, a hoodoo expert named Aunt Hannah, whose dual roles as grandmother and aunt mark her as the ultimate matriarch and custodian of African American culture. As such, Reuel brings her back with him to Telassar so that he can retain a connection to his African American roots. That he chooses to go back to Africa to rule the Ethiopian kingdom in the first place would seem to suggest that he lacks confidence in America's ability to dismantle the color line and create a more egalitarian system.

In Africa, Reuel is plagued by melancholia, and neither marriage nor kingship can lift the "shadows of great sins [that] darken his life" (621). And he views with "serious apprehension" the "advance of mighty nations penetrating the dark, mysterious forests of his native land" (621). As Deborah E. McDowell has observed, in its final pages the novel contemplates "the threat that European colonization poses to Telassar" to comment on the real-life situation that most African countries were in at the time (Introduction xviii), which distinguishes Hopkins's fantasy world from what M. Giulia Fabi calls the "traditional *ou-topoi*" (nonplace) of utopian fiction (*Passing* 47). In this regard, the end of Hopkins's postracial fantasy yields to a more mimetic realism. The oncoming tide of colonial invaders also connects the history of American slavery to a larger global system driven by imperialism, hegemony, and biopolitics. These historical forces exert so much pressure on the novel's utopian imaginings that they buckle under the weight of dystopian realities that prompted them in the first place.

This is a striking departure from the paradigmatic formula established by canonical works of utopian fiction like Edward Bellamy's *Look-*

ing Backward (1887). In the traditional narrative, the protagonist embarks upon a fantastic journey to an idealized world, meets a wise and influential guide, and soon encounters natives who explain all of their customs, institutions, and technologies—which are almost always more progressive or radical than those of the protagonist's native land. Toward the end of the story, the protagonist returns home, usually through a dream or time machine. Once home, the protagonist attempts to make use of the knowledge that was gained on the voyage. Combining the best of both worlds, real and imagined, the protagonist resolves his or her internal conflicts and appears to be a better and happier person for having made the journey. In terms of narrative closure, plot-level complications are neatly resolved, and cultural order and normative values are restored.[10]

Hopkins alters this traditional utopian blueprint in critical ways. She does not present her postracial Africa as a patently escapist fantasy that reverses the damage wrought by slavery and racism; rather, she offers Reuel's kingship as a trope that expands the horizon of African American political life beyond the immediate realities of Jim Crow. In doing so, she presents Telassar as an imaginative alternative to the American racial order, but her utopian vision never reaches the vanishing point of slavery and its effects, as it ultimately stops short of depicting true racial healing and ends with pessimism about the present and the future. Reuel's homecoming is not a happy one, and in actuality, it is more of a retrieval than a return. When he goes back to America he finds chaos and destruction everywhere, which is why he only stays long enough to collect his grandmother, and they soon flee for Telassar. Once there, it is not clear if Reuel has worked out his racial angst/trauma or if he is any better off as a result of his journey or the discovery of his hidden self. Insofar as narrative closure is concerned, the novel's ending is disappointing and, as a number of critics have pointed out, does not really resolve anything at all.[11]

In fact, the novel's final pages are permeated with a feeling of incompleteness and unresolvedness, illustrating seemingly contradictory desires for the dismantling of racial difference and the preservation of racial distinctiveness. On a formal level, this schism shows up in the aesthetic tension between romance and realism, utopia and dystopia, Africa and America. Thematically, this ambivalence registers as paradoxical plot points. If Hopkins's postracial fantasy wants us to believe that we are all "of one blood" and that we should stop fixating on race, then how can the novel logically conclude in Africa? Doesn't Reuel's second return to "the Motherland" reify the notion of distinct bloodlines? Why make the recovery of his "hidden self" synonymous with the discovery of an ancient African civilization in the first place? Don't these narrative choices compromise Hopkins's monogenetic argument?

To reconcile the sense of incongruity that dominates not just the novel's ending but its entire plot, we have to resist the temptation to define race in simplistic, either/or terms. Hopkins's enigmatic construction of race in *Of One Blood* is predicated on her simultaneous belief in the idea of the human family and in the idea of black cultural particularity. In this way, the novel is a highly inventive critique of race that anticipates and theorizes an important observation that Michael Eric Dyson has made, positing: "We should not be post-racial: seeking to get beyond the uplifting meanings and edifying registers of blackness. Rather, we should be post racist: moving beyond cultural fascism and vicious narratives of racial privilege and superiority that tear at the fabric of *e pluribus unum*" (231). Put another way, reading *Of One Blood* as postracial does not necessitate an erasure of blackness or a denial of its cultural meaning; rather, it demands that we consider what it might mean to read this novel (and American and African American literature in general) beyond the ideological and geographical borders of the American racial landscape to expand our own creative and critical horizons.

The Limits of Literary Realism

If *Of One Blood* rejects many of the tenets of mainstream literary realism, then it does so for good reason. As a number of critics have argued, implicit in the very term "American literary realism" lies a fundamental problem of representation and power that demands that we ask: Whose America? Whose literature? And whose reality?[12] In the process of sorting through these questions, critics have shown how realism is an ideologically driven discourse that is implicated in the very construction of the social landscape that it purports to merely describe and reflect. Under the guise of objectivity, realism manufactures a hegemonic perspective of the external world and human phenomena that attempts to pass itself off as authoritative, empirical, unbiased, and true. The problem with this is that such a worldview often reinforces the dominant class's attitudes and beliefs about society's most oppressed, disenfranchised, and vulnerable members, making their obviously biased and subjective accounts seem like accurate and legitimate forms of knowledge. In such a formation, realism functions less like a progressive practice committed to exposing social problems and more like a conservative rearticulation of the status quo.

Consequently, censures of mainstream literary realism have tended to emphasize the genre's failed mimesis and social program. While critics such as Amy Kaplan have attempted to recuperate realism by troubling its claims about the external world, insisting that realist writings show "a surprising lack of confidence in the capacity of fiction to reflect a solid world" and that they actively confront social problems (9), others, like Elizabeth Ammons, have revealed how such a defense of realism does not elucidate the unique challenges that African American writers faced at the turn of the twentieth century and how fraught the issue of representation was for them both in terms of aesthetics and politics ("Expanding" 97). Long before Ammons called for a more multicultural approach to realism, Albion W. Tourgée had pointed out the genre's limitations and rightly predicted that African Americans would be critical to the development of a national literature. From Tourgée's perspective, the realists were "the worst falsifiers" because they only told "the weakest and meanest part of the grand truth which makes up the continued story of every life" ("The South as a Field for Fiction" 411).

Tourgée also believed that the "life of the Negro as a slave, freedman, and racial outcast" offered "the richest mine of romantic material" ("The South as a Field for Fiction" 410). Deeply critical of the crude and narrow realism practiced by William Dean Howells, Tourgée felt that novel writing in general required a more comprehensive approach to human experience and that every novelist shared "the same obligation of truth-telling" regardless of formal considerations ("The 'Claim' of Realism" 388). In many ways, this outlook reflects African American writers' beliefs about the function of literature. Looking to revise distorted depictions of African Americans, black writers focused their efforts on creating authentic accounts of blackness (which is not to be confused with authentic blackness), and they mobilized multiple genres to do so. Because authenticity was, for them, less about mimesis and more about unbiased representation, African American writers freely deployed numerous narrative strategies and literary conventions to produce fiction that captured the full diversity and range of black experience. In this way, they advanced a definition of the novel that, in Raymond Williams's words, viewed the literary form as a "whole literature in itself," transforming realism from a singular prose style into a polygeneric strategy for initiating progressive social change (22).

Of One Blood displays this very expansiveness and idealistic approach toward novel-writing. More powerfully than any other work I have examined in this book, *Of One Blood* demonstrates the full aesthetic and political utility of Afro-realism. The novel makes use of mainstream realism's mimetic aesthetic to tell the truth about slavery and how it lives on in the present, but it also draws from more romantic and speculative forms to free African Americans from the shackles of this past, provide historical meaning to their current realities, and conceive of a more promising future. Although fiction, for Hopkins, served an important archival and pedagogical function—preserving tradition, recording cultural growth, and educating African Americans—it was also a tool to be used for political agitation and social transformation. As such, it needed to illustrate, with "fire and romance" all of the various experiences that comprised black life in America. And while mainstream realism's mimetic program gave her the representational power to depict the material conditions of black life, it could not render the more emotional and psychological dimensions of it—the horror, terror, and pain that black people have suffered since slavery. Neither could it foster a sense of race pride or capture African American hopes and dreams for a more inclusive world. To achieve these goals Hopkins would have to turn toward the gothic, sentimentalism, and utopia.

In this way, *Of One Blood*'s formal incoherence actually makes aesthetic and political sense. Instead of dismissing the text as flawed and failed as a result of its tangled plot, polygeneric makeup, and dizzying array of racial discourses, we should celebrate it as a significant accomplishment in African American literature for the simple fact that it defies the mainstream values of the white literary establishment in the service of expanding the possibilities for black representation in popular fiction.

In other words, realism alone would not have granted Hopkins the imaginative freedom to portray African Americans as the descendants of the highly skilled Africans she credits as having created civilization or to envision a world where African American life was not completely defined by race and racism. By definition alone, realism's mimesis would have called for temporal stasis as well as a more local treatment of black life, resulting in a narrative bound by the restrictions of the here and now and situated in the usual spaces of black America, such as the rural South or the urban North. Hopkins eschews these narrative expectations to elevate and globalize the black image and to break free from the assumption and expectation that black writers *can only or should only* produce purely mimetic works of racial realism. As Walter Mosely has argued, such narrow thinking keeps African American writers shackled to the "chains of reality" (34). As Mosely has explained, the "power" of more speculative genres is that they can "tear down the walls and windows, the artifice and laws by changing the logic, empowering the disenfranchised or simply by asking, What if? (34).

When read as a postracial fantasy, *Of One Blood* counters charges that it is escapist or somehow fraught with back-to-Africa baggage. Far from evading pressing political concerns or capitulating to political fads, the novel confronts the ways in which slavery lives on and continues to oppress African Americans. But it also foresees the arrival of a world or way of thinking in which slavery's racial divisions and hierarchies cease to define black experience and, perhaps more importantly, overdetermine how black people define and understand themselves. Toward this end, Hopkins's agenda is not incompatible with the aims of literary realism; rather, it revises mainstream realism to account for all of the suppressed and disavowed traumas of black life, to inspire black cultural pride, and to imagine a world where black identity is not constrained by race but enriched by it. This does not mean that the novel wants us to discard of the concept of race or to deny the existence of racism. Rather, *Of One Blood, or The Hidden Self* invites us to recalibrate our own relationship to race, to adopt more intricate models for theorizing racial identity, both in terms of the universal and the particular, the domestic and the transnational, and in relationship to the past, present, and future. In doing so, the novel implicitly asks us to contemplate how we will reconcile the persistence of race, its ideologies, and instruments of violence in an ever-increasingly diverse, racially mixed, global world that will inevitably give rise to new forms of blackness, being, and belonging.

Epilogue
Rethinking Blackness

In an essay published in the *Chronicle of Higher Education,* dated February 24, 2011, Kenneth W. Warren famously announced that African American literature was over. Appearing on the heels of Barack Obama's historic run for the White House, Warren's essay "Does African-American Literature Exist?" debuted the highly controversial thesis of his then-new book *What Was African American Literature?* Both works seemed orchestrated by the same postracial myopia that saw the election of the first black president as the end of race in America. After all, Warren not only relegated African American literature to the Jim Crow past, but he also argued that the racial conditions that gave rise to the literature belonged to a bygone era that is now behind us and better left so. Predictably, Warren's controversial claim ignited a firestorm of academic debate about just what the end of African American literature might mean for the future of the field. The debate between Warren, Henry Louis Gates Jr., and Gene Andrew Jarrett—which took place in the *Chronicle*—is a case in point.

Both Gates and Jarrett took issue with Warren's argument. Gates accused Warren of practicing a reductive historicism that limits African American literature to a one-hundred-year period and, more dangerously, seems to find solace in the idea that we are living in a "post–Jim Crow" era (Warren and Gates, "The End of African American Literature?"). Jarrett offered Obama's 1995 memoir, *Dreams from My Father: A Story of Race and Inheritance* (and its role in getting him elected), as proof that African American literature is alive and well, despite the passing of the "black-power and black-arts movement" politics that "helped elevate it to academic prominence" ("African American Literature Lives On"). In these final pages, I invoke these debates not so much in the hope of settling them, but primarily because I believe that they resonate with the arguments that I have made throughout *Afro-Realisms and the Romances of Race* and, perhaps more importantly, because they give us occasion to think about how we will define the larger historical project of African American literature going forward and further into the twenty-first century.

In a political environment where Obama's 2008 victory signified the passing of race, it is easy to see why Warren's book caused such an uproar. Growing antiblack violence, mass incarceration, and the rise of the alternative right clearly betrayed the postracial symbolism of his campaign. Although Warren's book made no such claims about our entering a postracial era, his argument did in fact loosen the historical ties that anchor the moorings of our present-day racial realities by drawing a distinction between Jim Crow and our contemporary moment. Warren's point was that the literature that we call African American literature today is not motivated by the same set of racial constraints: constitutionally sanctioned segregation and discrimination. Being a black writer today is largely a matter of choice, and one's work is generally not expected to represent the race. More troublingly, for Warren, this literature is written by black elites who profit from what he describes as the continuation of black particularity by exploiting the politics of racial solidarity. So, it is not that one cannot write African American literature anymore because race and racism are things of the past but, rather, that one cannot write African American literature today because the racial climate that demanded a separate, black literary tradition disappeared with desegregation.

While I am reluctant to consign African American literature to the literary past, primarily because I believe that it lives on in the rearticulation and reinvention of its central tropes and themes, Warren's concern with historical periodization resonates with the question of methodology under study in *Afro-Realisms and the Romances of Race*. More specifically, Warren's sense that the politics that initially inspired the project can no longer offer a coherent framework for analyzing contemporary black literature or making sense of our present moment is an astute assessment of the critical impasse at which we have arrived. To be sure, African American literature still exists, but in many respects, it has evolved past the politics of authenticity, protest, and racial solidarity that secured its academic foothold and has yet to fully articulate, with any scholarly consensus, where it is now and what comes next. As Rolland Murray has observed, we need to ask ourselves, "[W]hat happens to African American cultural expression once it is no longer an emergent subfield vying for legitimacy and becomes established at the center of dominant culture?" (727). While it may take several more decades before we can fully answer this question, my sense is that this shift has made the academic study of African American literature a paradoxical endeavor. The discipline is both settled and yet always in jeopardy of being eliminated. On the one hand, this can be attributed to faulty and racist assumptions about the field's legitimacy and ongoing relevance. On the other, it can be attributed to the fact that the humanities, in general, struggle to defend their enduring value in an increasingly corporate university system and world. To counteract the dangers of both positions—stasis and eradication—we need to adopt broader, more expansive, and unconventional heuristics for reading and writing African American literature as well as limning new understandings of what it means to be black and to participate in black expressive practices—past and present.

In some ways, Warren's intervention aimed to do just that by signaling a temporal break between Jim Crow and our contemporary moment. Warren's rationale was that African American literature was shaped by the pressures of disenfranchisement and the fight against it. While I wholeheartedly concur, I think that his truncated, linear approach to literary history ultimately gave a much longer and recursive genealogy short shrift. As Gates noted, in a live, online chat hosted by the *Chronicle,* Richard Wright anticipated Warren's argument in 1937, asserting that "Negro Literature" would fade away with desegregation but that a "funny thing happened on the way to the Civil Rights movement." African American writers "started reading and revising each other's works, situating their representations of their own experiences and those of other black people, in the tropes and metaphors of other black writers." As Gates explained, the entire corpus of black writing in America can be distinguished by these "signifying relations of revision." According to this view, African American literature "began in the 18th century with the trope of the talking book" and continues to exist today because the tradition is constantly being rewritten into existence. In the end, Gates conceded, and

I agree, that Warren's primary contribution was to periodization. That is, Warren was right to link postbellum/pre–civil rights black literature to the political necessities of Jim Crow, but wrong to locate the origins of the entire black literary tradition in this era, as calls for a distinct and separate literature occurred long before this time. Yet Gates's most incisive critique of Warren's thesis—which is in no small measure crucial to the argument that I make throughout this book—was his claim that what places a text inside or outside of the canon is not a matter of discrete historical periods or even race per se as much as it is a matter of "formal influence: trope-a-dope . . . Blackness is a use of language" (Warren and Gates, "The End of African American Literature?").

Of course, scholars working in African American literary studies have not tended to approach the work of canon formation in this radical, anti-essentialist way. Historically, scholars have insisted on using race as the metric by which a writer's work is judged. Indeed, as Jarrett noted in his response to Warren, this methodological tendency can be traced back to the emergence of black studies during the 1970s. Because African American literature was, in Jarrett's words, "an imprimatur of black politics," its subject matter had to meet the "tripartite standard of racial authenticity"—meaning that it "had to be by, about, and for African Americans." More specifically, the literature had to feature themes such as "African American empowerment, political self-determination, racial solidarity, and a shared history of racial oppression." While many scholars have since challenged the problematic assumptions and limitations of this older model of black studies, pushing back on concepts like authenticity and solidarity, as Jarrett has explained, the "remnants" of this past are "discernible even in today's most forward-looking anthologies." Many of these volumes are organized in such a way that overstates the significance of race in relationship to the literature, which of course then overdetermines how we assign value to the literary work ("African American Literature Lives On").[1] As I have argued here, such practices reinforce the assumption that African American literature must be written *by, for, and about* black people. This results in a marginalizing account of the canon, limiting it to works exclusively produced by black writers and that reflect the concerns of social realism, which almost always emphasizes a narrative of struggle, resistance, or protest.

Such assumptions are no longer tenable in our contemporary moment when black aesthetics are so deeply intertwined with mass culture and capitalism. Take, for example, Kendrick Lamar winning the Pulitzer for his 2017 rap album entitled *DAMN* or the commodification of the Black Lives Matter movement. As a number of popular commentators have noted, the notion of cultural ownership or cultural purity is a particularly fraught concept in a capitalist, free-market society. How do you own and police something so intangible and unfixed as "culture" considering that it circulates in a larger sphere of influence, supply, and demand? Moreover, black people, who have good reason to be anxious about cultural appropriation, sometimes appropriate other people's cultures too, while facilitating the commodification of their own. Consider the tiff between former Brooklyn Nets player Jeremy Lin, who is of Taiwanese descent, and his then teammate Kenyon Martin, who is African American. Martin accused Lin of cultural appropriation for wearing dreadlocks, and Lin *clapbacked* with a controversial Instagram post, which has since been deleted, displaying Martin's Mandarin tattoos, writing, "At the end of the day, I appreciate that I have dreads and you have Chinese tattoos [because] I think it's a sign of respect" (qtd. in Begley). As Lin's comments suggest, such borrowings are inevitable in a diverse and global economy, and they need not always be viewed as a form of cultural theft because sometimes they are the sincerest forms of flattery, gestures of allyship or cross-cultural solidarity.

Similarly, we cannot always assume that the commodification of black culture is something that other people do to black people, as if black people do not commodify their own culture. Indeed, as Blake Simons has rightly pointed out, black people have commodified the Black Lives Matter movement. In a recent online op-ed, Simons argued that the #BankBlackMovement, created by Kevin Cohee, the CEO of OneUnitedBank, the nation's largest black bank, is a primary example. Cohee lives in a $6 million oceanfront mansion paid for by his company, where he unconsciously promotes the message that "if we all #BankBlack and harness our 'spending power' that somehow we won't be shot dead by the racist right-wing police." Simons correctly identified the problem with thinking that black capitalism is the answer to the national assault on black bodies when he observed that: "OneUnitedBank operates no differently than any other white owned bank. It is owned by one person and has the same corporate for-profit structure as other banks, like Wells Fargo, that have harmed our communities. This corporate structure is capitalism with a Black face, and it does not provide material benefits to Black communities across the country" (Simons).

Notwithstanding the problematics of appropriation and commodification, examples such as the ones mentioned above underscore the extensive and influential reach of blackness in the twenty-first century. To be sure, appropriation and commodification can do real damage to historically oppressed peoples. These kinds of cultural and commercial transactions can allow those who have traditionally been in power to enjoy everything but the burden of being a part of a marginalized group or allow them to profit off the backs of people of color, capitalizing off of what Mark Anthony Neal has called the "corporate annexation of black popular expression" (102). But in an age of global blackness, in which what it means to be black is as expansive as the people who identify as such and the contours of blackness stretch wide and far, this kind of popular appeal can also be generative. This is to say that African American literary studies can benefit from these trends by developing a criticism that is equipped to make sense of what blackness is and what it can be in the broadest possible contexts so as to avoid delimiting its sphere of signification. Put another way, we need to engage in a form of self-critique that acknowledges how long-cemented notions of racial authenticity and cultural ownership have skewed our thinking about what it means to be African American and to write African American literature as well as our ideas about who has permission to read it, be influenced by it, and participate in its rhetorical practices. The intellectual payoff is that it can give us new ways of understanding the African Americanist literary project and its relationship to other cultural discourses.

Along these lines, the last decade has witnessed an emerging critical interest in black-authored narratives of white life. While white writers have, in Brian Norman's words, "long expounded on the life and times of black people in the U.S., to greater or lesser degrees of insight," "scholarship is only beginning to fully explore" the "inverse tradition" of black writers on white life (199).[2] This literary tradition—which includes Frank Yerby's *The Foxes of Harrow* (1946), Ann Petry's *Country Place* (1947),

Zora Neale Hurston's *Seraph on the Suwanee* (1948), and James Baldwin's *Giovanni's Room* (1956)—emerged in the postwar period amid the push for desegregation and as African American writers were looking to achieve greater commercial success in a literary marketplace that pigeonholed them by labeling them as "race writers" or "protest novelists." Hampered by the representational demands and expectations placed on their writings, African American authors produced white life novels to demonstrate their aesthetic range and to enjoy freedom of expression beyond the narrow categories that confined them. In this way, the white life novel gave black writers a vehicle to transcend racial taxonomies and allowed them to be seen as artists, not merely black artists. That the field is finally beginning to seriously examine this tradition points to the breakdown of well-established assumptions about African American literature.

Similarly, we should not be reluctant to engage with white-authored narratives of black life. One of the pervasive myths that continues to haunt our ostensibly postracial literary world is the idea that one must be black to write about black people with any knowledge or sensitivity. There is no denying that there is a long tradition of white writers who tried to write about blackness and racial issues to varying degrees of success: Harriet Beecher Stowe, Mark Twain, Harper Lee, and John Howard Griffin.[3] While it is true that their writings sometimes ambivalently reproduced the very inequality that they sought to condemn, it is also true that these writers bravely and boldly confronted racism at a time when most white people were oblivious to it or could not have cared less about African American issues. Not only were they trying to wake white people up from their racial complacency, but they were also looking to enhance our understanding of American culture writ large. As Stanley Crouch has rightly acknowledged, this kind of broad big-picture approach to writing about race regrettably disappeared from the American literary scene with the arrival of the cultural turn in the early 1970s. As the scholarly and creative community embraced ethnic, gender, and sexuality studies, people became obsessed with their identity and their culture—viewing both as forms of property that exclusively belonged to them and to people who looked like them or shared their way of life.

Consider the hostile reception that greeted the publication of William Styron's novel *The Confessions of Nat Turner* (1967). Written from the first-person perspective of Turner, the African American leader of one of the most significant slave revolts in American history, *Confessions* was part of a larger movement to recuperate African American agency and resistance in discussions about slavery. Appearing during the rise of the Black Power movement, the novel was promptly dismissed as a work of cultural theft and black misrepresentation. Styron was pilloried by the African American literary community in a collection of essays entitled *William Styron's Nat Turner: Ten Black Writers Respond,* edited by John Henrik Clarke. According to Crouch, the fallout from the ordeal dramatically altered the literary landscape: "The impact of the controversy was that white writers at large opted for folding instead of holding, convinced that the challenge of writing across the color line was too big a risk to their careers and their reputations" (23). With the advent of political correctness in the 1990s, the idea of cultural ownership became sacrosanct, and no one dared to violate the rules of racial conduct for fear of being labeled a "cultural imperialist" or, worse yet, a "racist." According to Crouch, the effects on the literary world have been disastrous, and popular fiction has become, for the most part, "dull and dismal" (18).

Thankfully, it appears that the tide is finally changing. The last decade has witnessed a stream of white-authored narratives that revise and extend a problematic genealogy and that, taken together, constitute a move in the right direction: Hillary Jordan's *Mudbound* (2008), Belle Boggs's *Mattaponi Queen* (2010), Stephen O'Connor's *Thomas Jefferson Dreams of Sally Hemings* (2016), C. E. Morgan's *The Sport of Kings* (2016), Thomas Mullen's *Darktown* (2016), and Brian Platzer's *Bed-Stuy Is Burning* (2017).[4] What is truly striking about these novels is that they demonstrate that white people can write about black people with thought, feeling, respect, and narrative depth. What is more, they also demonstrate *why* white writers should take on this task. Too often this responsibility falls on black writers, who have been boxed in by the expectation that the only way to achieve literary acclaim is by writing about race and race relations. This has left white writers mostly ignorant about black identity and racial formation in America and unfairly free to explore whatever captivates their interests. As Tanner Colby recently opined: "If you convince white people that they're not qualified to tackle race, if you scare them away from the issue, if you give them the slightest excuse to ignore it, they will be happy to ignore it. For as long as you let them" ("Can a White Writer Write Black Characters?"). Ultimately, the question may not be, Do white writers have the authority to write about black people?, but rather, Do they have the courage, empathy, and insight to write responsibly across the color line?

At its core, literature is about empathy. We cannot cultivate consideration for people who are different from ourselves if we do not attempt to see the world from their points of view. While it remains necessary and worthwhile to read literature written by African Americans (along with literature written by other racial and ethnic groups, women, and members of the LGBT community), it is also important for writers and critics to step outside of themselves to consider race and racialized experience in more complex ways. It is useful to examine race not simply as a narrative that belongs to a particular person or group but as a narrative that belongs to all of us. More specifically, this means that it is imperative for white writers to recognize that race is something that involves them too. In an America that is witnessing the frightening growth of an emboldened white nationalist movement, it is absolutely crucial for all white people to examine themselves and to acknowledge the ways in which race and racism have affected them. White writers, in particular, need to cast aside their white privilege and attempt to imagine life as African Americans and other people of color experience it. We cannot begin to close the racial gap until we try to walk in someone else's shoes and understand how they feel and how historical and social forces have shaped their realities.

Writing about people who are different from us may even bring about greater interracial intimacy. Although legal segregation officially ended with the Civil Rights Act of 1964, America remains deeply divided, and so does its fiction. Jonathan Franzen's controversial interview with *Slate* magazine underscored this point in a particularly vivid manner. When Isaac Chotiner asked Franzen if he had ever considered writing a book about race, Franzen replied: "I have thought about it, but—this is an embarrassing confession—I don't have very many black friends. I have never been in love with a black woman. I feel like if I had, I might dare" (Chotiner).[5] Although Franzen's remarks were obviously unsettling, for many reasons, his comments point to two stark truths about contemporary life in America and American fiction: (1) many people do not make friends with people outside of their own race, and (2) the task of creating a character of a different race requires that the writer attempt to inhabit that subjectivity. As Franzen clumsily tried to explain, this means that the writer has to really love the character or risk dehumanizing them. While such a lofty goal may not be obtainable on a large scale, it nevertheless remains a valuable endeavor for the rest of us. Another way to think about this is in terms of cultural awareness, that is, one's consciousness about the history of racial oppression. As my colleague Viet Thanh Nguyen has elucidated, "It is possible to write about others not like oneself, if one understands that this is not simply an act of culture and free speech, but one that is enmeshed in a complicated, painful history of ownership and division" (qtd. in Schulman). If Nguyen's remarks can be said to theorize what an ethical model of writing about other races and cultures might look like, then I believe that the white-authored novels I have studied here enact this kind of historical awareness.

Similarly, I believe the postbellum black novel provides us with a more progressive model for theorizing race, blackness, and African American literature. What especially interests me about the postbellum black novel is its visionary impulses, or what I call its *proleptic hermeneutics,* that is, the ways in which this literature seems to anticipate late twentieth- and twenty-first-century reassessments of blackness and black cultural production like the new black aesthetic, postsoul, and postblack. Acknowledging that there is little agreement among scholars about these terms, their temporal limits, and their specific aesthetic qualities, I invoke them as methodologies that attempt to historicize and contextualize black cultural production after the civil rights movement, emphasizing racial fluidity, or what Trey Ellis has called the "cultural mulatto archetype," and what Bertram D. Ashe has described as "exploration[s] of the boundaries of blackness" and "allusion-disruption" to trouble the traditional ways that blackness has been defined (613).[6] What most consistently unites these post–civil rights writings and cultural artifacts is a liberated attitude toward black subjectivity and its creative processes. These works view blackness more as a set of rhetorical tropes and representational strategies than as a racial essence bound to the artist. In this configuration, blackness functions as a kind of critical posture that enables the artist to explore the possibilities of being and expression beyond the boundaries of a fixed identity or a singular black community. By crossing traditional racial lines, these works draw from a vast and diverse range of artistic traditions, comfortably claiming a variety of cultural influences as the sources of inspiration for their representations, which typically aim to push back on narrow and reductive definitions of black identity or black art.

When we examine the postbellum black novel, specifically in terms of genre and representation, we find that it reflects these very concerns. Long before Greg Tate published "Cult-Nats Meet Freaky-Deke: The Return of the Black Aesthetic," black writers were challenging assumptions and expectations of who and what their work should depict and, in the process, aiming to undermine the racism of the literary marketplace and the larger culture.[7] Each of the black and white authors whom I have examined here attempts to deconstruct race outside of prevailing norms, challenging the idea of race as biology or essence as well as reductive and stereotypical approaches toward representing African Americans, in particular, and the American racial crisis, more generally, in popular fiction. In defying the literary and cultural establishments, not only were they trying to construct something new, something more realistic, but they were also tacitly thinking about a future beyond the narrow taxonomies of racial difference that dominated turn-of-the-twentieth-century American life.

All of the fiction that I have treated here features African American protagonists, albeit of mixed-race descent (like all African Americans in a larger sense), who in their respective experiments with racial passing or interracial intimacy struggle to resist one-drop regulations while also exploring the liberating possibilities of racial identity configured in decidedly progressive ways, as something deeply personal and a matter of choice. This represents neither an outright rejection or passive acquiescence to cultural norms but a series of complex negotiations, a mode of being that is more fluid and performative than it is authentic. While none of these narratives feature completely satisfying endings or the kinds of endings that many of us would associate with full agency and subjectivity, which may have more to do with the dystopian realities of their time of publication than with their authors' limited imaginations or personal views, these novels do in fact strive to posit a more optimistic and forward-looking portrait of race while remaining fiercely critical of present inequalities, making them more complex than what critics have generally recognized.

In a broader context, the postbellum black novel also gives us an intellectual history for understanding contemporary black cultural production beyond literature, such as television and film. In some ways, the novels that I have discussed here laid the groundwork for the innovative and unconventional approaches toward black representation and racial representation that we see in shows like Courtney Kemp's *Power* (Starz), Donald Glover's *Atlanta* (FX), Issa Rae and Larry Wilmore's *Insecure* (HBO), and Shonda Rhimes's *Grey's Anatomy, Scandal,* and *How to Get Away with Murder* (ABC), and in films such as Theodore Witcher's *Love Jones* (1997), Sanaa Hamri's *Something New* (2006), Barry Jenkins's *Medicine for Melancholy* (2008), Jenkins's *Moonlight* (2016), and Stella Meghies's *Everything, Everything* (2017). Most notable among these works are the television shows, where the episodic, multiseason format lends itself to greater narrative depth, character development, and nuance. In all of these shows, blackness is theorized beyond the stereotypical hood narrative of struggle and is explored and critiqued in relationship to other races as well as in terms of class and gender.

This is true even of a show like *Power,* a gritty crime drama that focuses on a black drug dealer turned legitimate businessman, James St. Patrick (a.k.a. Ghost), played by Omari Hardwick. The show revolves around James's conflicting loyalties to his black family, his white partner-in-crime, Tommy (who is not only positioned as James's "brother from another mother" and thus the whitest member of the St. Patrick family, but who also has a black girlfriend and appears to be more comfortable around blacks than whites), and his Latina mistress, Angela Valdes, a former around-the-way girl who left the neighborhood to attend Choate and who now works as an assistant United States attorney, much to James's dismay. Featuring a diverse cast comprised of black, white, and Latinx actors, Kemp, who is the show's creator and who is also black, has maintained: "Power is not a black show. It's not a white show. It's a New York show" (qtd. in Akingbade). Kemp's remarks demonstrate how a rethinking of race, genre, and authorship can alter how we delineate the field imaginary of black cultural production. When we let go of the idea that it is the author or creator who imbues a work with racial meaning to consider how a work's situatedness within a larger sphere of conditions and circumstances creates its own meaning, then we open up the possibilities for what counts as black art and where it can be found. This can give us a greater understanding of the diversity and range of black representation.

Similarly, Rhimes's network programming has also been a remarkable game-changer. By incorporating plenty of black folk amid a sea of other races, nationalities, and LGBT characters, Rhimes's television shows eschew tokenism. Rhimes's unique approach toward racial representation, particularly her use of the practice of color-blind casting (casting actors without taking into account their race or ethnicity) has significantly changed the face of prime-time television, resulting in multiracial casts that more accurately reflect the diversity of the real world. Rhimes's longest-running show, *Grey's Anatomy,* exemplifies this strategy, as the successful medical drama features multiple characters of color and frequently places them in interracial relationships without drawing attention to race or making it a plot point, which has the uncanny effect of "normalizing" such relationships. In vehicles such as *Scandal* and *How to Get Away with Murder,* Rhimes employs similar narrative approaches, but she more overtly focuses on exploring the lives of strong, smart, sexy, and powerful black women who are, in many ways, drawn from the realm of fiction rather than real life, but who are, paradoxically, more realistic than anything we have ever seen on television before because they are not beholden to the old politics of respectability, which demand that black characters adhere to white, middle- and upper-middle class heteronormative standards so as to represent the race in a positive light. In fact, what is so refreshing about black heroines such as Olivia Pope or Annalise Keating is that they are free to be just as damaged and vulnerable as anybody else.

Of course, in offering postbellum fiction as a point of origin for contemporary black cultural production, and more so, as the key to the future of African American literary studies, I understand that I invite a certain kind of scrutiny about the continued significance of literature in a world dominated by visual, social, and new media. I have no illusions about the diminishing influence of literary studies. Admittedly, the shift from a print-based culture to an electronic one has weakened the cultural power of the written word and ascribed greater cultural authority to television, film, and digital technologies. As Alvin Kernan argued in *The Death of Literature* (1990), traditional literature has ceased to provide practical meaning and value to society. As a result, what is needed is a new approach toward literature, one that engages the visual and electronic worlds. Similarly, I believe that African American literary studies can benefit from such an approach and that by engaging with popular culture and other media forms, the field can continue to enjoy great cultural relevance. In fact, I would even go so far as to say that African American fiction and criticism might take a cue from television and film, where there tends to be more complexity, as the best series challenge narrow ideas about black art and black identity. To be sure, the future of African American literature will be and already is being dramatically reshaped by television and film, as these visual forms will continue to introduce into our scholarly practice and lexicon a variety of pressing critical and theoretical issues pertaining to representation, reception, and cross-media adaptation and influence that will inevitably change the way that we read and make sense of traditional literary forms and devices. While such concerns ultimately go beyond the scope of this project, my claims about the postbellum black novel recognize these multimedia consequences and invite us to revisit this terrain as a source of critical inspiration for African American literary and cultural studies in the twenty-first century.

Perhaps more so now than ever we need a methodology that is animated by the postbellum black novel's fluidity, metacritique, and optimism. This is particularly true in a post-Obama world where hope has given way to cynicism amid Donald Trump's presidency and an epidemic of antiblack violence and shootings of unarmed African Americans. While I too proclaim that Black Lives Matter and am outraged beyond belief by recent events, I am reluctant to follow in Stephanie Li's footsteps by linking contemporary African American literature with this movement, as she does in her introduction to the 2017 *American Literary History* special issue entitled "What Is Twenty-First-Century African American Literature?" Responding to Bertram Ashe, who back in 2007 observed that there was "no organized or even loosely organized 'movement' that collects these post–Civil Rights movement artists and places them under any sort of overtly political banner" (618), Li argues that we now appear to have this kind of political cohesiveness, asserting that twenty-first-century African American literature "seconds the urgency, vision, and hope that we associate with the Black Lives Matter movement" (633).

I appreciate Li's endeavor to historicize and contextualize, but I worry that invoking Black Lives Matter as an organizing framework is simply trading one set of identitarian-based protest politics for another, ultimately reinscribing past paradigms. For far too long African American literature has been reduced to this specific genre and function, as if it were the most exalted form of black writing. As Brian Norman has explained, "to not engage the significant tradition of black writers" who rejected this standard "is to partake of an even longer tradition in African American literature that limits and patrols the imaginative boundaries of black writers" (206). Hence, I believe that African American literature should be defined in the widest way possible so as to avoid making facile and uncomplicated generalizations about blackness or the purview of black writing. Locating all of contemporary African American literature under the designation of Black Lives Matter ultimately reinforces the marginalizing expectation that African American writing should conform to the protocols of reflecting black social reality as well as the related idea that the most *woke* or socially conscious literature is that which is grounded in the protest tradition. The problem with this is that it undercuts the capaciousness of black expression and emancipating potential of self-determination. As Patricia Stuelke has cautioned us, declaring that Black Lives Matter can unwittingly align blackness with demonstrations, rallies, marches, oppression, and death, ultimately creating "a toxic racial narrative" that "locks black subjects into the infinitely recursive roles of universal tragic martyrs or pathological tragic victims" (754–55).

When I presented a version of this epilogue at the 2017 meeting of the American Studies Association, I was not entirely surprised to encounter pushback from skeptical colleagues: "Is a seemingly postblack/postracial framework such as yours compatible with a politics of rage in an era of Black Lives Matter?" As I explained, my desire to move away from the author-based system of racial/literary classification does not proceed from a longing to do away with blackness or race, or to disavow their continued significance; rather, it is motivated by a professional commitment to expand the possibilities for African American literary inquiry by moving beyond marginalizing modes of critique. While I believe that rage can be productive, particularly if it brings about social justice, I am hesitant to adopt this as a methodology for African American literature because it reinforces harmful stereotypes that cast black people as angry and violent. As Barbara Ransby has written in "The Class Politics of Black Lives Matter": "[R]age is the beginning, not the end point of movement building. . . . [R]age has to be coupled with compassion, critical generosity, and love." In my opinion, we need to challenge the politics of racial pessimism that have come to define not only our highly polarized political environment but also our intellectual practice. While these are very troubling times for our democracy and for our profession, we should not allow demoralizing conditions to demoralize us and overdetermine the content and direction of our scholarship. If anything, we need to approach our scholarship with greater optimism, viewing it as an opportunity to propose practical solutions to some of our most severe social problems.

Such is the argument of Christopher Castiglia's latest book, *The Practices of Hope* (2017). Pushing back on the "hermeneutics of suspicion" that have come to define critical methodologies in literary studies, Castiglia offers an alternative approach to literary analysis, a post-critique criticism animated by "idealism" and "imagination" (2). Motivated by a desire to recuperate critique from its conservative Cold War epistemology, Castiglia shows how the founders of American studies—many of whom are frequently dismissed and disparaged as the authors and agents of American exceptionalism—practiced a form of hopeful criticism that sought not only to oppose the homogeneity and hysteria of the Cold War period but also to illustrate how the idealism and imaginative quality of literature could be used to condemn social conditions, imagine alternative worlds and utopias, and thus advocate for a more egalitarian society. The true value of Castiglia's intervention is that it assigns greater moral and social value to critique, insisting on its centrality to efforts to strengthen our democracy:

> In offering critiques, we measure the present or the past against ideals. . . . Without ideals, there would be no critique. But our ideals are effaced by rituals of professionalization in a discipline that regards articulation of idealism as a sign of naïveté, triviality, or bad faith, making idealism cause for embarrassment. A critique that states our ideals, in contrast, would make clear what we are for, demonstrating how idealism is the basis for

> ethical judgement and encouraging the shaping and expression of ideals necessary to social engagement and change. (3)

In this way, Castiglia suggests that a criticism fueled by idealism can transform our civic and academic institutions for the better. This is an important corrective that not only has value for the way that scholars working in American studies approach criticism, but it also possesses great relevance for scholars in African American studies. For far too long, we have settled for a critique of despair and opposition. We have positioned boots-on-the-ground protest and activism as the most exalted forms of social action. While such activities remain highly effective ways of staging resistance to oppression, we should also come to see the political significance of other forms of expression that challenge prevailing power dynamics. Perhaps it is also time to add a little idealism and imagination to our work so that we might come to view both blackness and black writing in more uplifting and liberating ways.

That blackness is so frequently configured in terms of abjection, the object, and lack should prompt us to interrogate our critical commitment to invoking Afro-pessimism's discourses of abjectness, subjection, and social death in the service of theorizing black subjectivity. Here I am reminded of Li's observation that "[b]lackness in the twenty-first century is inseparable from acknowledging and confronting the dead . . . and envision[ing] a home for the living" ("What Is Twenty-First-Century African American Literature?" 638). Such a bleak and morbid assessment of black life demands that we ask ourselves some very urgent questions: Why is it that we constantly feel the need to turn toward a model of social death to analyze blackness and affirm black humanity? What about the critical possibilities of a black theory of social life? If we want to challenge the dominant cultural narrative that tells us over and over again that black life is cheap and that it does not matter, then is it not time for us to move beyond social death as our default critical paradigm? The problem with consistently choosing to view blackness through these dark lenses is that it can create a self-fulfilling prophecy that reinforces our most dangerous beliefs and expectations of the social world and how we walk in it. This in turn fashions a sort of feedback loop that becomes a totalizing heuristic. Now, more than ever, we need to tell a new narrative about what it means to be black and what the function of African American literature is in today's world. In many ways, what I am calling for in this book is a reinvigorated approach to African American literary studies, one that recognizes the transformative possibilities of optimism, life, and the diversity of blackness and black experience.

Indeed, I think that there is great value in looking to the postbellum black novel for a pathway to the future because it can give us a new purchase on old paradigms. In our current moment, which undoubtedly feels a lot like more of the same, we must be careful not to saddle black literature with the political demands of racial collectivity because it can forestall an appreciation for individuality and diversity. Similarly, we should not conflate the contemplation of futurity with a denunciation of the continued significance of blackness or race as conceptual categories. We should never stop thinking about what is involved and at stake in creating newer and more intricate models for thinking about race, culture, and politics in African American literary studies. To be sure, more work needs to be done—especially work that applies greater fluidity and nuance to the black literary past. The payoff will be that we create new ways of reading and discussing pre–civil rights movement black literature. Instead of privileging twentieth- and twenty-first-century writings as being more aesthetically sound and politically conscious than nineteenth-century works, we might come to see the undertheorized innovativeness and political work of earlier genres and literary periods. In these final pages, I offer this book as a model for what this kind of scholarship might look like as well as a provocative example of the possibilities that the postbellum black novel may offer African American literary studies.

Throughout this book, I have argued that some of the most conventional and established approaches to African American literature limit its archive and obscure its true complexity. Such methodologies are no longer able to provide cogent answers to the question of what, exactly, is "African American" about African American literature, certainly not in our twenty-first-century world where the task of defining blackness has never been more complicated or contested. When we take a longer view of literary history, we find that what has always defined African American literature is its ongoing dialectic with literary realism. From the truth-telling imperatives of the slave narrative to the flat-out rejection of the concept of racial authenticity that characterizes so many postsoul, post-black, and new black writings, black literature has been shaped alongside and against calls to, in more informal terms, *keep it one hundred.* In nineteenth-century literature, the conversation about race and realism is one of interracial exchange, and it finds its most compelling expression in the postbellum black novel. Writings by Twain, Howells, Harper, Chesnutt, and Hopkins demonstrate how realism could be repurposed not only to render blackness as a more fluid and interior subjectivity but also to serve as meta-criticism about fiction's ability to intervene in the larger cultural sphere and carry out the work of racial justice. Not in the simplistic, propagandistic style of the protest novel that James Baldwin famously excoriated, but as works of art, grounded in a representational and rhetorical domain.[8] In its treatment of black and white writers and their literary works, this book has tried to illuminate how questions of racial representation guided aesthetic experimentation during the nadir.

More than anything, I have tried to show how a literary history based on racial representation, as opposed to writers' racial identities, solves one of American and African American literature's greatest problems: the tendency to emphasize a writer's race over the content of their work. By focusing on the critique of race that is depicted in the literature, instead of the author's racial identity, we free black writing from the burden of representing race—both in terms of black racialized experience as well as the conceptual category itself. We also create new pathways of identification that go beyond skin-deep to contemplate what is involved and what is at stake in rendering race and racism in imaginative form. The benefit of such an approach is that it gives us a larger body of writing about black experience, as well as a more intricate paradigm for theorizing race and comprehending the various communities of writers, readers, and texts that make up African American literature. *Afro-Realisms and the Romances of Race* is ultimately a book that urges us to rethink the canonical narrative about race and realism in American and African American literary studies. Amid doomsday claims that we have reached the end of African American literature, as we have historically defined it, this book asks us to adopt a fresh perspective toward our interpretive practices in the hope that we might find more provocative and complex ways of theorizing blackness and race in the twenty-first century and beyond.

NOTES

Introduction: Race, Realism, and the Problem of Literary Classification

1. Toomer's views on race, art, and the literary marketplace were considerably ahead of their time. Not only did he posit a multiracial identity at a time when most Americans subscribed to the one-drop rule, but he also felt that what made *Cane* a black novel was its subject matter, not his Negro ancestry. In this same letter, Toomer told his publisher to "[f]eature Negro if you wish, but do not expect me to feature it in advertisements for you. . . . Whatever statements I give will inevitably come from a synthetic human and art point of view; not from a racial one" (Sept. 5, 1923, qtd. in Toomer, *Letters* 171).

2. My point here is that while *Cane* is clearly a work of American modernism, the novel has traditionally been viewed within the context of the Harlem Renaissance. The distinction that literary historians have made between the two movements, albeit largely false, has to with the fact that up until the late twentieth century, critics primarily understood modernism as a European aesthetic contemporaneous with the Harlem Renaissance but also separate from it. For more on the relationship between African American literature and modernism, see Houston Baker's essay "Modernism and the Harlem Renaissance"; Adrienne Johnson Gosselin's essay "Beyond the Harlem Renaissance: The Case for Black Modernist Writers"; and Shadi Neimneh and Marwan Obeidat's essay "Jean Toomer's *Cane:* The Harlem Renaissance, Modernism, and the Avant-Garde."

3. As Madhu Dubey has written: "Political claims about African-American literature have always depended on realist aesthetics, from the documentary impulse of the slave narratives to the reflectionist principles prescribed by the cultural nationalist program" (44). Nevertheless, canonical literary histories, white and black, have either ignored black contributions to realism or underassessed black writers' experiments with the genre altogether. Classic studies by white scholars such as V. L. Parrington's *The Beginnings of Critical Realism in America* (1930), Warner Berthoff's *The Ferment of Realism* (1965), and Michael Davitt Bell's *The Problem of American Realism* (1993) did not even acknowledge the existence of an African American literary tradition, let alone a black realist aesthetic. By contrast, during the 1930s and 1940s, black scholars such as Sterling Brown, Arthur P. Davis, and Ulysses Lee lauded realism for its potential to bring about racial reform, but they condemned virtually all literature prior to Richard Wright for being too feeble to perform this kind of radical cultural work. As Andreá N. Williams has noted, these critics located much of black literature

within the "romance tradition" and believed that "African American literature guaranteed its own critical neglect and commercial failure by clinging to sentimentalism rather than embracing the timely move towards realism" ("African American Literary Realism, 1865–1914" 186). Although more recent assessments of black postbellum literature, such as those by Williams, have since revised this theory, there are few full-length accounts of how African American writers created their own versions of realism.

4. For scholarship on race and realism, see Kenneth W. Warren, *Black & White Strangers;* Augusta Rohrbach, *Truth Stranger Than Fiction;* Cathy Boeckmann, *A Question of Character;* Ryan Simmons, *Chesnutt and Realism;* and Gene Andrew Jarrett, *Deans and Truants.* While these are all excellent studies, I concur with Simmons, who has written: "Few critics who theorize realism also contend with race, and vice versa. Although there are important exceptions to this rule . . . [rarely] is the literary production of an African American writer considered for more than a chapter. This is not mentioned to disparage these critics' work, but to point out that important work remains to be done" (7).

5. See *Clotel,* chapter 23, which is entitled "Truth Stranger Than Fiction." As a number of scholars have explained, this idiom was widely used in slave narratives as type of authenticating strategy, privileging the veracity of the story over its use of literary conventions from popular romantic fiction. For more on this expression, see John Ernest, *Chaotic Justice,* chap. 2; Augusta Rohrbach, *Truth Stranger Than Fiction,* chap. 2; and Andreá N. Williams, "African American Literary Realism, 1865–1914."

6. See Foucault, "What Is an Author?" In this essay, Foucault argues that the author, as an individual person who assigns meaning to a text, is a literary construct rooted in humanism. Instead of viewing authorship in this way, Foucault suggests that we approach authorship as a "function of discourse"—that is, something that is produced in relationship to language and social practices. According to Foucault, the idea of the discrete author is an invention of copyright law and is tied to questions of power, merit, and the privileging of certain discourses and systems of knowledge over others. The author does not refer to a real individual as much as it describes how we organize and make sense of texts (210–11).

7. For scholarship on slave narratives and their complicated publication histories, particularly the issue of white amanuenses, editors, and joint authorship, see William L. Andrews, *To Tell a Free Story;* John Ernest, *Chaotic Justice* 75–111; and Teresa A. Goddu, "The Slave Narrative as Material Text."

8. The term "nadir" was coined by the historian Rayford W. Logan in his 1954 book *The Negro in American Life and Thought: The Nadir, 1877–1901.* According to Logan, this period constituted the lowest point in African American history, as blacks witnessed the resurgence of a virulent white supremacy and political disenfranchisement. In the years since Logan's book appeared, scholars have taken issue with this particular usage of the term because it casts a pejorative shadow on African American life during this time that distorts how we view and make sense of it. Because we have placed too much emphasis on the discourses of violence and victimization, we have ignored and underassessed how African Americans resisted white supremacy and advocated for social change vis-à-vis literary and cultural production as well as through formal and informal politics. For more on this topic, see Barbara McCaskill and Caroline Gebhard's *Post-Bellum, Pre-Harlem* 1–6.

9. As Chesnutt observed: "At the time when I first broke into print seriously, no American colored writer had ever secured critical recognition except Paul Laurence Dunbar, who had won his laurels as a poet. Phillis Wheatley, a Colonial poet, had gained recognition largely because she was a slave and born in Africa, but the short story, or the novel of life and manners, had not been attempted by any one of that group." He also noted: "I have lived to see, after twenty years or more, a marked change in attitude of publishers and the reading public in regard to the Negro in fiction," adding that Harlem has "presented a new field for literary exploration" ("Post-Bellum—Pre-Harlem" 910).

10. See Warren's *Black and White Strangers,* chap. 3. Here, Warren explores the lasting influence of Stowe's *Uncle Tom's Cabin* and how it presented unique challenges to the task of defining realism during the postbellum period.

11. Canonical accounts of American literary history have almost always been structured by notions of linear time that depend upon the evolutionary discourse of progress, especially in discussions about genre (see Cathy Boeckmann's *A Question of Character,* 25–62; and Donald Pizer's *Realism and Naturalism,* esp. "The Evolutionary Foundation of W. D. Howells's Criticism and Fiction"). Reacting against this strain, I invoke anachronism as the methodology by which we can best assess the temporal maneuvers of African American writing during the nadir, and thus reappraise its formal and cultural value. In this context, my argument echoes Valerie Rohy's claim that "history is always ahistorical, progress is inextricable from backwardness, and that the time lines of the past live on in today's difficult conversations" (xvi).

12. More specifically, my book aims to join recent studies by Quashie, Levy-Hussen, and Freeburg, all of which propose a new line of inquiry for black literary studies, a line that seeks to upend assumptions about the political function of black literature to add greater nuance to our interpretive practices. Quashie argues that the tendency to view blackness through a "social public lens" undercuts our understanding of black subjectivity by placing too much emphasis on resistance, which ultimately dehumanizes black people and forestalls other methods of reading (4). Levy-Hussen intervenes in the debate about the function of neo–slave narratives, calling for an interpretive methodology that goes beyond the "therapeutic reading" (the idea that confronting the horrors of slavery will result in healing) and the "prohibitive reading" (which argues that revisiting the past is dangerous). Levy-Hussen's point is that neo–slave narratives "neither compel nor prohibit identification with the traumatic past. They desire identification while recognizing that the terms may be strained, disappointing, elusive, inhibiting, inassimilable with modern life, or otherwise non-cathartic" (6). Freeburg explores how black personhood destabilizes rather than upholds assumptions about the cohesiveness of collective political action. I see my work intersecting with all of these studies in its attempt to theorize blackness outside of the usual ways so as to arrive at a fuller sense of black experience and literary expression. My work departs from them in that I am interested in recuperating realism from its more negative associations with a white hegemonic worldview to demonstrate its aesthetic range and potential for expanding the archive of black representation in fiction.

13. Here I am specifically thinking about Warren's *Black and White Strangers;* Dubey's *Signs and Cities;* and Harper's *Abstractionist Aesthetics.* All of these studies demonstrate how

racial politics and debates about representation have shaped and defined American and African American literature and culture. These studies have also successfully challenged severely problematic assumptions and facile generalizations about race and authentic blackness, without which my intervention would not be possible. My work differs from theirs in its focus on African American literary realism, specifically the idea that it could serve as a powerful modality for challenging the external world and exposing its constructedness, thereby creating the conceptual space to reimagine it.

14. Here it might be productive to revisit Bernard W. Bell's account of African American literature: "Every American writer of African and European descent works within and against the dual tradition—oral and literary, African and European, romantic and realistic, male and female—that each inherits as part of his or her North American cultural legacy. . . . Each writer's contribution and significance are therefore influenced by his or her relationship to past and present writers, as well as by the relationship of his and her texts to others in the tradition, both in the Eurocentric sense of literary formalism and in the broader Afrocentric cultural sense" ("Women and Literature").

15. McKay begins her essay with Phillis Wheatley, the first person of African ancestry to publish a book in America. Because many whites at the time did not believe that blacks were capable of producing original literature, Wheatley was brought before a panel of eighteen white men to attest to the authenticity of her writing. As McKay explains, this dehumanizing experience illustrates how black writers have been discriminated against by white elites. It also speaks to a larger structural problem about the misperception of African American literature as an illegitimate academic enterprise.

16. See Morrison, "An Interview."

17. According to Marjorie Levinson, the last twenty years have witnessed a renewed interest among scholars in form and aesthetics. She calls this movement the "new formalism." As Levinson defines it, the new formalism differs from the old formalism in its bridging of the study of form to history and politics. In its "activist" strain, questions of form are subjected to historical reading in the style of Hegel, Marx, Freud, and Adorno, whereas its "normative" version returns to Kant to highlight the "disinterested," "playful," and "consensus-forming" aspects of form (559).

18. Acknowledging the new formalism's original engagement with early modern and Romantic aesthetics and its limited ability to speak to issues of race and racial formation, scholars working in race and ethnicity studies have adapted the methodology to address their specific concerns. The new formalism attempts to elucidate how we read race, how it is represented in literature, and how aesthetic forms can be racialized. For a critical overview, see Colleen Lye's *America's Asia: Racial Form and American Literature, 1893–1945;* Fred Moten's *In the Break;* and Elda E. Tsou's *Unquiet Tropes.*

19. For useful studies on late twentieth- and early twenty-first-century reassessments of blackness, see Trey Ellis, "The New Black Aesthetic"; Mark Anthony Neal, *Soul Babies;* and Margo Natalie Crawford, *Black Post-Blackness.*

* * *

1. The Long Hangover: Mark Twain's *Pudd'nhead Wilson* and the Ghosts of Slavery

1. The novelty of my argument finds some precedence in Henry Louis Gates's analysis of the slave narrative in *Figures in Black,* as he has argued that the slave narrative is the formal "negation" of the "plantation novel" (82). Gates suggests that the slave narrative's formal conventions challenge the false representation of slavery depicted in plantation novels, in that they debunk the fiction of "aristocratic, virtuous masters; beast-like, docile slaves; great manor houses; squalid field quarters; and idealized, alabaster womanhood" (82). In acknowledging the racist ideology implicit in the plantation form, Gates makes a broader argument about the relationship between form and ideology, upon which my argument builds.

2. See Cohen's essay "Aesthetic Anomalies in *Pudd'nhead Wilson,*" where he argues that Twain's sloppy revision resulted in textual incongruities that weakened the characters and the novel's critique of slavery.

3. See Fishkin's "Race and Culture at the Century's End," where she argues that the novel is flawed but that its flaws are the result of deteriorating race relations. See Gillman's "Sure Identifiers: Race, Science, and the Law in *Pudd'nhead Wilson,*" where she explores the social construction of race in relationship to genre and late nineteenth-century cultural discourses surrounding identity. See Sundquist's "Mark Twain and Homer Plessy," in which he reads the novel's flaws in the context of *Plessy v. Ferguson* (1896), contending that the narrative's divided form can be explained by the divisive logic of segregation. See Rowe's "Fatal Speculations: Murder, Money, and Manners in *Pudd'nhead Wilson,*" in which he argues that the novel is a historical romance that satirizes how little society has progressed since the antebellum days and, more specifically, that it implicates slavery in the development of a modern, postbellum, industrial economy.

4. Ferguson argues that slave narratives often feature similarly conflicting views about sin and salvation. In "Christian Violence and the Slave Narrative," she writes: "On the one hand, the authors stress the slave's spiritual liberation by willing obedience to a divinity they call Providence or Creator. . . . On the other, the narrators portray the slaveholders as new Adams and Eves who use the forgiveness resulting from the blood sacrifice and resurrection of Christ both to violate the Maker's original laws of human sanctity and to return themselves repeatedly and instantaneously to the moment of moral purity" (299). I think Ferguson's observation provides a useful lens for comprehending Roxy's inversion of the normal theological arrangement that we find in slave narratives and for grasping her subversive appropriation of white slave masters' use of religion.

5. The phrase "nature versus nurture" was first invoked by Francis Galton, who is considered the "father of eugenics," in 1869. The term refers to the late nineteenth-century debate about whether human behavior was more forcefully shaped by "nature," as in inherited traits (biological or genetic factors), or "nurture," as in acquired or learned characteristics, including environmental influences. Galton himself believed in heredity and the idea that society could be improved by "better breeding" (see Christine Rosen's *Preaching Eugenics: Religious Leaders and the American Eugenics Movement*).

6. In "The Ties That Bind: Race and Sex in *Pudd'nhead Wilson,*" Jehlen argues that *Pudd'nhead Wilson* is a "remarkable exploration of the anxieties aroused by a racist social structure" (109) but that, ultimately, Twain may have been "reluctant to see black men acquire the power of whites and may have viewed their bid for a share of power outright usurpation" (120). Thus, for Jehlen, the novel appears to vacillate between liberalism and conservatism, with the work ultimately ending in an impasse due to Twain's inability to imagine more radical change. While I agree with Jehlen's observations about the text's conflicting views about race, I believe that there is a more productive conversation to be had about the novel's tensions that does not discard its liberal critique of race on the basis of its racial cynicism or what may or may not be Twain's bigotry. More important than whether or not Twain was racist is the novel's overt criticism of the plantation romance's strategies for depicting slavery and African American identity at a time when the genre set the standard for authentic representation in fiction, despite the fact that such representations were rooted in racial stereotypes.

7. See, for example, Arthur G. Petit, *Mark Twain and the South;* Eric Lott, "Mr. Clemens and Jim Crow: Twain, Race, and Blackface"; and James S. Leonard, Thomas A. Tenney, and Thadious M. Davis, eds., *Satire or Evasion? Black Perspectives on Huckleberry Finn.*

8. For more on cross-dressing and slavery, see Kari J. Winter, *Subjects of Slavery, Agents of Change* 123–40; and Marjorie Garber, *Vested Interests: Cross-Dressing and Cultural Anxiety.*

9. I borrow the term "social death" from Patterson. In his seminal work *Slavery and Social Death,* he uses it to describe the condition of "natal alienation" and "isolation" suffered by enslaved black people. According to Patterson, since the enslaved person was considered property, and could be bought and sold, their ontological condition was one of "fungibility," resulting in a lack of agency and a denial of social relations (38). Drawing on Patterson's work, Afro-pessimists have argued that these same structures of racial oppression continue to organize black life, as they form the foundation of Western society. In *Red, White, and Black: Cinema and the Structure of U.S. Antagonisms,* Frank B. Wilderson provides what is perhaps one of the sharpest and most lucid definitions of Afro-pessimism: "The Afro-pessimists are theorists of Black positionality who share Fanon's insistence, that though Blacks are sentient, the structure of the entire world's semantic field . . . is sutured by anti-black solidarity" (58). For more on Afro-pessimism, see Jared Sexton's "The Social Life of Social Death"; Saidiya Hartman's *Scenes of Subjection;* and Hortense Spillers's *Black, White, and in Color.*

10. The novel's tension between race as an innate, inheritable, and corporeal condition and race as an arbitrary social construction with shifting and flexible boundaries has been widely explored. See, for example, Lee Clark Mitchell, "'De Nigger in You': Race or Training in Pudd'nhead Wilson?"; Andrea K. Newlyn, "Form and Ideology in Transracial Narratives: *Pudd'nhead Wilson* and *A Romance of the Republic*"; and Nancy Fredricks, "Twain's Indelible Twins."

11. In *Amalgamation!,* James Kinney makes a similar argument, positing: "This overblown assertion goes unchallenged by the author because we are supposed to see the irony of having Roxy—the best character in the novel, the only match for Wilson in intelligence, and 'Tom's' self-sacrificing mother—be the one to offer the obvious racial explanation in

such an exaggerated manner. Here, as elsewhere, Clemens uses exaggeration as a rhetorical clue to an intended irony" (221).

12. For an excellent overview of criminal anthropology, see Peter D'Agostino's essay "Craniums, Criminals, and the 'Cursed Race': Italian Anthropology in American Racial Thought, 1861–1914."

13. While the Civil War Amendments and the passage of the Civil Rights Act in 1866 may have put an end to slavery, granted equal protection, and extended suffrage to freedmen, the Slaughter-House ruling and *United States v. Cruikshank* severely curtailed the scope of the Thirteenth and Fourteenth Amendments by restricting federal protection and giving power back to southern states. For a good overview of this legal history, see Brook Thomas's introduction to the Bedford/St. Martin's edition of *Plessy v. Ferguson* 18–23.

14. Hall has argued that race is a discursive concept that operates like language in that it functions as part of a linguistic sign that can be made to signify many different things: "Its meaning is relational and it is constantly subject to redefinition in different cultures, different moments" (see Hall, "Race, the Floating Signifier").

2. Reimagining the Tragic Mulatta in Frances E. W. Harper's *Iola Leroy*

1. I borrow this description of the tragic mulatta plot from Anna Shannon Elfenbein's book *Women on the Color Line: Evolving Stereotypes and the Writings of George Washington Cable, Grace King, and Kate Chopin* (3). For more on the mulatta, see Teresa C. Zackodnik's *The Mulatta and the Politics of Race.*

2. For a discussion on African American writers and their shifting representational needs during this period, see Henry Louis Gates Jr.'s essay "The Trope of a New Negro and the Reconstruction of the Image of the Black."

3. Prior to *Iola Leroy*'s critical reappraisal by black feminist scholars such as Frances Smith Foster, Hazel Carby, and Deborah McDowell, African American male critics frequently dismissed the novel as lacking in artistic and political merit. For example, in *The Negro Caravan* (1941), Sterling Brown, Arthur P. Davis, and Ulysses Lee wrote that *Iola Leroy* was "as dull as it is pious" and described the novel as "inept" and derivative of William Wells Brown's *Clotel* (139–40). Years later, Robert Bone echoed a similar sentiment, lumping the novel in with a group of "Talented Tenth" texts he described as having "little artistic individuality" (29). Bone also singled *Iola Leroy* out as "lack[ing] the urgency of the other protest novels of the 1890's" (32). As Koritha Mitchell notes in her introduction to the new Broadview Press edition of *Iola Leroy,* such negative assessments continued well into the 1960s, when the Black Power movement gave rise to more militant criticism that viewed Harper's use of the tragic mulatta motif as proof of the novel's regressive politics. This trend endured through the 1980s and early 1990s in works such as Barbara Christian's *Black Feminist Criticism* and Houston Baker's *Workings of the Spirit* (Mitchell, Introduction 43). For positive assessments of the novel, see Elizabeth Ammons's *Conflicting Stories;* Hazel Carby's *Reconstructing Womanhood;* and Claudia Tate's *Domestic Allegories of Political Desire.* For more negative assessments, see Arlene Elder's *The Hindered Hand;* Blyden Jackson's *A*

History of Afro-American Literature; Alice Walker's *In Search of Our Mothers' Gardens;* and Kimberly A. C. Wilson's "The Function of the 'Fair' Mulatto."

4. Frustrated by reviews of *The Rise of Silas Lapham* (1885) and the cultural obsession with romantic fiction, Howells wrote to a friend that he planned to advance his views about literary realism by "banging the babes of Romance about." As Rosenthal maintains, the gendered connotations of the remark clearly point to Howells's disdain for what he perceived to be "women's fiction" (see Howells's letter to Edmund W. Gosse, dated Jan. 24, 1886, *Selected Letters,* vol. 3: *1882–1891* 152).

5. This term refers to black women's domestic fiction produced during the post-Reconstruction era. According to Tate, these narratives use "the gendered discourses of domestic civility as allegorical discourses of citizenship" (21) to express black women's desires for racial uplift configured as "moral development, spiritual maturation, professional aspirations, . . . economic advancement . . . and social justice for black Americans" (11). In this way, black women's domestic fiction is not merely a rearticulation of sentimental, white female norms, but a counterhegemonic representation of black people's desires for political enfranchisement.

6. The classic example of the conversion scene comes from *Uncle Tom's Cabin.* In this dramatic exchange, Topsy, an orphaned slave girl who, having internalized the racism of her environment, tells little Eva, the angelic child at the center of the novel, that she is wicked and unlovable, to which Eva replies: "O, Topsy, poor child *I* love you!," laying "her little thin, white hand on Topsy's shoulder" (409). In the act of expressing kindness to Topsy, little Eva functions as a redemptive figure whose compassion saves Topsy, and the conversion is complete: "[I]n that moment, a ray of real belief, a ray of heavenly love, had penetrated the darkness of her heathen soul! She laid her head down between her knees, and wept and sobbed,—while the beautiful child, bending over her, looked like the picture of some bright angel stooping to reclaim a sinner" (410). As scholars such as Lauren Berlant, Glenn Hendler, Julia Stern, and Marianne Noble have shown, appeals to the emotional sensorium were not employed to simply entertain audiences but rather to encourage them to take political action. For more on sentimentalism, see Berlant's *The Female Complaint;* Hendler's *Public Sentiments;* Stern's *The Plight of Feeling;* and Noble's *The Masochistic Pleasures of Sentimental Literature.*

7. In "The Cult of True Womanhood," Barbara Welter writes: "[The attributes] by which a woman judged herself and was judged by her husband, her neighbors and society could be divided into four cardinal virtues—piety, purity, submissiveness and domesticity. Put them all together and they spelled mother, daughter, sister, wife—woman" (152).

8. Interestingly enough, "Enlightened Motherhood" is also the title of an address that Harper gave before the Brooklyn Literary Society on November 15, 1892. In this speech, Harper advocates for a form of female political engagement that is more firmly situated within the domestic sphere, which would appear to be at odds with the facts of her very public political life as a female activist: "The school may instruct and the church may teach, but the home is an institution older than the church and antedates school, and that is the place where children should be trained for useful citizenship on earth and a hope of holy companionship in heaven" (Foster, *A Brighter Coming Day* 284–85). Rather than insist on

a separation between the public and private spheres, Harper's investment in both arenas encourages us to see them as underwriting each other and serving mutual ends in the campaign for black citizenship.

9. Although the first usage of the term "Talented Tenth" is frequently attributed to W. E. B. Du Bois and believed to have originally appeared in *The Negro Problem* (1903), a collection of essays edited by Booker T. Washington, he was not the true creator of the expression, but rather Henry Lyman Morehouse was, as Evelyn Brooks Higginbotham revealed in her book *Righteous Discontent: The Women's Movement in the Black Baptist Church, 1880–1920*. For more on Morehouse, see chapter 2 of *Righteous Discontent.*

10. In *Forgotten Readers,* McHenry writes: "Association with African American literary culture was considered fundamental to the agenda of racial uplift and social reform and one potential avenue to the assertion of political agency. Harper's *Iola Leroy* underscores this message in two ways: while it dramatizes the process of transformation to race consciousness and pious activism experienced by members of the fictional literary society, the novel offers itself as a means of making that process available to its readers. As a fictional heroine, Iola Leroy presented late nineteenth-century readers with an example of virtue, compassion, and high moral character; at the same time she is intelligent, ambitious, and committed to public service. By the end of the novel, Iola Leroy has not yet satisfied her desire to write a 'good, strong book' but her creator, Frances Harper, has; by stimulating the racial and sexual consciousness of her intended readers" (188).

11. It is worth noting that Victoria Earle Matthews also advocated for a similar approach to literature in her address delivered at the First Congress of Colored Women of the United States in Boston on July 30, 1895, entitled "The Value of Race Literature." By "race literature" Matthews did "not necessarily mean race matter" but more so a compendium of writing by black people so as to achieve a critical mass in letters. According to Matthews, the value of race literature lay in its ability to provide a "revelation to our people," "enlarge our scope, make us better known," and "undermine and utterly drive out the traditional Negro in dialect,—the subordinate, the servant as the type representing a race whose numbers are now far into the millions" (170, 173).

12. In 1893, as part of the World's Columbian Exposition, the World's Congress of Representative Women met in Chicago. Among others, Hallie Q. Brown, Anna Julia Cooper, Fannie Jackson Coppin, Sarah J. Early, Frances Harper, Fannie Barrier Williams, and Frederick Douglass—six black women and one black man—addressed the gathering. Harper told her audience that she felt they were standing "on the threshold of woman's era"; in 1894, *Woman's Era* was the name chosen for the journal run by the Woman's Era club in Boston. The club movement grew rapidly among Afro-American women and culminated in the first Congress of Colored Women of the United States, which convened in Boston in 1895. In 1896, the National Federation of Colored Women and the National League of Colored Women united in Washington, D.C., to form the National Association of Colored Women (NACW). For the first time, black women were nationally organized to confront the various modes of their oppression" ("On the Threshold" 264).

13. According to P. Gabrielle Foreman, *Iola Leroy*'s politics of naming links its characters to "previous and contemporaneous struggles for Black freedom and full citizenship rights"

by recuperating African American historical figures in its "homonymic and histotextual associations" (90). As Foreman explains, Lucille Delany's "most obvious possible paternal antecedent is Martin Delany" (99). Like the historical Delany, Lucille is cast as an ardent, dark-skinned lecturer-teacher-activist, committed to female education, community organization, and professional development. Foreman notes that for some historians, such a connection might seem strained, but in actuality, Harper and Delany operated in the same spheres of influence, lecturing and publishing in the same venues (102). Given their overlapping activities, it is highly likely that Delany informed Harper's depiction of Lucille.

3. Racial Fictions and the Cultural Work of Genre in Charles W. Chesnutt's *The House behind the Cedars*

1. Chesnutt penned this journal entry after reading Tourgée's novel *A Fool's Errand* (1879). Chesnutt was so inspired by Tourgée's success, especially in light of his lack of first-hand knowledge about the South, that he believed he too could capitalize on his outsider's viewpoint and write a realist novel about the region and its people that did not simply capitulate to racial stereotypes (Andrews, *Literary Career* 10–11).

2. Chesnutt's correspondence with George Washington Cable was highly influential in this regard. When Cable read an early draft of the manuscript entitled "Rena Walden," he encouraged Chesnutt to strengthen the melodramatic ending to initiate a greater emotional and sympathetic reaction in white readers. As Cable advised Chesnutt, the "grand finale should be made more powerful. . . . [It] ought to be simply tremendous" (*Letters* 47–48).

3. From the 1820s until the 1930s, the image of African Americans most consistently reflected in American literary and popular culture was steeped in what George M. Fredrickson has called "romantic racialism." As famously illustrated in Stowe's *Uncle Tom's Cabin* (1852), "romantic racialism" portrayed African Americans as docile, childlike, and feminine. In many representations, the so-called "pure Negroes" were portrayed as being inherently superior to mulattoes, who were believed to be tragically depressed, sterile, or untrustworthy owing to their "mixed blood" (see Fredrickson, *The Black Image in the White Mind,* specifically chap. 4). Despite the movement toward literary realism after the Civil War, American fiction continued to feature this romantic approach toward racial representation, as popular genres such as local-color and dialect fiction, regionalist writing, and the plantation tradition all utilized the practices of racial caricature, racial stereotyping, and minstrelsy to "realistically" depict racial differences. For more on racial representation and American literary realism, see Henry B. Wonham's *Playing the Races.*

4. For Cable, a literature that was both politically engaged and emotionally attuned had the best chance of awakening the dormant national consciousness to the ongoing plight of African Americans in the post-Reconstruction era. In his essay "The Freedman's Case in Equity" (1885), published in the *Century,* Cable argued that there was "a moral responsibility on the whole of the nation never to lose sight of the results of African-American slavery until they cease to work mischief and injustice" (409). More so than Cable, Tourgée was fiercely critical of Howells, with whom he carried on a running dispute during the 1880s.

In his essay "The 'Claim' of Realism" (1889), Tourgée condemned Howellsian realism not because its impartiality "inclines men to do evil, but because it does an infinitely worse thing in inclining them to do nothing" (387).

5. In his 1916 essay "The Negro in Books," Chesnutt suggested that a merger of realism and romance could create more diverse representations of African Americans that would not only combat and counter the overwhelmingly negative depictions of them but also perform the work of racial uplift: "And indeed, from the standpoint of the Negro himself, a little idealism, a little romanticism, would not at all be out of place. An occasional black or brown hero, a little braver, a little wiser, a little richer perchance, a little more sacrificing than one could reasonably expect to meet in real life; an occasional black or brown heroine—aside from the octoroon, who is always beautiful in books . . . would be something by way of example or inspiration" (180).

6. After *The Marrow of Tradition* (1901) failed to meet sales expectations, Chesnutt concluded that the fault lay not with him but with the reading public and the literary marketplace. In a letter to his publisher, Houghton Mifflin, Chesnutt remarked, "I am beginning to suspect that the public as a rule does not care for books in which the principal characters are colored people, or written with a striking sympathy with that race as contrasted to the white race" (*Letters* 171).

7. As Fabi explains it, in addition to presenting readers with the theme of racial passing, Chesnutt also participates in a form of narrative passing in which he "foregrounds the limited point of view of John Walden, whose racial identity is not specified and who is perceived as white by the other characters in the novel, and initially by the reader as well" to challenge readers' assumptions about race and the larger cultural order that regulates it (*Passing* 73).

8. I borrow this term from Hartman, who invokes it to call attention to the ways in which slavery continues to exert force on contemporary life. As Hartman explains in *Lose Your Mother,* this phenomenon can be attributed to the continuation of the slave episteme and structures of oppression: "If slavery persists as an issue . . . it is not because of an antiquarian obsession with bygone days or the burden of a too-long memory, but because black lives are imperiled and devalued by a racial calculus and a political arithmetic that were entrenched centuries ago" (6).

9. John's insistence that marriage is a "reciprocal arrangement, by which the contracting parties give love for love," also underscores Brook Thomas's argument that realism can only be fully understood in relationship to notions of consent and contract as a result of societal shift from "status relations," such as race and class, to "consensual ones," as in relations of "mutual benefit and trust" (see *American Literary Realism* 5, 135, 49).

10. In discussions of realism, moral agency refers to the individual's ability to make important decisions in the absence of a clear moral arbiter or guide. For discussions on realism and moral agency, see Gregg Crane's *The Cambridge Introduction to the Nineteenth-Century Novel* 162; and Phillip J. Barrish's *The Cambridge Introduction to American Literary Realism* 114–33.

11. I borrow this phrase from William Faulkner's novel *Requiem for a Nun* (1951).

12. Michael Davitt Bell, June Howard, and Steven Belluscio argue that making sharp dis-

tinctions between realism and naturalism is not entirely helpful, given the sheer capaciousness of these terms and the diversity of understandings about them among practitioners and critics alike. That said, however, there are some key differences between the two pertaining to theme and subject matter. For example, realists tend to emphasize the significance of consent and human agency, whereas naturalists tend to depict agency and consent as elusive ideals that are ultimately at the mercy of social forces and trends, or circumstances beyond the individual's control (see Bell's *The Problem of American Realism* 110–14; Howard's *Form and History in American Literary Naturalism* 10–14; and Belluscio's *To Be Suddenly White* 45–54).

13. For an interesting reading on Frank's unacceptableness and colorism, see Dean McWilliams's *Charles W. Chesnutt and the Fictions of Race* 138–39.

4. The Limits of Literary Realism: Pauline Hopkins's Postracial Fantasy in *Of One Blood*

1. It is interesting to consider *Of One Blood* within the context of Gilroy's remarks in *Against Race: Imagining Political Culture beyond the Color Line* (2000), where he argues that the great challenge of the twenty-first century will be the achievement of a global democracy that promotes "planetary humanism," a new political ethics of identity that emphasizes the inherent humanity and equality of all human beings and that rejects modernity's "raciology." "Raciology" is Gilroy's term for what he calls the nineteenth-century "world of discourse" that made race real in an empirical way, using the methodologies of anthropology, geography, law, science, and philosophy. As Gilroy explains, modernity inaugurated a "distinctive regime of truths" that substantiated the idea of racial difference by introducing "novel ways of understanding embodied alterity, hierarchy, and temporality. It made human bodies communicate the truths of an irrevocable otherness that were being confirmed by a new science and a new semiotics just as the struggle against Atlantic racial slavery was being won" (58). *Of One Blood* attempts to conceive of a world outside of raciology to imagine a fully realized black subjectivity and racial progress.

2. My use of the term "postracial" does not render race a thing of the past, and neither does it suggest that race is not a crucial concept in the novel. Rather, I deploy the prefix "post" to signify that the novel deconstructs race and slavery much in the same way that postcolonialism interrogates colonialism and creates a counterhegemonic discourse. I also use the term to account for the ways in which the novel attempts to envision an alternative to the American racial order that exists both within and outside of its turn-of-the-twentieth-century milieu.

3. Although Hopkins was intrigued by the idea of black repatriation to Africa, she did not believe that large-scale emigration was necessary: "Are we obliged to emigrate to Africa?—No. Friendly intercourse and mutual aid and comfort are all that are necessary at the present time. The future is in God's hands and will take care of itself" (*Primer* 20).

4. For more on the romance, see Richard Chase's *The American Novel and Its Tradition;* Joel Porte's *In Respect to Egotism: Studies in American Romantic Writing;* and George Dekker's *The American Historical Romance.*

5. In his highly influential essay "The Novelization of Voice," Andrews showed how during the 1850s African American writers began to experiment with narrative voice, which resulted in three major developments: (1) "a harsher, more extreme form of address"; (2) a movement away from the "monologic voice" of autobiography in favor of greater "dialogization"; and (3) the creation of the fictive voice, which he argued was the most "radical vocal experiment" in all of nineteenth-century African American literature (24).

6. Beard was a medical doctor who specialized in neurology. He is credited with developing the clinical and diagnostic profile for neurasthenia, which he believed was brought about by the depletion of nervous energy or the impairment of the nervous system. Because Beard believed that the illness was triggered by the pressures and demands of contemporary life, his prescribed cure called for withdrawal from one's fast-paced, hectic routines. For more on Beard and neurasthenia, see Beard's *American Nervousness, Its Causes and Consequences* (1881) and A *Practical Treatise on Nervous Exhaustion* (1880).

7. See, for example, Yogita Goyal's book *Romance, Diaspora, and Black Atlantic Literature,* where she argues that "Dianthe carries out the role of the doomed mulatta to the letter" and at "no point in the novel does Dianthe gain any form of agency (33). In "Fate Has Linked Us Together," Jennie A. Kassanoff posits that "Dianthe is unable to exert any agency of her own and falls into complete submission to masculine mandates" because she is "unable to retrieve her original identity" (173). Similarly, in *Domestic Allegories of Political Desire,* Claudia Tate writes that in the figure of Dianthe, Hopkins "seems to have silenced the discourse of female agency, which was a very important feature of the 1890's domestic novels" (208).

8. As Valerie Rohy has written: "Coupling scientific claims to futurity, the literary time line framed realism as a modern language, a writing of the present. Inspired by the ideology of progress, it dismissed mere literariness as a thing of the past, leaving earlier nonrealist writing to hold the place of an abject, less rigorously factual discourse. The gothic and the romance appeared at best outmoded, at worst corrupt" (79).

9. For an excellent reading of incest in *Of One Blood,* see Shawn Salvant's reading of the novel in *Blood Work.*

10. I draw this overview of the utopian novel's basic trajectory from Jean Pfaelzer's account in *The Utopian Novel in America* (18). See also Robert C. Elliott, *The Shape of Utopia: Studies in a Literary Genre.*

11. For example, Yogita Goyal has written that *Of One Blood* "ends with a great deal of uncertainty, appealing to God to resolve the conflicts that find no resolution within the novel itself" (57). John J. Kucich has argued that the novel's "dissatisfying ending illustrates the dangers of looking beyond a politics of identity. Rather than fashion a coherent New Negro ideology by mixing notions of mainstream America with a Pan-African worldview, *Of One Blood* opts to undermine the very terms of racial and cultural identity itself, returning to a point of mythic origin . . . [pointing to a] lack of closure in American racial ideology at the beginning of the twentieth century" (147). Valerie Rohy has rightly noted that the "tension of Hopkins's compromises remains in play at the novel's conclusion, which refuses to resolve, indeed scarcely slows, the dizzying reversals the narrative has set in motion. . . . As ending, *Of One Blood* has only the question of ending, the placeholder of a missing end [i.e., Reuel's "Where will it stop? "What will the end be?]" (97).

12. See Elizabeth Ammons's essay "Expanding the Canon of American Realism" (1995), where she links such questions to issues of canonicity, pedagogy, and the representation of voices in literary studies, ultimately arguing for a more diverse literary realism. See also Andreá N. Williams's essay "African American Literary Realism, 1865–1914," where she posits that the protocols of realist representation necessitated that African American writers ask: "Whose reality determines the 'real'? What are the limits of a realist approach to representation? How do race and realism influence each other?" (186).

Epilogue: Rethinking Blackness

1. For an anthology of African American literature that challenges traditional assumptions about race, subject matter, and genre focus, see Jarrett's *African American Literature beyond Race,* which is, as far as I know, the only one of its kind.

2. See John C. Charles's *Abandoning the Black Action Hero;* Stephanie Li's *Playing in the White;* and Veronica Watson's *The Souls of White Folk.*

3. As Brian Platzer has explained, the "theme running among these grand works that 'created and inhabited black characters' is that they did not fully inhabit them. For the most part, these authors gave black characters speech and action but not thought" ("When Are You Going to Write about Black People?").

4. I borrow this list of works from Platzer, who describes these novels as "standout" titles that have "taken on the challenge of inhabiting Black characters with a goal of better understanding and expressing their experience" (see "When Are You Going to Write about Black People?").

5. In this same interview, Franzen goes on to say, "I write about characters, and I have to love the character to write about the character. If you have not had direct first-hand experience of loving a category of person—a person of a different race, a profoundly religious person, things that are real stark differences between people—I think it is very hard to dare, or necessarily even want, to write fully from the inside of a person" (Chotiner, "Jonathan Franzen on Fame, Fascism, and Why He Won't Write a Book about Race").

6. See Ellis's essay "The New Black Aesthetic," in which he describes the "cultural mulatto" as a kind of hybrid subjectivity that claims a "multi-racial mix" of influences and that can easily maneuver in a variety of contexts and settings (235). See also Ashe's essay "Theorizing the Post-Soul Aesthetic: An Introduction." Here, Ashe provides a useful explication of the term and identifies its basic narrative strategies, positing that postsoul work often aims to push the limits of blackness by interrogating the idea of an authentic black subject and by signifying (or what Gates calls repetition with a difference) on familiar tropes from the Black Power and civil rights movements to "oppose reductive iterations of blackness" (616).

7. Tate's essay, which was originally published in the *Village Voice* in 1986, is widely viewed as the first expression of the postsoul aesthetic. Here, Tate charts the demise of the black cultural nationalist movement—which he shortens to "cult-nats"—and the rise of what he describes as a "freaky-deke"—meaning free-spirited or kinky—approach toward black cultural expression (198). Tate argues that in spite of the problematic, almost laughable as-

pects of the cult-nats program—for example, the "sexist, anti-Semitic, black supremacist, pseudo-African mumbo-jumbo, paramilitary adventurist parts"—what they made possible was the very idea of a black aesthetic, which was fully realized in the "provocative avant-garde black art of the '70's and early 80's" (200). Tate's point was that while black artists had successfully expanded the possibilities for black art, black critics had failed to produce criticism as "fecund, eclectic, and freaky-deke as the art . . . and the culture itself" (200). Hence, Tate posits that what is needed in black culture is a kind of black postmodernism that can deconstruct contemporary black cultural production. Considering the overwhelmingly sober and sociological orientation of much of contemporary black criticism, I would argue that Tate's remarks are just as apropos today as they were back in the mid-1980s.

8. In his essay "Everybody's Protest Novel" (1949), James Baldwin famously indicted social protest fiction, rejecting its contrived pathos and crude conflation of literature and sociology. Baldwin argued that it was the responsibility of the writer to abandon this kind of pamphleteering in favor of greater narrative and emotional complexity, ambiguity, and paradox. In particular, Baldwin's critique about *Native Son* (1940), which is worth quoting at length here, resonates with my arguments about the limitations of Afro-pessimist scholarship in African American literary studies: "For Bigger's tragedy is not that he is cold or black or hungry, not even that he American, black; but that he has accepted a theology that denies him life, that he admits the possibility of his being sub-human and feels constrained, therefore, to battle for his humanity according to those brutal criteria bequeathed him at his birth. . . . The failure of the protest novel lies in its rejection of life, the human being, the denial of his beauty, dread, power, in its insistence that it is his categorization alone which is real and which cannot be transcended" (1704–5).

WORKS CITED

Abdur-Rahman, Aliyyah I. *Against the Closet: Black Political Longing and the Erotics of Race.* Durham, N.C.: Duke University Press, 2012.

Akingbade, Tobi. "Power Creator Insists 50 Cent's Series is 'Not a Black Show' as Season Premiere Hits Screens." *Metro UK.* July 2, 2018. metro.co.uk/2018/07/02/power-creator-insists-50-cents-series-not-black-show-season-premiere-hits-screens-7675378.

Alden, William Livingston. Rev. of *Pudd'nhead Wilson,* by Mark Twain. *Idler,* August 1894, 222–23.

Alger, Horatio. *Ragged Dick.* 1868. Ed. Hildegard Hoeller. New York: Norton, 2007.

Ammons, Elizabeth. *Conflicting Stories: American Women Writers at the Turn into the Twentieth Century.* New York: Oxford University Press, 1992.

———. "Expanding the Canon of American Realism." *The Cambridge Companion to American Realism and Naturalism.* Ed. Donald Pizer. Cambridge: Cambridge University Press, 1995. 95–114.

Andrews, William L. *The Literary Career of Charles W. Chesnutt.* Baton Rouge: Louisiana State University Press, 1980.

———. "The Novelization of Voice in Early African American Narrative." *PMLA* 105.1 (Jan. 1990): 23–34.

———. *To Tell a Free Story: The First Century of Afro-American Autobiography, 1760–1865.* Urbana: University of Illinois Press, 1986.

Ashe, Bertram. "Theorizing the Post-Soul Aesthetic: An Introduction." *African American Review* 41.4 (2007): 602–23.

Baker, Houston, Jr. "Modernism and the Harlem Renaissance." *American Quarterly* 39.1 (1987): 84–97.

———. *The Workings of the Spirit: The Poetics of Afro-American Women's Writing.* Chicago: University of Chicago Press, 1991.

Baldwin, James. "Everybody's Protest Novel." *The Norton Anthology of African American Literature.* 2nd. ed. Ed. Henry Louis Gates Jr. and Nellie Y. McKay. New York: Norton, 2004. 1699–1705.

———. *Giovanni's Room.* 1956. New York: Vintage, 2013.

Barrish, Phillip J. *American Literary Realism, Critical Theory, and Intellectual Prestige, 1880–1995*. Cambridge: Cambridge University Press, 2001.

———. *The Cambridge Introduction to American Literary Realism*. Cambridge: Cambridge University Press, 2012.

Baym, Nina. "Concepts of the Romance in Hawthorne's America." *Nineteenth-Century Fiction* 38 (1984): 426–43.

———. *Woman's Fiction: A Guide to Novels by and about Women, 1820–70*. 2nd ed. Urbana: University of Illinois Press, 1993.

Beard, George M. *American Nervousness, Its Causes and Consequences*. New York: G. P. Putnam's Sons, 1881.

———. *A Practical Treatise on Nervous Exhaustion (Neurasthenia): Its Symptoms, Nature, Sequences, Treatment*. New York: W. Wood, 1880.

Begley, Ian. "Jeremy Lin Takes Kenyon Martin Jabs on Hair, Race in Stride." *ESPN*. Oct. 6, 2017. www.espn.com/nba/story/_/id/20925633/jeremy-lin-brooklyn-nets-all-good-kenyon-martin-remarks-hair-race.

Bell, Bernard W. "Women and Literature: The Dual Tradition of African American Fiction." *OUPblog*, Sept. 7, 2006. www.blog.oup.com/2006/09/women_and_liter-5/.

Bell, Michael Davitt. *The Problem of American Realism: Studies in the Cultural History of a Literary Idea*. Chicago: University of Chicago Press, 1993.

Bellamy, Edward. *Looking Backward: From 2000 to 1887*. 1888. New York: Dover, 1996.

Belluscio, Steven J. *To Be Suddenly White: Literary Realism and Racial Passing*. Columbia: University of Missouri Press, 2006.

Berlant, Lauren. *The Female Complaint: The Unfinished Business of Sentimentality in American Culture*. Durham, N.C.: Duke University Press, 2008.

Berthoff, Warner. *The Ferment of Realism: American Literature, 1884–1919*. 1965. Cambridge: Cambridge University Press, 1981.

Blight, David. *Race and Reunion: The Civil War in American Memory*. Cambridge: Belknap Press of Harvard University Press, 2001.

Boeckmann, Cathy. *A Question of Character: Scientific Racism and the Genres of American Fiction, 1892–1912*. Tuscaloosa: University of Alabama Press, 2000.

Boggs, Belle. *Mattaponi Queen*. Minneapolis: Graywolf, 2010.

Bone, Robert. *The Negro Novel in America*. 1958. New Haven: Yale University Press, 1965.

Bonner, Sherwood. *Suwanee River Tales*. Boston: Roberts Brothers, 1884.

Botting, Fred. *Gothic*. London: Routledge, 1996.

Boucicault, Dion. *The Octoroon, or Life in Louisiana*. New York: Samuel French, 1859.

Bradbury, Malcom. Introduction. *Pudd'nhead Wilson and Those Extraordinary Twins*. By Mark Twain. 1969. New York: Penguin, 2004. 7–44.

Braithwaite, William Stanley. "The Negro in American Literature." *The William Stanley Braithwaite Reader.* Ed. Philip Butcher. Ann Arbor: University of Michigan Press, 1972. 68–84.

Brodhead, Richard. *Cultures of Letters: Scenes of Reading and Writing in Nineteenth-Century America.* Chicago: University of Chicago Press, 1993.

Brooks, Daphne A. *Bodies in Dissent: Spectacular Performances of Race and Freedom, 1850– 1910.* Durham, N.C.: Duke University Press, 2006.

Brown, Lois. *Pauline Elizabeth Hopkins: Black Daughter of the Revolution.* Chapel Hill: University of North Carolina Press, 2008.

Brown, Sterling A., Arthur P. Davis, and Ulysses Lee, eds. *The Negro Caravan.* New York: Dryden, 1941.

Brown, William Wells. *Clotel, or The President's Daughter: A Narrative of Slave Life in the United States.* 1853. Ed. Robert S. Levine. Boston: Bedford/St. Martin's, 2000.

Bulwer-Lytton, Edward. *The Last of the Barons.* London: Saunders and Otley, 1843.

Cable, George Washington. "The Freedman's Case in Equity." *Century Magazine* Jan. 1885: 409–18.

Cady, Edwin. *The Realist at War: The Mature Years, 1885–1920.* Syracuse: Syracuse University Press, 1958.

Cagidemetrio, Alide. "A Plea for Fictional Histories and Old Time 'Jewesses.'" *The Invention of Ethnicity.* Ed. Werner Sollors. New York: Oxford University Press, 1989.

Carby, Hazel V. Introduction. *The Magazine Novels of Pauline Hopkins.* By Hopkins. New York: Oxford University Press, 1988. xxix–l.

———. "On the Threshold of Woman's Era: Lynching, Empire, and Sexuality in Black Feminist Theory." *Critical Inquiry* (Autumn 1985): 262–77.

———. *Reconstructing Womanhood: The Emergence of the Afro-American Woman Novelist.* New York: Oxford University Press, 1987.

Carton, Evan. "*Pudd'nhead Wilson* and the Fiction of Law and Custom." *American Realism: New Essays.* Ed. Eric Sundquist. Baltimore: Johns Hopkins University Press, 1982. 42–65.

Castiglia, Christopher. *The Practices of Hope: Literary Criticism in Disenchanted Times.* New York: New York University Press, 2017.

Castronovo, Russ. *Necro Citizenship: Death, Eroticism, and the Public Sphere in Nineteenth-Century United States.* Durham, N.C.: Duke University Press, 2001.

Chakkalakal, Tess, and Kenneth W. Warren, eds. *Jim Crow, Literature, and the Legacy of Sutton E. Griggs.* Athens: University of Georgia Press, 2013.

Charles, John C. *Abandoning the Black Hero: Sympathy and Privacy in the Postwar African American White-Life Novel.* New Brunswick, N.J.: Rutgers University Press, 2013.

Chase, Richard. *The American Novel and Its Tradition.* 1957. Baltimore: Johns Hopkins University Press, 1980.

Chesnutt, Charles W. *The Colonel's Dream.* New York: Doubleday, Page, 1905.

———. *The Conjure Woman and Other Conjure Tales.* 1899. Ed. Richard Brodhead. Durham, N.C.: Duke University Press, 1993.

———. "The Future American." 1900. *Charles W. Chesnutt: Stories, Novels, and Essays.* Ed. Werner Sollors. New York: Library of America, 2002. 845–63.

———. *The House behind the Cedars.* 1900. New York: Penguin, 1993.

———. *The Journals of Charles W. Chesnutt.* Ed. Richard Brodhead. Durham, N.C.: Duke University Press, 1993.

———. *The Marrow of Tradition.* 1901. Ed. Werner Sollors. New York: Norton, 2012.

———. "The Negro in Books." 1916. *The New Negro: Readings on Race, Representation, and African American Culture, 1892–1938.* Ed. Henry Louis Gates Jr. and Gene Andrew Jarrett. Princeton: Princeton University Press, 2007. 173–82.

———. "Post-Bellum—Pre-Harlem." 1931. *Charles W. Chesnutt: Stories, Novels, and Essays.* Ed. Werner Sollors. New York: Library of America, 2002. 906–12.

———. *"To Be an Author": Letters of Charles W. Chesnutt, 1889–1905.* Ed. Joseph R. McElrath Jr. and Robert C. Leitz III. Princeton: Princeton University Press, 1997.

———. "What Is a White Man?" 1889. *Charles W. Chesnutt: Stories, Novels, and Essays.* Ed. Werner Sollors. New York: Library of America, 2002. 837–44.

———. *The Wife of His Youth and Other Stories of the Color Line.* 1899. Ann Arbor: University of Michigan Press, 1968.

Chotiner, Isaac. "Jonathan Franzen on Fame, Fascism, and Why He Won't Write a Book about Race." *Slate.* July 31, 2016. http://www.slate.com/articles/arts/interrogation /2016/07/a_conversation_with_novelist_jonathan_franzen.html.

Christian, Barbara. *Black Feminist Criticism: Perspectives on Black Women Writers.* New York: Pergamon, 1985.

Clarke, John Henrik, ed. *William Styron's Nat Turner: Ten Black Writers Respond.* Boston: Beacon, 1968.

Cohen, Philip. "Aesthetic Anomalies in *Pudd'nhead Wilson.*" *Studies in American Fiction* 10.1 (Spring 1982): 55–59.

Colby, Tanner. "Can a White Writer Write Black Characters?" *Slate.* Sept. 19, 2012. https://slate.com/culture/2012/09/michael-chabons-telegraph-avenue-can-a-white-guy-write-about-black-characters.html.

Cooper, Anna Julia. *A Voice from the South.* 1892. New York: Oxford University Press, 1988.

Crafts, Ellen, and William Crafts. *Running a Thousand Miles for Freedom: The Escape of William and Ellen Craft.* 1860. Athens: University of Georgia Press, 1999.

Crane, Gregg. *The Cambridge Introduction to the Nineteenth-Century American Novel.* New York: Cambridge University Press, 2007.

Crane, Stephen. *Maggie: A Girl of the Streets.* 1893. Ed. Thomas A. Gullason. New York: Norton, 1979.

Crawford, Margo Natalie. *Black Post-Blackness: The Black Arts Movement and Twenty-First- Century Aesthetics.* Urbana: University of Illinois Press, 2017.

Crouch, Stanley. "Segregated Fiction Blues." *The Artificial White Man: Essays on Authenticity.* New York: Basic Civitas, 2004. 15–50.

D'Agostino, Peter. "Craniums, Criminals, and the 'Cursed Race': Italian Anthropology in American Racial Thought, 1861–1914." *Comparative Studies in Society and History* 44.2 (2002): 319–43.

Davidson, Adenike Marie. *The Black Nation Novel: Imagining Homeplaces in Early African American Literature.* Chicago: Third World, 2008.

Dawson, Melanie V. *Emotional Reinventions: Realist-Era Representations beyond Sympathy.* Ann Arbor: University of Michigan Press, 2015.

De Voto, Bernard. *Mark Twain's America.* Boston: Little, Brown, 1932.

Delany, Martin R. *Blake, or The Huts of America.* 1859. Ed. Jerome McGann. Cambridge: Harvard University Press, 2017.

Dixon, Thomas. *The Clansman: An Historical Romance of the Ku Klux Klan.* 1905. Lexington: University of Kentucky Press, 1970.

———. *The Leopard's Spots: A Romance of the White Man's Burden—1865–1900.* 1902. New York: Wessels, 1908.

Douglas, Ann. *Terrible Honesty: Mongrel Manhattan in the 1920s.* New York: Farrar, Straus and Giroux, 1995.

Du Bois, W. E. B. *Black Reconstruction in America, 1860–1880.* 1935. New York: Free Press, 1998.

———. "Howells and Black Folk." *Crisis: A Record of the Darker Races* 6.7 (November 1913): 338.

———. *The Souls of Black Folk.* 1903. Ed. Brent Hayes Edwards. New York: Oxford University Press, 2007.

Dubey, Madhu. *Signs and Cities: Black Literary Postmodernism.* Chicago: University of Chicago Press, 2003.

duCille, Ann. *The Coupling Convention: Sex, Text, and Tradition in Black Women's Fiction.* New York: Oxford University Press, 1993.

Dyson, Michael Eric. *April 4, 1968: Martin Luther King, Jr.'s Death and How It Changed America.* New York: Basic Civitas, 2008.

Elam, Michele (née Birnbaum). *Race, Work, and Desire in American Literature, 1860–1930.* Cambridge: Cambridge University Press, 2003.

———. *The Souls of Mixed Folk: Race, Politics, and Aesthetics in the New Millennium.* Stanford: Stanford University Press, 2011.

Elder, Arlene. *The "Hindered Hand": Cultural Implications of Early African-American Fiction.* Westport, Ct.: Greenwood, 1978.

Elfenbein, Anna Shannon. *Women on the Color Line: Evolving Stereotypes and the Writings of George Washington Cable, Grace King, and Kate Chopin.* Charlottesville: University of Virginia Press, 1989.

Elliot, R. S. "The Story of Our Magazine." *Colored American Magazine* (May 1901): 43–77.

Elliott, Robert C. *The Shape of Utopia: Studies in a Literary Genre.* Chicago: University of Chicago Press, 1970.

Ellis, Trey. "The New Black Aesthetic." *Callaloo* 38 (Winter 1989): 233–43.

Ernest, John. *Chaotic Justice: Rethinking African American Literary History.* Chapel Hill: University of North Carolina Press, 2009.

———. "From Mysteries to Histories: Cultural Pedagogy in Frances E. W. Harper's *Iola Leroy.*" *American Literature* 64.3 (1992): 497–518.

Fabi, M. Giulia. *Passing and the Rise of the African American Novel.* Urbana: University of Illinois Press, 2001.

———. "Reconstructing Literary Genealogies: Frances E. W. Harper's and William Dean Howells's Race Novels." *Soft Canons: American Women Writers and the Masculine Tradition.* Ed. Karen L. Kilcup. Iowa City: University of Iowa Press, 1999. 48–66.

Faulkner, William. *Requiem for a Nun.* 1951. New York: Random House, 2012.

Ferguson, Sally Ann. "Christian Violence and the Slave Narrative." *American Literature* 68.2 (1996): 297–320.

Fiedler, Leslie A. *Love and Death in the American Novel.* New York: Scarborough, 1960.

Fishkin, Shelley Fisher. "Race and Culture at the Century's End: A Social Context for *Pudd'nhead Wilson.*" *Essays in Arts and Sciences* 9 (May 1990): 1–27.

Foner, Eric. *Forever Free: The Story of Emancipation & Reconstruction.* New York: Vintage, 2005.

Foreman, P. Gabrielle. *Activist Sentiments: Reading Black Women in the Nineteenth Century.* Urbana: University of Illinois Press, 2009.

Foster, Frances Smith. Introduction. *A Brighter Coming Day: A Frances Ellen Watkins Harper Reader.* By Harper. New York: Feminist Press at CUNY, 1990. 3–40.

Foster, Frances Smith, and Kim D. Green. "Ports of Call, Pulpits of Consultation: Rethinking the Origins of African American Literature." *A Companion to African American Literature.* Ed. Gene Andrew Jarrett. Malden, Mass.: Wiley-Blackwell, 2013. 45–58.

Foucault, Michel. "What Is an Author?" *Aesthetics, Method, and Epistemology.* Trans. Robert Hurley et al. Ed. James D. Faubion. New York, NY: New Press, 1998. 205–22.

Fredricks, Nancy. "Twain's Indelible Twins." *Nineteenth-Century Literature* 43 (1989): 484–99.

Fredrickson, George M. *The Black Image in the White Mind: The Debate on Afro-American Character and Destiny, 1817–1914*. Middleton, Ct.: Wesleyan University Press, 1971.

Freeburg, Christopher. *Black Aesthetics and the Interior Life*. Charlottesville: University of Virginia Press, 2017.

Gaines, Kevin K. *Uplifting the Race: Black Leadership, Politics, and Culture in the Twentieth Century*. Chapel Hill: University of North Carolina Press, 1996.

Garber, Marjorie. *Vested Interests: Cross-Dressing and Cultural Anxiety*. New York: Routledge, 1992.

Gardner, Eric. *Unexpected Places: Relocating Nineteenth-Century African American Literature*. Jackson: University Press of Mississippi, 2009.

Gates, Henry Louis, Jr. *Figures in Black: Words, Signs, and the "Racial" Self*. New York: Oxford University Press, 1987.

———. "The Trope of a New Negro and the Reconstruction of the Image of the Black." *Representations* 24 (Autumn 1988): 129–55.

Gillman, Susan. *Blood Talk: American Race Melodrama and the Culture of the Occult*. Chicago: University of Chicago Press, 2003.

———. "'Sure Identifiers': Race, Science, and the Law in *Pudd'nhead Wilson*." *Mark Twain's "Pudd'nhead Wilson": Race, Conflict, and Culture*. Ed. Gillman and Forrest G. Robinson. Durham, N.C.: Duke University Press, 1990. 86–104.

Gillman, Susan, and Forrest G. Robinson. Introduction. *Mark Twain's "Pudd'nhead Wilson": Race, Conflict, and Culture*. Ed. Gillman and Robinson. Durham, N.C.: Duke University Press, 1990. vii–xvii.

Gilroy, Paul. *Against Race: Imagining Political Culture beyond the Color Line*. Cambridge: Belknap Press of Harvard University Press, 2000.

Ginsberg, Elaine K. "The Politics of Passing." Introduction. *Passing and the Fictions of Identity*. Ed. Ginsberg. Durham, N.C.: Duke University Press, 1996. 1–18.

Goddu, Teresa A. *Gothic America: Narrative, History, and Nation*. New York: Columbia University Press, 1997.

———. "The Slave Narrative as Material Text." *The Oxford Handbook of the African American Slave Narrative*. Ed. John Ernest. New York: Oxford University Press, 2014. 149–64.

Goldfield, David R. *Still Fighting the Civil War: The American South and Southern History*. Baton Rouge: Louisiana State University Press, 2002.

Goldsby, Jacqueline. *A Spectacular Secret: Lynching in American Life and Literature*. Chicago: University of Chicago Press, 2006.

Goldstein, Philip. "Reading *Pudd'nhead Wilson:* Criticism and Commentary from the Gilded Age to the Modern, Online Era." *Reception: Texts, Readers, Audiences, History* 9.1 (2017): 4–22.

Gosselin, Adrienne Johnson. "Beyond the Harlem Renaissance: The Case for Black Modernist Writers." *Modern Language Studies* 26.4 (1996): 37–45.

Goyal, Yogita. *Romance, Diaspora, and Black Atlantic Literature.* New York: Cambridge University Press, 2010.

Greene, J. Lee. *Blacks in Eden: The African American Novel's First Century.* Charlottesville: University of Virginia Press, 1996.

Griggs, Sutton E. *Imperium in Imperio.* 1899. New York: Modern Library, 2003.

Gruesser, John Cullen. "Pauline Hopkins's *Of One Blood:* Creating an Afrocentric Fantasy for a Black Middle-Class Audience." *Modes of the Fantastic: Selected Essays from the Twelfth International Conference on the Fantastic in the Arts.* Westport, Ct.: Greenwood, 1995. 74–83.

Hall, Stuart. "Race, the Floating Signifier." https://www.mediaed.org/assets/products/407/transcript_407.pdf.

Harper, Frances E. W. "Enlightened Motherhood." 1892. *A Brighter Coming Day: A Frances Ellen Watkins Harper Reader.* Ed. Frances Smith Foster. New York: Feminist Press, 1990.

———. *Forest Leaves.* 1845. Ed. Alex W. Black, Brigette Fielder, and Johanna Ortner. Just Teach One: Early African American Print Project. http://dx.doi.org/10.17613/M68P0H.

———. *Iola Leroy, or Shadows Uplifted.* 1892. New York: Penguin, 2010.

———. *"Minnie's Sacrifice," "Sowing and Reaping," "Trial and Triumph": Three Rediscovered Novels by Frances E. W. Harper.* Ed. Frances Smith Foster. Boston: Beacon, 1994.

———. *Moses: A Story of the Nile.* 1869. *A Brighter Coming Day,* 138–65.

———. *Poems on Miscellaneous Subjects.* Boston: J. B. Yerrington and Son, 1854. Schomburg Center, The New York Public Library, Digital Collections. http://digitalcollections.nypl.org/items/a99f2422-237e-46bf-e040-e00a18066b09.

———. "The Two Offers." 1859. *A Brighter Coming Day,* 105–14.

Harper, Phillip Brian. *Abstractionist Aesthetics: Artistic Form and Social Critique in African American Culture.* New York: New York University Press, 2015.

Harris, Joel Chandler. *Uncle Remus: His Songs and Sayings.* 1880. New York: Hawthorn, 1921.

Harris, Trudier. "Chesnutt's Frank Fowler: A Failure of Purpose?" *CLA Journal* 22 (1979): 215–28.

Hartman, Saidiya V. *Lose Your Mother: A Journey along the Atlantic Slave Route.* New York: Farrar, Straus and Giroux, 2006.

———. *Scenes of Subjection: Terror, Slavery, and Self-Making in Nineteenth-Century America.* New York: Oxford University Press, 1997.

Hattenhauer, Darryl. "Racial and Textual Miscegenation in Chesnutt's *The House behind the Cedars.*" *Mississippi Quarterly* 47 (1993–94): 27–45.

Hendler, Glenn. *Public Sentiments: Structures of Feeling in Nineteenth-Century American Literature.* Chapel Hill: University of North Carolina Press, 2001.

Henson, Josiah. *The Life of Josiah Henson, Formerly a Slave, Now an Inhabitant of Canada, as Narrated by Himself.* Boston: Arthur D. Phelps, 1849.

Higginbotham, Evelyn Brooks. *Righteous Discontent: The Women's Movement in the Black Baptist Church, 1880–1920.* Cambridge: Harvard University Press, 1993.

Hildreth, Richard. *The Slave, or Memoirs of Archy Moore.* Boston: John H. Eastburn, 1836.

Hopkins, Pauline E. *Contending Forces: A Romance Illustrative of Negro Life North and South.* 1900. Ed. Henry Louis Gates Jr. New York: Oxford University Press, 1988.

———. *Daughter of the Revolution: The Major Nonfiction Works of Pauline E. Hopkins.* Ed. Ira Dworkin. New Brunswick, N.J.: Rutgers University Press, 2007. 335–52.

———. "Famous Men of the Negro Race." 1900–1901. *Daughter of the Revolution,* 9–110.

———. "Famous Women of the Negro Race." 1901–2. *Daughter of the Revolution,* 111–98.

———. "The Mystery within Us." *Colored American Magazine,* May 1900. *Short Fiction by Black Women, 1900–1920.* Ed. Elizabeth Ammons. New York: Oxford University Press, 21–26.

———. *Of One Blood, or The Hidden Self.* 1902–3. Ed. Henry Louis Gates Jr. New York: Oxford University Press, 1988.

———. *A Primer of Facts Pertaining to the Early Greatness of the African Race and the Possibility of Restoration by Its Descendants—with Epilogue.* 1905.

Horvitz, Deborah. "Hysteria and Trauma in Pauline Hopkins's *Of One Blood, or The Hidden Self.*" *African American Review* 33.2 (Summer 1999): 245–60.

Rev. of *The House behind the Cedars,* by Charles W. Chesnutt. *Boston Evening Transcript* Oct. 31, 1900: 12.

Rev. of *The House behind the Cedars,* by Charles W. Chesnutt. *Zion's Herald* Nov. 28, 1900: 1526.

Rev. of *The House behind the Cedars,* by Charles W. Chesnutt. *Peoria Evening Star* Nov. 27, 1900:10.

Howard, June. *Form and History in American Literary Naturalism.* Chapel Hill: University of North Carolina Press, 1985.

Howells, W. D. *Criticism and Fiction.* 1891. New York: Hill and Wang, 1962.

———. *A Hazard of New Fortunes.* 1890. New York: Meridian, 1994.

———. *An Imperative Duty.* 1891. Ed. Paul R. Petrie. Toronto: Broadview, 2010.

———. "Mr. Charles W. Chesnutt's Stories." *Atlantic Monthly* 85 (May 1900): 699–700.

———. *My Literary Passions.* 1891. New York: Harper and Brothers, 1895.

———. "A Psychological Counter-Current in Recent Fiction." *North American Review* 173 (1901): 872–88.

———. *The Rise of Silas Lapham.* 1885. New York: Penguin, 1983.

———. *Selected Letters of W. D. Howells,* Vol. 3: *1882–1891.* Ed. Robert C. Leitz III and Christoph K. Lohmann et al. Boston: Twayne, 1980.

———. *Selected Letters of W.D. Howells,* Vol. 4: *1892–1901.* Ed. Thomas Wortham. Boston: Twayne, 1981.

Hughes, Langston. "Mark Twain's *Pudd'nhead Wilson.*" *Interracialism: Black-White Intermarriage in American History, Literature, and Law.* Ed. Werner Sollors. New York: Oxford University Press, 2000. 326–30.

Hurston, Zora Neale. *Seraph on the Suwanee.* 1948. New York: Harper Perennial Modern Classics, 2008.

Rev. of *Iola Leroy,* by Frances E. W. Harper. *Christian Recorder* Jan. 12, 1893: n. pag., "Publications Reviewed."

Rev. of *Iola Leroy,* by Frances E. W. Harper. *Nation* Feb. 23, 1893: 146–47.

Rev. of *Iola Leroy,* by Frances E. W. Harper. *Friends' Review* June 22, 1893: 758.

Jackson, Blyden. *A History of Afro-American Literature: The Long Beginning, 1746–1895.* Baton Rouge: Louisiana State University Press, 1989.

Jacobs, Harriet. *Incidents in the Life of a Slave Girl.* 1861. Ed. Jean Fagan Yellin. Cambridge: Harvard University Press, 2000.

Jameson, Fredric. *The Seeds of Time.* New York: Columbia University Press, 1994.

Jarrett, Gene Andrew. "Addition by Subtraction: Toward a Literary History of Racial Representation." *Legacy* 24.2 (2007): 315–21.

———. *African American Literature beyond Race: An Alternative Reader.* Ed. Jarrett. New York: New York University Press, 2006.

———. "African American Literature Lives On, Even as Black Politics Expire." *Chronicle of Higher Education.* Mar. 27, 2011. www.chronicle.com/article/African-American-Literature/126867.

———. *Deans and Truants: Race and Realism in African American Literature.* Philadelphia: University of Pennsylvania Press, 2007.

Jehlen, Myra. "The Ties That Bind: Race and Sex in *Pudd'nhead Wilson.*" *Mark Twain's "Pudd'nhead Wilson": Race, Conflict, and Culture.* Ed. Susan Gillman and Forrest G. Robinson. Durham, N.C.: Duke University Press, 1990. 105–20.

Johnson, Edward A. *Light Ahead for the Negro.* New York: Grafton, 1904.

Johnson, James Weldon. *The Autobiography of an Ex-Coloured Man.* 1912. Ed. Jacqueline Goldsby. New York: Norton, 2015.

Jordan, Hillary. *Mudbound.* Chapel Hill, N.C.: Algonquin, 2008.

Kaplan, Amy. *The Social Construction of American Realism.* Chicago: University of Chicago Press, 1988.

Kassanoff, Jennie A. "Fate Has Linked Us Together: Blood, Gender, and the Politics of Representation in Pauline Hopkins's *Of One Blood.*" *The Unruly Voice: Rediscovering Pauline Elizabeth Hopkins.* Ed. John Cullen Gruesser. Urbana: University of Illinois Press, 1996. 158–81.

Kerman, Cynthia Earl, and Richard Eldridge. *The Lives of Jean Toomer: A Hunger for Wholeness.* Baton Rouge: Louisiana State University Press, 1987.

Kernan, Alvin B. *The Death of Literature.* New Haven: Yale University Press, 1990.

Kinney, James. *Amalgamation! Race, Sex, and Rhetoric in the Nineteenth-Century American Novel.* Westport, Ct.: Greenwood, 1985.

Kucich, John J. *Ghostly Communion: Cross-Cultural Spiritualism in Nineteenth-Century American Literature.* Hanover, N.H.: Dartmouth College Press, 2004.

Larsen, Nella. *"Quicksand" and "Passing."* 1928/1929. Ed. Deborah E. McDowell. New Brunswick, N.J.: Rutgers University Press, 1986.

Lazarus, Emma. "The New Colossus." 1883. https://www.poetryfoundation.org/poems/46550/the-new-colossus.

Leonard, James S., Thomas Tenney, and Thadious M. Davis, ed. *Satire or Evasion? Black Perspectives on "Huckleberry Finn."* Durham, N.C.: Duke University Press, 1992.

Levine, Robert S. "African American Literary Nationalism." *A Companion to African American Literature.* Ed. Gene Andrew Jarrett. Malden, Mass.: Wiley-Blackwell, 2013. 119–32.

———. *Dislocating Race and Nation: Episodes in Nineteenth-Century American Literary Nationalism.* Chapel Hill: University of North Carolina Press, 2008.

Levinson, Marjorie. "What Is New Formalism?" *PMLA* 122.2 (2007): 558–69.

Levy-Hussen, Aida. *How to Read African American Literature: Post–Civil Rights Fiction and the Task of Interpretation.* New York: New York University Press, 2016.

Lewis, R. W. B. *The American Adam: Innocence, Tragedy, and Tradition in the Nineteenth Century.* Chicago: University of Chicago Press, 1955.

Li, Stephanie. *Playing in the White: Black Writers, White Subjects.* New York: Oxford University Press, 2014.

———. "What Is Twenty-First-Century African American Literature?" Introduction to spec. issue of *American Literary History* 29.4 (Winter 2017): 631–39.

Lombroso, Cesare. *Criminal Man.* 1876. Trans. Mary Gibson and Nicole Hahn Rafter. Durham, N.C.: Duke University Press, 2006.

Lott, Eric. "Mr. Clemens and Jim Crow: Twain, Race, and Blackface." *Criticism and the Color Line: Desegregating American Literary Studies.* Ed. Henry B. Wonham. New Brunswick, N.J.: Rutgers University Press, 1996. 30–42.

Luciano, Dana. “Passing Shadows: Melancholic Nationality and Black Critical Publicity in Pauline Hopkins’s *Of One Blood.*” *Loss: The Politics of Mourning.* Ed. David L. Eng and David Kazanjian. Berkeley: University of California Press, 2003. 148–87.

Lutz, Tom. *American Nervousness 1903: An Anecdotal History.* Ithaca, N.Y.: Cornell University Press, 1991.

Lye, Colleen. *America’s Asia: Racial Form and American Literature, 1893–1945.* Princeton: Princeton University Press, 2004.

———. “Racial Form.” *Representations* 104.1 (2004): 92–101.

Matthews, Victoria Earle. “The Value of Race Literature: An Address.” 1895. *Massachusetts Review* 27.2 (Summer 1986): 161–91.

McCaskill, Barbara, and Caroline Gebhard. Introduction. *Post-Bellum, Pre-Harlem: African American Literature and Culture, 1877–1919.* Ed. McCaskill and Gebhard. New York: New York University Press, 2006. 1–14.

McDowell, Deborah E. Introduction. *Of One Blood, or The Hidden Self.* New York: Washington Square Press, 2004. v–xvi.

McElrath, Joseph R., Jr., “W. D. Howells and Race: Charles W. Chesnutt’s Disappointment of the Dean.” *Nineteenth-Century Literature* 51.4 (1997): 474–99.

McHenry, Elizabeth. *Forgotten Readers: Recovering the Lost History of African American Literary Societies.* Durham, N.C.: Duke University Press, 2002.

McKay, Nellie Y. “Naming the Problem That Led to the Question ‘Who Shall Teach African American Literature?’ Or, Are We Ready to Disband the Wheatley Court?” *PMLA* 113.3 (May 1998): 359–69.

McWilliams, Dean. *Charles W. Chesnutt and the Fictions of Race.* Athens: University of Georgia Press, 2002.

Mitchell, Koritha. Introduction. *Iola Leroy, or Shadows Uplifted.* 1892. Toronto: Broadview, 2018. 13–50.

———. “Why Americans Know Frederick Douglass but Not Frances Harper.” Blog post. *Koritha Mitchell.* Jan. 25, 2018. www.korithamitchell.com/americans-know-frederick-douglass-not-frances-harper.

Mitchell, Lee Clark. “‘De Nigger in You’: Race or Training in *Pudd’nhead Wilson*?” *Nineteenth-Century Fiction* 42 (1987): 295–312.

Mitchell, Michele. *Righteous Propagation: African Americans and the Politics of Racial Destiny after Reconstruction.* Chapel Hill: University of North Carolina Press, 2004.

Morehouse, Henry Lyman. “The Talented Tenth.” *American Missionary* 50.6 (June 1896): 182–84.

Morgan, C. E. *The Sport of Kings.* New York: Farrar, Straus and Giroux, 2016.

Morrison, Toni. *Playing in the Dark: Whiteness and the Literary Imagination.* New York: Vintage, 1992.

Morrison, Toni, and Nellie McKay. "An Interview with Toni Morrison." *Contemporary Literature* 24 (1983): 413–29.

Mosley, Walter. "Black to the Future: Science Fiction May Have a Special Allure for African Americans." *New York Times Magazine* Nov. 1, 1998: 33–34.

Moten, Fred. *In the Break: The Aesthetics of the Black Radical Tradition.* Minneapolis: University of Minnesota Press, 2003.

Mullen, Thomas. *Darktown: A Novel.* New York: Atria/37 INK, 2016.

Murray, Rolland. "Not Being and Blackness: Percival Everett and the Uncanny Forms of Racial Incorporation." *American Literary History* 29.4 (Winter 2017): 726–52.

Neal, Mark Anthony. *Soul Babies: Black Popular Culture and the Post-Soul Aesthetic.* New York: Routledge, 2002.

Neimneh, Shadi, and Marwan Obeidat. "Jean Toomer's Cane: The Harlem Renaissance, Modernism, and the Avant-Garde." *Journal of Foreign Languages, Cultures, and Civilizations* 3.1 (June 2015): 58–66.

Nelson, Dana D. *The Word in Black and White: Reading "Race" in American Literature, 1638–1867.* New York: Oxford University Press, 1992.

Newlyn, Andrea K. "Form and Ideology in Transracial Narratives: *Pudd'nhead Wilson* and *A Romance of the Republic.*" *Narrative* 8.1 (2000): 43–65.

Noble, Marianne. *The Masochistic Pleasures of Sentimental Literature.* Princeton: Princeton University Press, 2000.

Norman, Brian. "Write Like Me: Black Fictions of White Life." *American Literary History* 28.1 (January 2016): 199–209.

Norris, Frank. *McTeague: A Story of San Francisco.* 1899. New York: Penguin, 2012.

Obama, Barack. *Dreams from My Father: A Story of Race and Inheritance.* New York: Crown, 1995.

O'Connor, Stephen. *Thomas Jefferson Dreams of Sally Hemings: A Novel.* New York: Penguin, 2016.

Otten, Thomas J. "Pauline Hopkins and the Hidden Self of Race." *ELH* 59.1 (Spring 1992): 227–56.

Pace v. State of Alabama 106 U.S. 583 (1883).

Page, Thomas Nelson. *In Ole Virginia, or Marse Chan and Other Stories.* New York: Scribner's, 1887.

———. *Red Rock: A Chronicle of Reconstruction.* New York: Scribner's, 1898.

Parker, Hershel. *Flawed Texts and Verbal Icons: Literary Authority in American Fiction.* Evanston, Ill.: Northwestern University Press, 1984.

Parrington, V. L. *The Beginnings of Critical Realism in America.* New York: Harcourt, Brace, 1930.

Parrott, T. M. Rev. of *Pudd'nhead Wilson,* by Mark Twain. *Booklover's Magazine* Feb. 1904: 145–54.

Patterson, Orlando. *Slavery and Social Death: A Comparative Study.* Cambridge: Harvard University Press, 1982.

Peterson, Carla. "Capitalism, Black (Under)development, and the Production of the African American Novel in the 1850's." *American Literary History* 4.4 (1992): 559–83.

———. "Commemorative Ceremonies and Invented Traditions: History, Memory, and Modernity in the 'New Negro' Novel of the Nadir." *Post-Bellum, Pre-Harlem: African American Literature and Culture, 1877–1919.* Ed. Barbara McCaskill and Caroline Gebhard. New York: New York University Press, 2006. 34–56.

Petit, Arthur G. *Mark Twain and the South.* Lexington: University Press of Kentucky, 1974.

Petrie, Paul R. Introduction. *An Imperative Duty.* By William Dean Howells. 1891. Toronto: Broadview, 2010.

Petry, Ann. *Country Place.* 1947. Evanston, Ill.: Northwestern University Press, 2019.

Pfaelzer, Jean. *The Utopian Novel in America, 1886–1896: The Politics of Form.* Pittsburgh: University of Pittsburgh Press, 1984.

Pizer, Donald. *Realism and Naturalism in Nineteenth-Century American Literature.* 1966. Carbondale: Southern Illinois University Press, 1984.

Platzer, Brian. *Bed-Stuy Is Burning: A Novel.* New York: Atria, 2017.

———. "When Are You Going to Write about Black People?" *Literary Hub.* July 11, 2017. lithub.com/when-are-you-going-to-write-about-black-people.

Plessy v. Ferguson 163 U.S. 537 (1896). *Plessy v. Ferguson: A Brief History with Documents.* Ed. Brook Thomas. Bedford Series in History and Culture. Boston: Bedford/St. Martin's, 1997. 41–60.

Rev. of *Pudd'nhead Wilson,* by Mark Twain. *Atheneum* Jan. 19, 1895: 83–84.

Quashie, Kevin. *The Sovereignty of Quiet: Beyond Resistance in Black Culture.* New Brunswick, N.J.: Rutgers University Press, 2012.

Ransby, Barbara. "The Class Politics of Black Lives Matter." *Dissent Magazine* Fall 2015. www.dissentmagazine.org/article/class-politics-black-lives-matter.

Richardson, Samuel. *Pamela.* 1740. New York: Norton, 1958.

Riis, Jacob A. *How the Other Half Lives.* 1890. Ed. Hasia R. Diner. New York: Norton, 2009.

Ritzenberg, Aaron. "The Dream of History: Memory and the Unconscious in Charles Chesnutt's *The House behind the Cedars.*" *Passing in the Works of Charles W. Chesnutt.* Ed. Susan Prothro Wright and Ernestine Pickens Glass. Jackson: University Press of Mississippi, 2010. 51–66.

Robbins, Hollis. Introduction. *Iola Leroy.* By Frances E. W. Harper. 1892. Ed. Hollis Robbins and Henry Louis Gates Jr. New York: Penguin, 2010. xix–xxxiii.

Rogin, Michael. "Francis Galton and Mark Twain: The Natal Autograph in *Pudd'nhead Wilson." Mark Twain's "Pudd'nhead Wilson": Race, Conflict, and Culture.* Ed. Susan Gillman and Forrest G. Robinson. Durham, N.C.: Duke University Press, 1990. 73–85.

Rohrbach, Augusta. *Truth Stranger Than Fiction: Race, Realism, and the US Marketplace.* New York: Palgrave, 2002.

Rohy, Valerie. *Anachronism and Its Others: Sexuality, Race, Temporality.* Albany: State University of New York Press, 2009.

Rosen, Christine. *Preaching Eugenics: Religious Leaders and the American Eugenics Movement.* New York: Oxford University Press, 2004.

Rosenthal, Debra J. "The White Blackbird: Miscegenation, Genre, and the Tragic Mulatta in Howells, Harper, and the 'Babes of Romance.'" *Nineteenth-Century Literature* 56.4 (Mar. 2002): 495–517.

Rowe, John Carlos. "Fatal Speculations: Murder, Money, and Manners in *Pudd'nhead Wilson." Mark Twain's "Pudd'nhead Wilson": Race, Conflict, and Culture.* Ed. Susan Gillman and Forrest G. Robinson. Durham, N.C.: Duke University Press, 1990. 137–54.

Russell, Irwin. "Christmas-Night in the Quarters." *Scribner's* 15 (1877): 445–46.

Saks, Eva. "Representing Miscegenation Law." *Interracialism: Black-White Intermarriage in American History, Literature, and Law.* Ed. Werner Sollors. New York: Oxford University Press, 2000. 61–81.

Saldívar, Ramón. "Historical Fantasy, Speculative Realism, and Postrace Aesthetics in Contemporary American Fiction." *American Literary History* 23.3 (Fall 2011): 574–99.

Salvant, Shawn. *Blood Work: Imagining Race in American Literature, 1890–1940.* Baton Rouge: Louisiana State University Press, 2015.

Santamarina, Xiomara. "'Are We There Yet?' Archives, History, and Specificity in African- American Literary Studies." *American Literary History* 20.1/2 (Spring–Summer 2008): 304–16.

Schrager, Cynthia D. "Pauline Hopkins and William James: The New Psychology of Race." *The Unruly Voice: Rediscovering Pauline Elizabeth Hopkins.* Ed. John Cullen Gruesser. Urbana: University of Illinois Press, 1996. 182–209.

Schulman, Sarah. "White Writer." *New Yorker* Oct. 21, 2016. https://www.newyorker.com/culture/cultural-comment/white-writer.

Scott, Sir Walter. *Ivanhoe: A Romance.* 1819. New York: Modern Library, 2001.

Sexton, Jared. "The Social Life of Social Death: On Afro-Pessimism and Black Optimism." *InTensions* 5 (Fall/Winter 2011): 1–47. http://www.yorku.ca/intent/issue5/articles/jaredsexton.php.

Shi, David E. *Facing Facts: Realism in American Thought and Culture, 1850–1920.* New York: Oxford University Press, 1995.

Shih, Shu-Mei. "Comparative Racialization: An Introduction." *PMLA* 123.5 (2008): 1347–62.

Simmons, Ryan. *Chesnutt and Realism: A Study of the Novels.* Tuscaloosa: University of Alabama Press, 2006.

Simons, Blake. "Yes, Black Liberals Commodify Black Lives Matter Too, and It's a Major Problem." *Black Youth Project.* May 12, 2017. http://blackyouthproject.com/yes-black-people-commodify-black-lives-matter-too-and-its-a-major-problem.

Sinclair, Upton. *The Jungle.* 1906. Ed. Clare Virginia Eby. New York: Norton, 2002.

Smith, Valerie. "Reading the Intersection of Race and Gender in Narratives of Passing." *Diacritics* 24.2/3 (Summer–Autumn 1994): 43–57.

Spillers, Hortense. *Black, White, and in Color: Essays on American Literature and Culture.* Chicago: University of Chicago Press, 2003.

Stern, Julia. *The Plight of Feeling: Sympathy and Dissent in the Early American Novel.* Chicago: University of Chicago Press, 1997.

Stowe, Harriet Beecher. *Uncle Tom's Cabin, or Life among the Lowly.* 1852. New York: Penguin, 1986.

Stuelke, Patricia. "Trayvon Martin, Topdog/Underdog, and the Tragedy Trap." *American Literary History* 29.4 (Winter 2017): 753–78.

Styron, William. *The Confessions of Nat Turner.* 1967. New York: Vintage, 1992.

Sundquist, Eric. "Mark Twain and Homer Plessy." *Mark Twain's "Pudd'nhead Wilson": Race, Conflict, and Culture.* Ed. Susan Gillman and Forrest G. Robinson. Durham, N.C.: Duke University Press, 1990. 46–72.

———. *To Wake the Nations: Race and the Making of American Literature.* Cambridge: Belknap Press of Harvard University Press, 1993.

Tate, Claudia. *Domestic Allegories of Political Desire: The Black Heroine's Text at the Turn of the Century.* New York: Oxford University Press, 1992.

Tate, Greg. "Cult-Nats Meet Freaky-Deke: The Return of the Black Aesthetic." *Flyboy in the Buttermilk: Essays on Contemporary America.* New York: Simon and Schuster, 1992. 198–210.

Thomas, Brook. *American Literary Realism and the Failed Promise of Contract.* Berkeley: University of California Press, 1997.

Tompkins, Jane. *Sensational Designs: The Cultural Work of American Fiction, 1790–1860.* New York: Oxford University Press, 1985.

Toomer, Jean. *Cane.* 1923. New York: Penguin, 2019.

———. *The Letters of Jean Toomer, 1919–1924.* Ed. Mark Whalan. Knoxville: University of Tennessee Press, 2006.

Tourgée, Albion W. "The 'Claim' of Realism." *North American Review* 148.388 (Mar. 1889): 386–88.

———. *A Fool's Errand.* New York: Fords, Howard, and Hulbert, 1879.

———. "The South as a Field for Fiction." *Forum* (Dec. 1888): 404–13.

Tsou, Elda E. *Unquiet Tropes: Form, Race, and Asian American Literature.* Philadelphia: Temple University Press, 2015.

Twain, Mark. *Adventures of Huckleberry Finn.* 1885. 3rd ed. Ed. Thomas Cooley. New York: Norton, 1998.

———. *The Gilded Age.* 1873. Ed. Louis J. Budd. New York: Penguin, 2001.

———. *Life on the Mississippi.* 1883. New York: Harper and Brothers, 1917.

———. *Pudd'nhead Wilson and Those Extraordinary Twins.* 1893–94. 2nd ed. Ed. Sidney E. Berger. New York: Norton, 2005.

Walker, Alice. *In Search of Our Mothers' Gardens.* New York: Harcourt, Brace, Jovanovich, 1983.

Warren, Kenneth W. *Black and White Strangers: Race and American Literary Realism.* Chicago: University of Chicago Press, 1993.

———. "Does African-American Literature Exist?" *Chronicle of Higher Education* Feb. 24, 2011. https://www.chronicle.com/article/Does-African-American/126483.

———. *What Was African American Literature?* Cambridge: Harvard University Press, 2011.

Warren, Kenneth W., and Henry Louis Gates Jr. "The End of African American Literature?" Live Chat. *Chronicle of Higher Education* Feb. 24, 2011. www.chronicle.com/article/Live-Chat-The-End-of/126492.

Washington, Booker T., ed. *The Negro Problem.* New York: James Pott, 1903.

———. *Up from Slavery.* 1901. Ed. William L. Andrews. New York: Oxford University Press, 1995.

Washington, Mary Helen. "Uplifting the Women and the Race: The Forerunners—Harper and Hopkins." *Invented Lives: Narratives of Black Women, 1860–1960.* Ed. Washington. New York: Doubleday, 1987. 73–86.

Watson, Veronica T. *The Souls of White Folk: African American Writers Theorize Whiteness.* Jackson: University Press of Mississippi, 2013.

Webb, Frank J. *The Garies and Their Friends.* 1857. Ed. William Huntting Howell and Megan Walsh. Toronto: Broadview, 2016.

Weinauer, Ellen M. "'A Most Respectable Looking Gentleman': Passing, Possession, and Transgression in *Running a Thousand Miles for Freedom.*" *Passing and the Fictions of Identity.* Ed. Elaine K. Ginsberg. Durham, N.C.: Duke University Press, 1996. 37–56.

Welter, Barbara. "The Cult of True Womanhood." *American Quarterly* 18 (Spring 1966): 151–74.

Wells, Ida B. *Southern Horrors and Other Writings: The Anti-Lynching Campaign of Ida B. Wells, 1892–1900.* Ed. Jacqueline Jones Royster. Boston: Bedford/St. Martin's, 1997.

Wharton, Edith. *The House of Mirth.* 1905. Ed. Elizabeth Ammons. New York: Norton, 1990.

Wilderson, Frank B. *Red, White, & Black: Cinema and the Structure of U.S. Antagonisms.* Durham, N.C.: Duke University Press, 2010.

Williams, Andreá N. "African American Literary Realism, 1865–1914." *A Companion to African American Literature.* Ed. Gene Andrew Jarrett. Malden, Mass.: Wiley-Blackwell, 2013. 185–99.

———. *Dividing Lines: Class Anxiety and Postbellum Black Fiction.* Ann Arbor: University of Michigan Press, 2013.

Williams, Raymond. "Realism and the Contemporary Novel." *Universities & Left Review* 4 (Summer 1958): 22–25.

Wilson, Kimberly A. C. "The Function of the 'Fair' Mulatto": Complexion, Audience, and Mediation in Frances Harper's *Iola Leroy.*" *Cimarron Review* 106 (1994): 104–13.

Winter, Kari J. *Subjects of Slavery, Agents of Change: Women and Power in Gothic Novels and Slave Narratives, 1790–1865.* Athens: University of Georgia Press, 1992.

Wonham, Henry B. *Playing the Races: Ethnic Caricature and American Literary Realism.* New York: Oxford University Press, 2004.

Yerby, Frank. *The Foxes of Harrow.* New York: Dial, 1946.

Zackodnik, Teresa C. *The Mulatta and the Politics of Race.* Jackson: University Press of Mississippi, 2004.

Zafar, Rafia. *We Wear the Mask: African Americans Write American Literature, 1760–1870.* New York: Columbia University Press, 1997.

INDEX